Our Short Story

Writers

Blanche Colton Williams

Alpha Editions

This edition published in 2020

ISBN : 9789354021374

Design and Setting By
Alpha Editions
email - alphaedis@gmail.com

Our Short Story Writers

BY

BLANCHE COLTON WILLIAMS, Ph.D.

*Instructor in Story Writing, Columbia University (Extension Teaching
and Summer Session); Associate Professor of English,
Hunter College of the City of New York.*

*Author of "A Handbook on Story Writing"; "How to Study 'The Best
Short Stories'"; "Gnomic Poetry in Anglo-Saxon";
Editor "A Book of Short Stories."*

NEW YORK
DODD, MEAD AND COMPANY
1929

TABLE OF CONTENTS

CHAPTER I   AGE

Alice Brown   1

CHAPTER II

James Branch Cabell 22

CHAPTER III

Dorothy Canfield 41

CHAPTER IV

Robert W. Chambers 55

CHAPTER V

Irvin Shrewsbury Cobb 73

CHAPTER VI

James Brendan Connolly 85

CHAPTER VII

Richard Harding Davis 105

CHAPTER VIII

Margaret Wade Deland 129

CHAPTER IX

Edna Ferber 146

CHAPTER X

Mary Wilkins Freeman 160

TABLE OF CONTENTS

CHAPTER XI   PAGE

Hamlin Garland 182

CHAPTER XII

William Sidney Porter ("O. Henry") 200

CHAPTER XIII

Joseph Hergesheimer 223

CHAPTER XIV

Fannie Hurst 237

CHAPTER XV

Jack London 256

CHAPTER XVI

James Brander Matthews 278

CHAPTER XVII

Melville Davisson Post 293

CHAPTER XVIII

Mary Roberts Rinehart 309

CHAPTER XIX

Booth Tarkington 322

CHAPTER XX

Edith Wharton 337

CHAPTER XXI

Maxwell Struthers Burt 358

CHAPTER XXII

Wilbur Daniel Steele 372

FOREWORD

A T the risk of supererogation I desire to state emphatically that these twenty authors are only representative of our short story writers. I labor under no delusion that they are all we have of high rank, rather am I inclined to suspect that the first prospective reader will find his favorite story teller missing. Some of my own preferred stylists are conspicuously absent; and, although for the most part I have included those whom within prescribed limits I place first, I regretfully record the absentees. The short story is the literary medium that supersedes all others in America; one small volume is a container too exiguous for even its chief authors.

According to the dominant principle working throughout the series of which this book is a unit, the writers discussed should be living or at least contemporary. If, by request of the publishers, Jack London and "O. Henry" were to be replevined from the famous dead, I was of the opinion that Richard Harding Davis should not be omitted. Henry James, from a literary point of view, would precede any of these three. For reasons later forthcoming, however, he is not among those present. The seventeen

FOREWORD

living writers I have chosen on three counts: significance of work in time or theme or other respect; weight or actual value of work, and quantity of work measured by the number of stories or story volumes. It happens that certain significant writers may have been left out because of their having turned, after one momentous contribution to the short story, to the novel, or for other reason having failed to produce a corpus of short story material. George W. Cable's place in literature was established primarily through *Old Creole Days;* but in the opinion of the present writer the niche he occupies is that of novelist. "Octave Thanet" one might rightly expect to find here. But only her first volume had been published when Hamlin Garland's *Main-Travelled Roads* appeared, and there were stronger arguments for his inclusion. Many recent writers have published in leading periodicals stories which have not yet found preservation between the covers of a book. There are enough of these writers alone to justify a volume of reviews.

Herein are Alice Brown and Mary Wilkins Freeman, interpreters of New England; Irvin Cobb, humorist, Southerner and journalist successor to R. H. D.; Edith Wharton, representative of culture and the Henry James school; Dorothy Canfield, lover of humanity and democracy; Robert W. Chambers, imaginative artist, superior to Chambers the novelist; Melville Davisson Post, detective story writer, and Brander Matthews, New York realist, technicians who

FOREWORD

have held out for the *story;* Mary Roberts Rinehart,
product of the motion picture era; James Brendan
Connolly, author of sea stories pronouncedly individual; Hamlin Garland, realist of the Middle West;
Margaret Deland, witness through her Pennsylvania
tales that religion and truth are not incompatible with
dramatic effect; Booth Tarkington, satirist, argus-
eyed reader of life; Fannie Hurst, stylist of distinction and, with Edna Ferber, portrait painter of the
middle class of New America; James Branch Cabell
and Joseph Hergesheimer seekers after beauty, per-
formers of "the old gesture toward the stars."

So ends the first score; and, on demand there are
these toward a second: Mary Raymond Shipman An-
drews, Wilbur Daniel Steele, George W. Cable, "Oc-
tave Thanet", Katharine Fullerton Gerould, Rupert
Hughes, Clarence Budington Kelland, Gouverneur
Morris, "Charles Egbert Craddock", Annie Trumbull
Slosson, Mary Synon, Will Allen White, Josephine
Daskam Bacon, Mary Heaton Vorse, Lawrence Perry,
Willa Cather, Henry Van Dyke, with your own prefer-
ences to complete the twenty.

This volume must conform, in a measure, to the
series, of which several numbers have already appeared. But one difference will be noticed: there are,
comparatively, fewer names of authors, and they are
treated at proportionately greater length. An entire
volume, by George Gordon, is devoted to *The Men
Who Make Our Novels,* and another, by Grant Over-

FOREWORD

ton, to *The Women Who Make Our Novels.* Forty-seven names are included in the first of these; thirty-five in the second.

The biographical data have been secured from the highest available sources, and when I have drawn considerably upon one source as I have done in *Adventures and Letters of Richard Harding Davis* (Edited by Charles Belmont Davis), or Dr. C. Alphonso Smith's *O. Henry Biography,* I have been scrupulous to indicate the fact.

It is a pleasure here to express sincere thanks to my friend and colleague, Mrs. J. H. Temple, Jr. ("E. K. T."), who contributed the chapter on James Brendan Connolly.

BLANCHE COLTON WILLIAMS

New York City,
October 22, 1920.

OUR SHORT STORY WRITERS

CHAPTER I

MR. GRANT OVERTON in *The Women Who Make Our Novels* says discriminatingly about the lady whose name heads this chapter: "It is perhaps unfortunate that in a book dealing with American women novelists it should be necessary to confine the consideration of Alice Brown to her novels." Novelist, essayist, poet, dramatist, Alice Brown has done her best work in the short-story. On looking over certain of her earlier collections, however, one might well ask, "Would the content of these tales not gain if organized into novel form?" Whether Miss Brown's first short-stories are to be regarded as tentative efforts toward noveldom or whether her novels must be viewed as the work of a short-story writer straying afield is a moot question. Not inconceivably she is one of those rare authors destined to comparative success in two literary types.

The New Hampshire scenes and persons in *Meadow Grass* and *Tiverton Tales,* obviously direct from her memory and observation, occur and recur throughout the volumes. One lays them down and with slight effort constructs a neighborhood history. If not quite novels in embryo or even in the amorphous state, they are at least prophecies. Beginning with *High Noon,* Miss Brown entered into constructive fiction. Her previous building rested on the knowledge and inheritance of childhood. The *High Noon* accomplishment is that of an artist finding herself, uncertainly, gropingly, in her chosen form. For this reason the stories are not real nor convincing as are those in the earlier volumes. They are trials toward a new goal. In *The County Road, Vanishing Points,* and *The Flying Teuton* the author has arrived. She is sure of her manner, her invention and her technic. She has mellowed to maturity. This is by no means to say that her first books may not be so valuable. From the point of view of literary history they are superior. No historian of New England writing henceforth may afford to neglect her studies—not more than he might omit those of Sarah Orne Jewett or the first work of Mary Wilkins Freeman. On the other hand, no account of the short-story would be complete without emphasis upon the greater art of her second and third periods.

Had Alice Brown so elected she might have ranked higher as essayist or poet than story writer. It is not too much to add that she may be remembered as dramatist. Something of her own feeling about the medium of expression she probably put into the letter Zoe Montrose wrote Francis Hume (in *The Day of His Youth*) : "Do not write verse until you fail to express yourself in prose. Verse should glide full-winged over the surface of the waters where the spirit of God lies sleeping." Her versatility has meant breadth and variety; it has not favored, even if it has not hindered, her intensification in any one of the literary forms. If it has conduced to mixture rather than subtile differentiation of type, then the glory is greater to her short-stories that they have emerged triumphant.

Alice Brown was born in Hampton Falls, New Hampshire, December 5, 1857. "Her home was not so far from the sea," says Harriet Prescott Spofford, "that the swift sea-turn did not creep in with its salt dews; and there the sound of the rote after great storms reached her ears and startled her imagination." She went to a district school, which she has undoubtedly commemorated in *Number Five,* the opening essay in *Meadow Grass.* "Up to the very hollow which made its playground and weedy garden the road was elm-bordered and lined with fair meadows, skirted in the background with shadowy pines, so soft they did not even wave; they only seemed to breathe." The treasures of the road she touches with lingering hand: the watering trough, the lichened fence, the pasture; the forget-me-not and the milk-weed; the little river, the bridge and the meadows.

There her environment was not unlike that of her compeers over America; there history repeated itself. There was the boy who led his class (he does his hayin' now by hand); there was the youngster who ran away (he has become the shif'less citizen); there the insepa-rable friends fell in love with the same girl (only one remains); there was the little girl who lived with the selec'man's wife and who had only one beautiful thing to remember all her life—a pink cambric dress given her by the lady who "boarded" a few weeks in the neighborhood.

It is deducible from her Tiverton stories that, apart from her school life, Miss Alice absorbed all the cus-toms of the country and saw everything. She watched the making of rugs, hand-woven coverlets, occasionally the carding of wool into rolls and the spinning of rolls into thread; she knew how to make "riz doughnuts" and pies and biscuits; she knew what it was to visit in the "sullar" barrels of Bald'ins and barrels of pork. She knew how butter was kept cool (for she has re-corded an instance of a napkin lost in the well); she knew how to churn and how to "make the butter come." She observed the hogsheads under the eaves, where insects came daily to their death. She officiated at the winding of grandfather's clocks, took sharp note of false teeth, and knew that chewing cloves or wearing cracker poultices supposedly abated the pain of an aching molar. She was aware that a medicated stock-ing-leg is soothing to a sore throat. She was familiar with the cinnamon rose, the clove pink and the currant worm; she must have loved the larkspurs and ladies' delights, for she uses them over and again; she took note of hollows under syringa bushes where hens had bathed. She walked lanes bordered with raspberry and rose; roaming the fields and woods, she learned thoroughwort, spearmint, pennyr'yal, wormwood and tansy. She loved the forest under the sun and under the moon. Always she has loved trees; from her first stories to her latest, she is a Druid.

With adjoining communities she was on terms of acquaintance. Penrith figures occasionally; Horn o' the Moon frequently; Sudleigh often. Sudleigh, rival of Tiverton! The name is no mask for the initiated; it serves as well as the real for others. It is perhaps an example of unconscious humor or native shrewd-ness that New England thrift is illustrated in the Sud-leighites (not by the Tivertonians) who sold ice water on a memorable occasion for a penny a glass.

Above all, Alice Brown knew people. Her picture of an old lady climbing upon an antiquated steed by means of chair and "cricket" one would take oath is memory drawn; her village witch is reminiscent, albeit speaking, we doubt not, Miss Brown's own philosophy: "There's a good deal missed when ye stay at home makin' pies an' a good deal ye can learn if ye live out-door." Some years have passed since we saw her

Children of Earth at Mr. Ames's Little Theatre; but
we have not forgotten the village fool whose presence
in the play testifies to his creator's kinship with Shakespeare. Miss Dyer and Mrs. Blair, of *Joint Ownership* (in *Meadow Grass*) are true neighborhood types.
Then there are Parson True and his daughter, Farmer
Eli Pike and his family, including Hattie's Sereno,
and the Mardens, who, though types, are individual-
ized, and we hazard, all of them, from originals.
There is the old lady who, despoiled of youth's desire,
approached octogenarianhood wearing a hat that proud-
ly sported lavender roses; there is the vexatious Widow
Poll, who tagged along where she was not wanted and
who thrust her heavy foot by accident, premeditated
or unpremeditated, into Heman's violin case (if she
did not wear Congress gaiters, with elastic sides, some
of her sisters did); there are the comforters of the
sick who talk of death under circumstances similar
to those attending the comfortee; there are those who
immolate themselves on the shrine of ancestor worship
and drag out barren lives—if service is ever barren.

Her nomenclature is redolent of New England:
Caleb (Kelup), Eli, Cyrus, David, Elkanah, Solon,
Liddy, Luceba, 'Mandy, Dorcas, Delilah.

And if her characters are not idealized portraits of
childhood acquaintances they may well have been. If
we go up Tiverton way we believe we shall find them
all—older, perhaps, or even in the churchyard or recognizable in their descendants " 'Ain't you Rufe

Gill?' Fielding made the concession of his verb to place and time. The other straightened himself. 'Well, no,' he said, 'I ain't. But father is.' " (From *A Runaway Match*, in *High Noon.*)

In *The End of All Living*, her final sketch in *Tiverton Tales*, Miss Brown pictures the churchyard behind the First Church, on a sloping hillside, "Overrun with a briery tangle, and relieved by Nature's sweet and cunning hand from the severe decorum set ordinarily about the dead." For interest, the burial ground in Plymouth offers fit comparison with the spot described by Miss Brown, as Irving's Westminster Abbey is its companion-piece in literature.

About 1871 or '72, Miss Brown began her course at Robinson Seminary in Exeter. During the hardest winter months she lived in Exeter, but the rest of the year she walked to and from her home, nearly four miles.

It is less easy to determine from her work what she gathered in that period of advanced schooling. But she must have tucked away a good bit from the English poets, Wordsworth, Keats, Milton, Rossetti and Tennyson; in those days she was training to teach. Her first essays are touched with unconscious rhythm of poetry. "—or when the board was set, what faces smiled," ends a sentence in *Number Five*, "a haunting spirit in perennial bliss" closes *The End of All Living*. Perfect iambic pentameters, each. It was from her poetic power, Harriet Prescott Spofford said some years ago, her friends expected the most.

Miss Brown taught for a few years in the country and Boston, but "hating it more and more every minute," as she herself has said, she gave up teaching for writing. After working for a time on the *Christian Register*, she became, in 1885, a member of the staff of *The Youth's Companion*. There she ground out stuff from the latest books and magazines and wrote stories. Eventually she resigned to devote herself entirely to writing.

In 1886 she first went abroad, spending the greater part of the year in France; in 1890 she went again, "enjoying five months of gentle vagabondage in England." Part of the time she spent in London, but more of it in Devon and Cornwall, regions for which she was made eager through the history of her native village. It will be recalled by those who have read *The Flat-Iron Lot (Tiverton Tales)*, "the first settlers came from Devon." Six years later, *By Oak and Thorn*, a collection of travel reminiscences, incorporated Miss Brown's reaction to her pleasant holiday.

In 1895 she made another journey, in the companionship of Louise Imogen Guiney, walking all of ten weeks in Wales, Shropshire and Devon, and going up to London for a season with the younger English poets. In collaboration with Miss Guiney, she published a booklet on Robert Louis Stevenson, a study which is also an appreciation.

In 1895 *Meadow Grass* appeared.* Reviews of
the book favored *Farmer Eli's Vacation.* C. M.
Thompson, writing in the *Atlantic Monthly*, July, 1906,
states that he regards it as Miss Brown's best achievement. But in story value and structure it is inferior
to *Told in the Poorhouse, A Righteous Bargain,* or
Joint Owners in Spain, not to go outside of the same
covers. As has been indicated in reconstructing the
early days of Miss Brown's life, these are tales, presumably, of the Hampton Falls neighborhood. The
homely dialect of this and her succeeding collection,
Tiverton Tales (1899) contributes to verisimilitude
and drama as it inspires the reader with sympathy for
the dramatis personæ. In English fiction one must
go to George Eliot for fit comparison; Mary Ann
Evans, one of, and yet apart from, Warwickshire folk,
saw their oddities and foibles. Miss Brown stands
in the same relation to her Tivertonians. She is one
of them at heart, and yet she is not quite democratic.
Not that she feels aloofness or means to convey superiority. She suffers from or profits by a point of
view, native to her and strengthened by absence, which
recognizes them as "characters." In so recognizing
them she unconsciously aligns herself with the external
standards of conventionality and culture. Now and
then she drops into an "I" use which brings her singu-
larly back into the magic circle of her own. Mr. C. M.
Thompson liked her dialect stories because he knew

* Preceded by her early novel, *Fools of Nature.*

her class of people; a writer in *Reedy's Mirror* later remarked that if one cannot sympathize with her people it is because he is so saturated with the New England atmosphere. The combined comment offers two somewhat contradictory angles from which results agreement that she is successful.

The technique of these stories reveals the tryer-out. *After All,* for example, maintains unity by a nice emphasis upon character; it works out its theme. But the "story" falters. So the dramatic note occurs, but by fits and starts, showing that the author has the sense of drama but has not learned properly to subdue the unimportant, to graduate to scale and to point up her climaxes. She sees the universally dramatic and pathetic in human relations, however small the revealing occurrence. *Told in the Poorhouse* will illustrate as well as any of the tales her early inclination to the dramatic:

Josh Marden and his wife Lyddy Ann have been married for "fifteen year" when Josh's second cousin 'Mandy comes to help with the work. She starts trouble. Josh "looked at 'Mandy an' he got over seein' Lyddy Ann, that's all." On Josh's birthday 'Mandy gave him a present of a bill folder. He discarded the old one. Lyddy took it back for her own. "An' arterwards it come out that the old pocket-book was one she'd bought for him afore they was married—earned in bindin' shoes." Later, when 'Mandy presumed to sit in Lyddy's place at table, the wife ordered her up.

"You've took my husband away, but you shan't take my place at table." Josh orders Lyddy into the fore-room. 'Mandy leaves. For some years Lyddy keeps to her side of the house, Josh to his. At last he falls sick, suffers a stroke, and Lyddy tends him. Before he dies he makes trial of speech. Lyddy thinks she understands, " 'Yes, Joshuay, yes, dear!' An' she got up an' took the pocket-book 'Mandy had gi'n him off the top o' the bureau an' laid it down on the bed where he could git it. But he shook his head, an' said the word ag'in, an' a queer look—as if she was scairt an' pleased—flashed over Lyddy Ann's face. She ran into the parlor, an' come back with that old pocket-book he'd give up to her, an' she put it into his well hand. That was what he wanted. His fingers gripped it up, an' he shet his eyes. He never spoke ag'in."

The stories in *Meadow Grass* and *Tiverton Tales* reveal, in the complimentary sense, their feminine authorship. Miss Brown sees events through the woman's eyes, which means that she sees them more truly than if she attempted the masculine point of view. For the sexes rarely envision correctly other than through their respective lenses. And although Miss Brown's later stories succeed in assuming the masculine angle, she grew in years and in practice before attempting it. Whether, therefore, playing up a woman heroine or villain Miss Brown's earlier stories emphasize the woman's outlook. Her men are convincing, but slightly drawn; they appear infrequently, as men on a New England farm are infrequently at the house. Her children are shadowy. Either they are cowed and humble, like Rosie of the *March Wind,* or they are well-behaved and inconspicuously demure, like Claribel of *After All.* Yet, later on, Miss Brown was to show her sympathy with girlhood in *The Secret of the Clan* (1912).

If Miss Brown's mental attitude challenges comparisons with that of George Eliot, her characters bring back memories of *Cranford.* Deacon Pitts, mentioned in *Dooryards,* prefatory sketch in *Tiverton Tales,* had a ghoulish delight in funerals. This morning the butcher had brought him news of death in a neighboring town. Suddenly, as he turned back toward the house, bearing a pan of liver, his pondering eye caught sight of his aged wife toiling across the fields. "He set down his pan and made a trumpet of his hands. 'Sarah!' he called piercingly. 'Sarah! Mr. Amasa Blake's passed away! Died yesterday!'" Who can forget the Cranford lady, threatened to surrender by a fit of coughing, her delicious morsel of gossip! And if the gentleman evokes the thought, "At least Tiverton is not composed altogether of Amazons!" still he betrays his kinship with the females of Mrs. Gaskell's species.

Tiverton Tales can hardly be described as elaborating the sentiment of love; yet the greater number of them embody the passion as it slighted or glanced at or enveloped her people. *The Mortuary Chest,* most delightful of the series, introduces the elderly maiden and her old lover—the clergyman who had married elsewhere and who now recalls the past with his first love; *Horn o' the Moon* presents Doctor Mary, self-appointed to nurse Johnnie Veasey, and left forlorn when Johnnie goes away to marry the other girl; *A Stolen Festival,* which tells something about the first wedding anniversary of Letty and David, betrays his forgetfulness of the day, Letty's pitiful attempt to celebrate, and her early schooling to the difference between the ways of men and women; *A Last Assembling,* comparable only to Miss Wilkins's *A New England Nun,* with a glint of Cornelia Comer's *Long Inheritance* threading through it, psychologizes the refusal of Dilly to marry Jethro after many years; *A Second Marriage* unmistakably reveals the hidden springs of Amelia's decision not to marry the love of her boyhood, Laurie Morse.

But the most individual story in the volume is *The Way of Peace,* which recounts the sorrow of a daughter for her mother and her successful attempt to impersonate that mother. When she saw herself in the mirror she was comforted. And her way of peace was assured when the youngest of her nephews and nieces crept up to her and asked, "Grandma, when'd you get well?" Pathological and nostalgic, perhaps, but saved by its uncompromising honesty.

In making a study of Alice Brown's development, her novels and other works should be taken into account. It is to be regretted that the present comment must omit them, with only suggestions here and there, which may be traced out to the fuller completion of the tapestry.

Her early story-writing was diversified, then, by a historical study, *Mercy Otis Warren,* in connection with which she did much research work acquainting herself fully with the revolutionary era. A volume of poems, *The Road to Castaly,* also marks her productivity before 1900. *King's End* and *Margaret Warrener* were published in 1901.

The volume of stories succeeding *Tiverton Tales* marks a distinct change in her subject-matter and her method, or more accurately a reversion to the novelette experiment, *The Day of His Youth.* In *High Noon* (1904) sentiment is pronounced and increased, love dominates, and the business of marriage provokes the author's analytical powers. Admirers confessed of Miss Brown's work, we think it not too harsh to say that such stories as *The Book of Love* are Myrtle Reedian, at best—in the language of the hero, Graham —"a kind of divine nonsense." *A Meeting in the Market Place, His Enemy, Natalie Blayne, A Runaway Match, Rosamund in Heaven, The Miracle, The Map of the Country,* and *The End of the Game* all are permeated by a scientific sentimental interest in love. The disappointed, the hope of union after death, the adjustment of temperaments, the salvation through service of those love has passed by—these and similar themes constitute the illuminatingly subjective side of the volume.

Prominent among her characters, now, are literary men and women. Her own attitude is more consciously literary. The title, *High Noon,* she follows out by a proverb from the Persian, "One instant only is the sun at noon," and indicates thereby her recognition of the crucial moment. She is studying the nature of the short-story and short-story writers. In *The End of the Game* she speaks of the short-story as "perfect of form and sonnet-like in finish," mentions Prosper Merimee—the earliest of *conte* writers—and concludes *The End of the Game* in a Lady-or-Tiger manner, which certainly points to study of Stockton. Her local color, save for the marsh, is disappearing. The best of the lot is *Natalie Blayne,* in that it is more objective and is possessed of sufficient humor to redeem the sentiment elsewhere overstrained.

In *The County Road* (1906) the author returns to her country folk but creates with a noticeably freer hand than in *Meadow Grass* and *Tiverton Tales.* In ten years her Tiverton friends have advanced, with the rest of the world. Blue coverlets still exist, but the book telling how to make them Cynthia of *Bachelor's Fancy* finds in the attic. Nancy of the masculine pipe and tobacco still wanders, Sudleigh stage runs, and shoe-binding continues. But she looks forward, not backward. Her young people meet on nearly equal terms with the old folk. It is true that Abigail and

Jonathan in *A Day Off* are the protagonists and their
daughter plays a secondary rôle, but the daughter provides causation for the mother's acts throughout. It
is also true that *Old Immortality*, the most distinctive
story in the volume, has an old couple for its chief
actors. But *A Winter's Courting, The Looking Glass,
The Twisted Tree,* and *Bachelor's Fancy* have for
heroines young and beautiful women. If her study of
love is still pathological, it is also more sane and hopeful. By logical growth and development Miss Brown
uses old scenes in a novel way. Her temperament has
become pronounced and her art has advanced at the
expense of locale. The creator has displaced the copy-
ist. Oddly enough, the sea has gained hold upon Miss
Brown. Cynthia of *Elephant's Mountain,* worn thread-
bare, obsessed by her husband's much greasing of his
boots, leaves the country and takes refuge with her
sister by the sea. The scene is Fastnet, and the Captain of the tale is one after Miss Jewett's order.

Her dramatic power has grown. *A Day Off,* for
example, is constructed in scenes, the action of which
is developed through dialogue. Her characters stand
on their own feet, here as in the other stories.

She elaborates her theories of soul-communion. *The
Cave of Adullam* emphasizes the joy of living in spirit
beside the heart's love; *Bankrupt* (of *Meadow Grass*)
is its prototype. Miss Lucretia of one is Dorcas of the
other in a similar situation.

A new note of allegory enters *The County Road,*

extended in her subsequent stories. Sylvia of *The Twisted Tree* in her sick-soul condition is obsessed with the idea that the tree symbolizes herself. (O. Henry touched the theme in *The Last Leaf*). Haven, who loves Sylvia, grafts new shoots upon the tree; Sylvia recovers. It is worth while following out Miss Brown's interest in this *motif* as expressed in *A Homespun Wizardry (Harper's,* October, 1913) and *A Mind Cure (Harper's,* August, 1914).

We have emphasized the beginning of Miss Brown's work, for in it lies the germ of all her subsequent development. We may pass over *Country Neighbors* (1910), *The One-Footed Fairy and Other Stories* (1911) and study her perfect orientation in *Vanishing Points* (1913). This collection was also preceded by her novels, *Rose McLeod* and *Paradise*.

Her setting may be, now, Boston or Darjheeling; her characters may be young, middle-aged or old; they may be curates, editors or autocrats of civic affairs; they may be Aunt Harriets of Overland, or Elisha Porsons of commercial circles. She may set her stage for men, alone, as she does in *The Master*—one of the best "man" stories ever written by a woman; for the actors in young love, as in *The Discovery* or *The Flight of the Mouse;* for millionaires and journalists, as in *The Lantern.* She may write in the person of a man-narrator or as the camera-author. It matters not. Her people act and interact so as to give the illusion of life.

She breasts out against new subjects, swimming with the times. She makes, for instance, a case of social theories and practices in *The Man in the Cloister* and concludes that human kindness is the solution of the problem presented. She has advanced in the plot or "fable." She has a story to tell, not merely a thesis to illustrate, a "character" to hit off. She is adept at creating suspense, pause, climax; she weaves the fabric of her plot by clues and forecast and their fulfillment. Whole scenes may be lifted and acted on the stage with but slight changes for "directions." In *The Master,* for example, the table scene; in *The Lantern,* the scene between Porson and the Marshalls. She is not always skillful with coincidence; the double one in *The Clue* will strain the reader's credulity. So the poor architecture of *The House With the Tower* (*Harper's,* May, 1914), is righted by a storm that rises all too easily. But she apologizes for coincidence in a later volume: "It is true that the most extraordinary and exact coincidences happen, as if pieces in the mosaic of life, made to fit together in some mysterious forecast of destiny, rush toward each other and are finally joined."* Perhaps she is colder and remoter in some of her later tales. If so, the reason lies largely in the truth that she leaves her characters to declare themselves: the story is more objective than her earlier and comparatively subjective interpretations.

March 21, 1913, Winthrop Ames, of The Little

* *The Flying Teuton,* page 48.

Theatre, New York, inaugurated a drama contest. One thousand six hundred and forty-six plays were submitted. In 1914, the award of ten thousand dollars was made to Alice Brown for *Children of Earth.* It is not a good acting play, as the published version may show to those who did not see it while on the boards. But the fidelity to New England life is not less than that evinced in *Meadow Grass* and *Tiverton Tales;* it is imaginative and poetic. It illustrates in its non-success the paradox that some of the most dramatic story-writers fall short on the actual stage.

The Flying Teuton (1918), following *Bromley Neighborhood* and *The Prisoner,* carries on the method of *Vanishing Points,* with an emphasis upon the supernatural. She had already touched it in *The Tryst* and *There and Here* of *High Noon.* Her *Tryst* of the *Flying Teuton* is the companion piece of the former *Tryst* in that the earlier story looks mystically into the future and the life beyond, while the later illustrates the theory of transmigration of souls and hints at remote pasts of two who meet in Paestum. *The Flying Teuton,* the story lending its name to the book, is a sort of modern Flying-Dutchman that has been classed among the great short-stories produced by the World War. *A Citizen and His Wife* is not far behind it— a spy story combined with a unique love motive: a traitor is betrayed by his wife who loved him only a little less than her country. *The Island* emphasizes Miss Brown's favorite thesis, that life and love are

continuous in a vast and beautiful way, touched long
before in *A Meeting in the Market-Place (High Noon)*.
It conceives the ideal as one where Keats's magic case-
ments are part of the mansion of the soul, where
Shelley's *Skylark* is real and where invisible colonies
reach out to aid England. It is but a step from this
story content to *The Wind Between the Worlds* (1920)
and its theme of whether or not communication with the
dead is possible. It also finds reverberation in *Old
Lemuel's Journey (Atlantic Monthly,* June, 1920),
which takes the dying man upon a mysterious visit
before his final demise.

A quarter century has elapsed between Miss Brown's
first stories and her latest. She has become a citizen
of the world; her story people have become citizens of
the world. And yet as a world-weary traveler returns with joy to his native heath, she occasionally
writes of her home folk. Her flavor is less strong as
the cosmopolite is less remarked than the villager.
There are readers who prefer the meadow and Tiverton, those who prefer the denizens of the world—burning laurel leaves idly for ceremonial, pasting book-
plates in volumes newly arrived from England, telling
stories in French and referring easily to "roses from
Paestan rosaries." It is perhaps a trifle to be lamented
that some of us like the author so well in all her phases
we cannot tell which Alice Brown we fain would see
immortal. But we are content to leave all her works
on the knees of the gods.

Volumes of stories by Miss Brown:

Meadow Grass, 1895.
Tiverton Tales, 1899.
High Noon, 1904.
The County Road, 1906.
Country Neighbors, 1910.
The One-Footed Fairy, 1911.
Vanishing Points, 1913.
The Flying Teuton, 1918.
Homespun and Gold, 1920.

CHAPTER II

IN *The Cream of the Jest,* Chapter VI, Mr. James Branch Cabell writes: "Besides, it was droll to read the 'literary notes' which the Baxon-Muir people were industriously disseminating, by means of the daily journals, concerning Felix Kennaston's personality, ancestry, accomplishments, recreations and preferences in diet. And then, in common with the old woman famed in nursery rhyme, he was very often wont to observe, 'But lawk a mercy on me! This is none of I!'"

Tentative conclusions reached in this article might prompt Mr. Cabell to reiterate the rhyme with respect to himself. His readers see him differently; and since he has reminded us of the sardonic point of every human story, that "the person you or I find in the mirror is condemned eternally to misrepresent us in the eyes of our fellows," he will assuredly not find himself in this particular mirror perfectly and whole. But it would be labor well worth the pains to effect a brief appreciation that Mr. Cabell might notice with approval however reserved, one that revealed a modicum of understanding of his artistic problems and his solution of them, or that evinced apprehension of what he is saying through his novels and short stories.

That he says impeccably his say is indisputable; that he says it for only a few is undebatable, though this limitation—provided the few be of a definite class of readers—is one he seeks. It is perhaps to be regretted that he cannot express himself for a large number. They, though unaware, need him. But he is unintelligible to many readers who are intelligent; he is dismissed by many who are scholars without interest in narrative, the medium which transmutes Mr. Cabell's acquisition of fact into art. He is, in short, enjoyed only by those who possess a certain scholarship plus a but slightly secondary interest in fiction plus a mental kinship that recognizes the aptness of his means. "Leave hope behind" might be inscribed for all others who seek to enter; for to them his Paradise is metamorphosed, in very truth, to an Inferno.

Lest we seem to set ourselves high among the elect, let us state with all frankness that at times we are in doubt whether we wander in fields of asphodel or are caught in a mirage of delusion, scorned while we admire. The legend, "Thou fool!" may face us; but we fondly fancy it leers at the traveler far behind. . . .

Mr. Cabell desires "to write perfectly of beautiful happenings," and the intensity of this desire burns purposefully throughout his works. He knows, as every artist knows, that art has beauty for its province.

But he has outstripped most of his brother-craftsmen in pursuing that ideal beauty all artists follow after. He might have expanded, consciously, Poe's theories in *The Philosophy of Composition* were it not that he independently discovered the truth. As Poe knew that for harmony of effect beauty is best allied with the passion of love, so Mr. Cabell knows. He cites Gautier's words to the point that "everything passes but art," and he enumerates clarity, beauty and symmetry among the auctorial virtues that contribute to literary permanence. To these, he adds tenderness, truth and urbanity. The great body of his work celebrates undying love and imperishable beauty.

This love which he celebrates he figures through Mr. Erwyn, in *Love at Martinmas (Gallantry)*: "Dear lady, surely you would not confound amour with love? Believe me, the translation is inadequate. Amour is but the summer wave that lifts and glitters and laughs in the sunlight, and within the instant disappears; but love is the unfathomed eternal sea itself." And this beauty he celebrates is the soul of beauty. It is what Ettarre meant to Kennaston: "And it is the cream of a vile jest that I am ·forbidden ever to win quite to you, ever to touch you, ever to see you even save in my dreams!"

His world of Art is, therefore, not the real world. In *Beyond Life* he says, "Really there should be no trifling with facts, for always the ever present danger exists that, in treating of the life immediately about him, even the unobservant literary genius may notice that this life for the most part consists of ugly and stupid persons doing foolish things, and will take a despondent view of the probable outcome."

Again, Charteris surely speaks for him in *The Lady of all Our Dreams (The Certain Hour)*. Charteris confesses to having made some joyous tales which "prevaricate tenderly about the universe and veil the pettiness of human nature with screens of verbal jewel-work.

"It is not the actual world they tell about, but a vastly superior place where the Dream is realized and everything which we knew was possible comes true. It is a world we have all glimpsed, just once, and have not entered, and have not ever forgotten." . . . And once more, "I was born with the desire to make beautiful books—brave books, that would preserve the glories of the Dream untarnished, and would recreate them for battered people, and re-awaken joy and magnanimity."

Ideal Beauty, Ideal Love, and a Dream World belong to the romanticist. And it is through his concepts of these terms and the exercise of his talents with them that James Branch Cabell overtops to-day all other romantic writers in America.

To watch his progress, to trace it through his works, is to observe how he cast off shackle after shackle of limitation, to ultimate unhampered movement over the earth, in the zenith that is Heaven or the pit that is Hell.

In *The Eagle's Shadow* (1904), he sought to escape the world of fact by intrusions into the land of fancy. But it was insufficient for his needs—this land peopled with imaginary folk of the present. By entering the door of the past he removed himself further from the actual. From historical data he wove fictive tapestries of dreams figuring Francois de Montcorbier, Sir John Falstaff, the gay Falmouths and the noble Puysanges. Those tales he gathered up after their appearance in *Harper's Magazine,* covering a period of some three years, in *The Line of Love* (1905). But he essayed a more difficult task. He turned to a past between the late middle ages and the present, and recreated the era of the Second George of England. It is true that he modestly disclaims, by suggestion, what he has attempted to do; but his success is the more pronounced. In the Epistle Dedicatory he quotes Thackeray, "I have said, *Show me some good person about that Court; find me, among those selfish courtiers, those dissolute gay people, some one being that I can love and regard,"* and he hints at hesitating to try that wherein the giant failed. He says, further, in the Epilogue, that his pictures of that time, "Aim little at the lofty and sublime." . . .

> "He merely strove to find
> And fix a faithful likeness of mankind
> About its daily business—and secure
> Far less a portrait than a miniature."

At first blush, then, it would appear that he had abandoned idealism for realism or at best a dissolute reality. Let not his speciousness betray you! Read, instead, *Simon's Hour*, and marvel at the sacrificial act of the debauched vicar who died for the lady he had loved; or *In the Second April*, and thrill at the parlous adventures Jean Bulmer, otherwise the Duke of Ormskirk, endured for the Lady Claire; or *The Scapegoats*, and know the heart of the old Prince de Gâtinais, who so loved France that he murdered his son's love, Nelchen, and then, having prayed that for his crime he might dwell eternally in the nethermost pit of hell, ended his own life with the same poison-brew.

But Mr. Cabell found the age of gallantry insufficient to his needs—whether he had exploited it by way of "taking a dare" or for contrast. He reverted to the remoter past, where he found greater satisfaction, and published, in *Harper's*, from 1905 to 1908, a series of masterpieces later collected under the appropriate title, *Chivalry* (1909). The science of love, the art of versifying, the making of chansons, the pleasant custom of singing sestinas or tensons beneath the window of the fair, the jongleur disguise assumed by princes and kings that they may woo for their own sakes the ladies they would serve, the trappings and the local color of the age—all this he has subordinated to his purpose: the relation of beautiful happenings.

Yet, after two volumes of stories and part of a

third, setting forth this age in a chain of poignantly beautiful climaxes, he found it inadequate. He had tried the romance of the imaginary in the present time, of the imaginary in past time; there was left to him the romance of a world imagined by the past. What the vision and the dream meant to Geoffrey of Monmouth, Robert of Wace, and Sir Thomas Mallory; what the worlds peopled by their own creation meant to them they have meant, and more, to James Branch Cabell, who but for the grace of God might have been compeer to him who wrote *Gawain and the Green Knight,* or to those who perfected the tale of Tristram and Iseult and knew the City of Camelot. But here he is. And whether he is a reincarnation of Shakespearian wisdom, of Chaucerian cynical humor and Puckish malice, or whether he is properly of the twentieth century is beside the point. Praise be, he is ours!

It must be remembered that Mr. Cabell's mystic concept sees reality in the dream, even as it recognizes in reality a mysticism all its own. Felix Kennaston's reflections convey as much, and in a manner that inevitably carries conviction they are the author's. He penetrates to the heart of the vague feeling that art is irreligious. Only in the passing moment, he reminds himself, and through its evanescent emotions and sensations is man brought into contact with reality. The ideal of religion is disregard of the present. But art strives to make the sensation of a moment soul-satisfying. It performs what religion promises. . . .

He is sensitive to the fact that the artist's life is seldom regarded seriously. It is, perhaps, this recognition which lends to his latest works an increasing cynicism acquired at no loss of his ideal. "You would be at one with all fat-witted people", he asserts, "if you concede that the perfection of any art . . . is at best a by-product of life's conduct." He asseverates that phrase-spinning is the most profitless of all pursuits. He observes in *The Lady of All Our Dreams*: "Fairhaven was proud of John Charteris now that his colorful tales had risen from the semi-oblivion of being cherished merely by people who cared seriously for beautiful things, to the distinction of being purchasable in railway stations." And in *April's Message* the Earl apologetically remarks: "I do not understand poetry. It appears to me unreasonable to advance a statement simply because it happens to rhyme with a statement you have previously made."

But the artist *is*, because he must be. In *The Second April*, Jean Bulmer remarks: "In every man as I now see quite plainly, there is a god. And the god must judge, and the man himself be but the temple and the instrument of the god. And whether to go to church or no is a matter of trivial importance so long as the man obey the god which is within him." However great the exactions of art, he will meet them because of the god. These exactions mean sacrifice of time and friends. Even Shakespeare suffered from realization of the fact, "Lord what a deal of ruined life

it takes to make a little art!" *(Judith's Creed)*. And
latter-day John Charteris says, "My books, such as
they are, have been made at the dear price of never
permitting myself to care seriously for anything else.
I might not dare to dissipate my energies by taking
any part in the drama I was attempting to re-write,
because I must jealously conserve all the force that was
in me for the perfection of my version." He served
his dream and he got his books; but at the expense of
"fifteen years of human living and human intimacy."
Charteris admits they are hardly worth so much; but
it was necessary to obey the god within him; he must
have done so had he known they were worth far less.

So it was, by this obedience, Mr. Cabell wrote
Jurgen. In this return to the dream world of the past
he accepts Guinevere, let us say, as a real personage.
Heaven and Hell as actual kingdoms. But in his
scorn of illusions that satisfied the earlier dreamers, he
practises his casual cynicism even while he tells the
story artistically as he may. *Jurgen* becomes for some
of us, then, not the positive expression of beauty that
some critics declare it to be; but a vent for feelings
that turn in revulsion from old and false ideals. Or,
paradoxically, it is beautiful in so far as it destroys
decrepit foundations to make way for new towers of
the spirit. Tenderness remains, however, with the
cynicism; for Jurgen avoided that "part of Heaven
wherein were his grandmother's illusions; and this
was accounted for righteousness in Jurgen. That part

of Heaven smelt of mignonette, and a starling was singing there."

So, finally, fulfilment of all ideals lies "beyond life" . . . "The Universe was life's big barren studio, which the Artist certainly had neither planned nor builded, but had, somehow, occupied to make the best of its limitation." So Kennaston reflected, and so the author, through him, envisions all life as a struggle to artistic attainment: "Living may become symmetrical, well-plotted, coherent and rational" . . . But the day is not yet.

To be a renowned story teller forms only a part of Mr. Cabell's ambition. Therefore, he easily compasses perfection in the art, around which he has struck a circle so much greater. More specifically, in *The Line of Love* he attains the first requirements of the modern raconteur. He entertains by detailing a struggle or conflict (motivated by love, having its climax in love, in conformity with his artistic principle), satisfying the reader by the sense of finish only with his final word. Even in these early stories the hand of the 'prentice is guided by unmistakable genius; and although he is obviously indebted to predecessors, his own contribution is no less patent.

The *Love-letters of Falstaff* reveals him an artist in contrasts. Sir John, as he himself admits, is without honor; his face is bloated; his habits are vulgar. But he recalls the time, under the stimulus of Sylvia Vernon's visit, when "I was wont to sigh like a leaky bellows; to weep like a wench that hath lost her grandam; to lard my speech with the fag-ends of ballads like a man milliner; and, indeed, indite sonnets, canzonets, and what not of mine own." In this memory sounds the strain of the Bard of Avon, transmitted through James Branch Cabell. Reminiscent of Sonnet LXIII are the following lines, extracted from a poem ostensibly by Sir John:

"For without thy door
Now stands with dolorous cry and clamoring
Faint-hearted love, that there hath stood of yore.
Though winter draweth on, and no birds sing
Within the woods, yet as in wanton spring
He follows thee and never will have done,
Though nakedly he die, from following
Whither thou leadest."

Even the wreck that was Sir John had dwelt in Arcady; and Mr. Cabell's art restores that period of love and beauty. . . .

The best of this lot of impartially French and English backgrounds is *In Necessity's Mortar*, which challenges comparison with Stevenson's *A Lodging for the Night*. Yet, notwithstanding that Mr. Cabell profited by the older writer's work, his own narrative is superior. He retails the mutual love of Francois Villon and Catherine de Vaucelles. Having left her one evening, Francois was attacked by Gilles Raguyer, egged on by Ysabeau Montigny. Ysabeau's charge was unfounded, but so much the worse for Francois. Back to the wall he fought, finally killing one of his antagonists. The result was outlawry and his oath to drag the name of Villon in the dust. The years spent with the swine, suggested in the final scene with Catherine, work to an inevitable end. No one who has read the tale can forget Francois's pleading with Catherine, to kill her love for him—because he knows he is not worthy—nor his success. When he sees loathing supplant love in her eyes, he goes. And then, outside, he falls on his knees. "Dear God," he prays, "let me not live long." . . .

This first volume makes use of all the romanticist's tools: in *Ursula's Garden* and *The Conspiracy of Arnaye* disguise is the chief means of interesting the reader. *The Castle of Content* rests its dramatic climax upon the burning of papers which would have established Tom Allonby's title as Marquis of Falmouth. In most of the stories the lovers surrender wealth, fair name or life—or all—for the ladies they serve. Mr. Cabell's types of heroine, which persist in his later writings, are becoming established. They have an abundance of corn-colored, honey-colored, or golden hair; their eyes are sapphires or emerald-green, or sea-green; their mouths are small, "and thereto soft and red", perhaps "red wounds"; their faces are of a startling whiteness; they are unbelievably slender and willowy. "Rose of all the world" is a favorite comparison, which, likewise, endures for subsequent works. Already, the author has become intoxicated with the picture of the lark soaring to meet his love, the sun, and falling dizzy from his divine passion. . . .

The suitors seek perfection, and presumably they find it in the ladies they valiantly fetch off after durance, tribulation or strife:

> "I am weary of love that is pastime
> And gifts that it brings!
> I pray thee, O Lord, at this last time,
> Ineffable things . . ."

So sings Raoul, the page, otherwise Monsieur de Puysange.

Mr. Cabell's stories are recalled through pictures: We think of Katherine, Princess of France, perched in an apple-tree, while young Henry V looks up at her *(Chivalry);* of Olivia and Wycherley awaiting death on the rock that must be inundated by the tide; of Francois Villon's bleeding lip. The author is at pains to etch these pictures: "Francois felt the piercing cold of the steel, the tingling of it against his teeth, then the warm grateful spurt of blood; through a red mist he saw Gilles and Ysabeau run screaming down the Rue St. Jacques." And more recently, as Mr. Cabell might say, "His split lip was a clammy dead thing that flapped against his chin as he ran." So, *In the Second April (Gallantry),* one remembers that the

Duke of Ormskirk and the Lady Claire stand on the tower, where he engages with the brigand Cazaio. And one remembers that after a swift battle, the brigand meets his doom:

"Then his feet flipped upward, convulsively, so that John Bulmer saw his spurs glitter and twitch in the moonlight, and there was a snapping and crackling and swishing among the poplars, and immediately the slump of his body upon the turf below."

Chivalry pushes romanticism to the furthest bounds in making lovers of kings and queens, kings and queens of lovers. These stories purport to be told from the French of Nicolas de Caen and most of them begin: "I abridge, as heretofore, at discretion; and the result is that to the Norman cleric appertains whatever the tale may have of merit, whereas what you find distasteful in it you must impute to my delinquency in skill rather than in volition." There is Alianora, the Queen of Henry III, whose wreckage of England led to the Barons' War. *The Sestina* tells how she called upon the pedant, Osmund Heleigh, brother to the Earl of Brudenel, and how he brought her safely to her own place, then fell in duel with Gui Camoys; how, afterward, Alianora became a good queen reigning with wisdom. *The Scabbard* relates an episode in the history of Richard II. He had relinquished England and become the playmate of the world; but anon returned to the Welsh border, where he lived in humble guise. There he loved Branwen, for whose sake he

slew his igonminious rival and for whose sake he
surrendered the throne to King Henry. The author
repeats this motive of surrender in a better story,
The Navarrese, the tale of Antoine Riczio and Jehane,
Countess of Rougemont, later Duchess of Brittany,
later Queen of England, wife of Henry IV. But the
choice of most readers of this perfectly wrought collection of beautiful happenings is *The Fox Brush,* the
romance of Henry V and Katherine of France. Per-
sonally, we prefer *The Housewife,* a story of the good
Queen Philippa, wife to Edward III. The author's
sense of humor agreeably emerges in the letter the
Queen writes her royal husband and, previously, in her
management of Prince Lionel.

So in this volume Mr. Cabell approached more
nearly his ideal. But he begins to comprehend that
the Lady Ettarre may not be touched by mortal
man . . .

The Certain Hour (1916) is the latest volume of
this author's short stories. Its ten numbers are ar-
ranged chronologically, beginning with the year 1210
and progressing by easy stages to the present. The
first, *Belhs Cavaliers,* rehearses in flawless narrative
the climactic episode between Beatritz, sister-in-law of
William Prince of Orange, and her lover Raimbaut
de Vaquieras. The refinement of ideal love is vitalized
in the crucial moment. He will not permit her to
take her own life, great though the need; for the Church
declares suicide a deadly sin. In order, therefore, that

he may suffer for her throughout eternity, he kneels
to beg her forgiveness for the act he is about to com-
mit. He will kill her, and then himself. But the
author prevents the extreme sacrifice and gives the
lovers a happy end.

The reader will observe that nearly all the characters
in this volume are drawn from history; that love is
the dominant passion, as in former collections; that
all the adventures are excursions in Beauty. The title
may indicate a growing interest in short story technique; but it was hardly necessary for Mr. Cabell to
improve upon his art after the initial *The Line of Love.*
One curious point is that the quality of Shakespeare's
passion is different from that of others, and that the
dedication of the book is in harmony with *Judith's
Creed.*

Mr. Cabell's discriminating workmanship may best
be indicated by a passage which reveals, also, his joy
in the working:

"Kennaston never in his life found any other playthings comparable to those first wide-margined 'galley-
proofs' of *The Audit at Storisende.* Here was the
word, vexatiously repeated within three lines, which
must be replaced by a synonym; and the clause which,
when transposed, made the whole sentence gain in
force and comeliness; and the curt sentence whose addition gave clarity to the paragraph, much as a pinch
of alum clears turbid water; and the vaguely unsatisfactory adjective, for which a jet of inspiration sug-

gested a substitute, of vastly different meaning, in
the light of whose inevitable aptness you marveled over
your preliminary obtuseness. . . ."

It is not by chance that his earlier works challenge
comparison with Maurice Hewlett's in theme and manner, that sprightly passages of *Gallantry* recall Anthony Hope's *Dolly Dialogues*. He served his apprenticeship, but with swiftness. It is not by chance
that the story in his latest volume wherein he presents
a word artificer at his task is a story about William
Shakespeare. The woman was "quite certain perdur-
able writing must spring from a surcharged heart,
rather than from a re-arrangement of phrases." But
the Master was exclaiming on a harsh and ungram-
matical clash of sibilants—that Master who would have
said, "to live untroubled and weave beautiful and win-
some dreams is the most desirable of human fates."

It will not be forgotten that Mr. Cabell is a gene-
alogist, and that his labors of research have strengthened his knowledge of the past. The list of his books
shows a nice balance between his constructive work
and his investigations in family history. *Branchiana,
A Record of the Branch Family in Virginia* (1906)
was succeeded in 1911 by *Branch of Abingdon,* and in
1915 by *The Majors and Their Marriages.* Nor, although he is primarily an artist in narrative, will it
be forgotten that he is both poet and essayist. For
his short stories abound in verse specimens of the

sort which the age of chivalry affected, and which cleverly contributed reality to various scenes. And the fact may be gathered independently from his *From the Hidden Way* (1916). And, briefly, as to his essays, he has expressed opinions upon a variety of subjects in *Beyond Life* (1919).

Other longer works not herein mentioned previously are *Cords of Vanity* (1909), *The Soul of Melicent* (1913), reprinted in 1920 under the title *Domnei,* and *The Rivet in Grandfather's Neck* (1915).

It is cause for rejoicing that Mr. Cabell's stories appear with increasing frequency, in *McClure's* and *The Century.* In general, they carry on the traditions of his earlier volumes, with a leaning to the Jurgenesque. His *Porcelain Cups (The Century,* 1919*)* was adjudged by the Committee from the Society of Arts and Sciences one of the best stories published in the year and is reprinted in the Society's first volume of *O. Henry Memorial Award Prize Stories* (1920).

This author should only have just begun his career, since he is not yet forty-two years of age. He was born in Richmond, Virginia, April 14, 1879. His life has offered the variety a writer of the studio finds helpful; after graduation at the College of William and Mary, 1898, he worked on *The Richmond Times, The New York Herald* and *The Richmond News.* He has been historian of the Virginia Society of Colonial Wars and of the Virginia Society of the Sons of the

American Revolution. In connection with his researches, he has travelled much, in America, France and England. He was married in 1913, since which time he has lived for the most part at Dumbarton Grange, Dumbarton, Virginia.

Mr. Cabell's Short Stories:

> *The Line of Love*, 1905.—Revised Edition, 1921.
> *Gallantry*, 1907.—Revised Edition, 1922.
> *Chivalry*, 1909.—Revised Edition, 1921.
> *The Certain Hour*, 1916.
> *Figures of Earth*, 1921.

CHAPTER III

IN the twentieth century it is possible for one, before she is forty years of age, to be a doctor of philosophy, master of half a dozen languages, a successful novelist, story-writer, wife, mother, and war worker. Dorothy Canfield is all of these, and in addition, after much travel and living abroad, she is an American of Americans. Her Americanism is the essence of her greatness and her significance for the literature of to-day and to-morrow. It is the foundation on which rise her achievements.

How has she managed to do so much? First, the circumstances of her birth were favorable. Daughter of the late James Hulme Canfield, who was President of the University of Kansas at the time she was born, and his wife Flavia Camp Canfield, artist, Dorothea Frances made her entry dowered with unusual intelligence and æsthetic sensibility. She was born, February 17, 1879, in perhaps the most American region of America, if the land of the free be symbolized by wind-blown skies and boundless plains. The Mid-West setting, however, was balanced by the girl's

academic activities at Lawrence and later at the Ohio
State University, of which her father was President
when she took her A. B. degree in 1899. Thus briefly
are indicated the Americanism and the general culture
which made possible a Dorothy Canfield. The
languages, German, Italian, Spanish, and Danish are
explained by her travel; French she acquired in her
mother's studio in Paris. When her father accepted
the Chair of Librarian at Columbia University, she
extended her researches in the graduate school recently
opened, and in 1904 took the doctorate degree in Comparative Literature. She combined her knowledge of
French and English in her thesis: *Corneille and Rac-
ine in England* (1904).

Meantime, in 1902, Miss Canfield while working
on her dissertation, served as Secretary of the Horace
Mann School, connected with the Teachers College of
Columbia University, a position she held for three
years. Then out of her association with the late Professor George R. Carpenter, she was urged to further
writing. With Professor Carpenter she compiled a
text-book, *English Rhetoric and Composition* (1906),
and about the same time began to publish stories in
magazines. Mr. Grant Overton remarks in *The
Women Who Make Our Novels*: "Before *The Squirrel Cage* [published in 1912], Mrs. Fisher was merely
the author of a few text-books. After it she was an
important figure in American fiction." From the angle
of the public, and in a deeply sardonic sense this is

more than true. For the reading public would be as indifferent to the scholar who produced a work on the French dramatists as to the technician who contributed to a book on the art and business of writing. It should be stated, however, that many of Mrs. Fisher's stories were published years before they were gathered up into *Hillsboro People* and *The Real Motive*. Some of them appeared as early as 1906: *The Bedquilt, The Philanthropist and the Peaceful Life* —reprinted, 1915, under the title *Fortune and the Fifth Card*—and *The Great Refusal*. Undoubtedly the success of *The Squirrel Cage* hastened their preservation in book form.

On May 9, 1907, Dorothy Canfield was married to John Redwood Fisher, of New York. Shortly after the event, they went to Arlington, Vermont, where they found far removed from city commerce and pandemonium a house adapted to the art of living and working. No one can read *At the Foot of Hemlock Mountain*, the essay that introduces *Hillsboro People* (1915), and fail to be convinced of the real life that Dorothy Canfield Fisher experiences in the town of Arlington. For the essay is reflective of her own village. Acording to her sentiments, "Like any other of those gifts of life which gratify insatiable cravings of humanity, living in a country village conveys a satisfaction which is incommunicable. . . ." "City dwellers make money, make reputations (good and bad), make museums and subways, make charitable institutions, make with a hysteric rapidity, like excited spiders, more and yet more complications in the mazy labyrinths of their lives, but they never make each others' acquaintances . . . and that is all that is worth doing in the world. . . ."

It is proof of her wisdom and of her fathoming the meaning of the verb *to live* that, after the great cities New York, Paris, and Rome, she turned, a single-hearted American, to the country, not to escape from but to mingle with her fellow beings. All novels, she says, seem badly written, faint and faded, in comparison with the life which palpitates up and down the village street. She commiserates the city dweller who lives through "canned romances, adventures, tragedies, farces," as one who passes blindfold through life.

Yet it is not to be forgotten that Mrs. Fisher is a product of balance, and she continues to maintain that balance. With her husband and children she adventures away from Arlington and seeks what she needs by way of change. In 1911-1912 they spent the winter in Italy. In Rome, Mrs. Fisher met Madame Montessori and worked with her at the Children's House at the same time she was translating the works later published under the titles *A Montessori Mother* (1913) and *Mothers and Children* (1914).

Her mounting fame rose with a greater climax, the world war. The years from 1914 to 1919 are crowded with the work of the woman as of the writer. In Paris, she edited a magazine for soldiers; she took care of the

refugees; she organized two children's homes at Gue-
thary, in the south of France; she organized at Meudon
a home and day nursery for munition workers' children; she ran a camp on the edge of the war zone.
Meantime, *Hillsboro People* (1915) and *The Bent
Twig* (1915), were followed by *The Real Motive*
(1916), *Fellow Captains* (1916) and *Understood
Betsey* (1917). *Home Fires in France* (1918) and
The Day of Glory (1919) placed a gold laurel-leaf
crown on the author's work in France. The sketches
and stories under these two titles are among the most
popular of the many works written during the war
and immediately after the armistice.

Although Mrs. Fisher is first of all a novelist she is
next a short-story writer. In the future, the literary
historian will class her tales, in all probability, as
of three periods: before the war, during the war, and
after the war. At the moment, the first two divisions
are the ones which concern us.

Hillsboro People (1915) and *The Real Motive*
(1916) may be discussed as if the titles were merged
in one volume; for the stories divided between the two
cover the years from 1906 to 1915, with the over-
flow of 1916 in the latter volume. To read these collections is to feel the invigorating influence of a fresh
buoyant optimism, to catch glimpses of a generous
sympathy, to come face to face with a democracy which
in the best sense is no respecter of persons, whether
differentiated by age or social conditions or culture

The stories have their settings in the Middle West, in and near New York, in Paris, and in Hillsboro. (All in the collection of 1915 are connected in one way or other with Hillsboro). The range of time is from the eighteenth century, for example, *In New New England* (first published in 1910), to the present, the time of the greatest number. The characters reflect the author's many-sided interests: the librarian is represented in J. M., hero of *Avunculus* (1909), and in Miss Martin (*Hillsboro's Good Luck,* 1908); the artist is found in Fallères, who painted the college president *(Portrait of a Philosopher,* 1911), in *An April Masque* (1910), in *The Deliverer* (1909), and triumphantly in *The Artist* (1911). The college professor figures in *An Academic Question* (1910), and *A Thread without a Knot* (originally entitled, when first published in 1910, *An Unframed Picture*). A baby is the hero of *Vignettes from a Life of Two Months* (1915), old men are heroes of *The Heyday of the Blood* (1909), and *As a Bird Out of the Snare* (1908); an old lady is the humble heroine of *The Bedquilt* (1906). Nor does this list exhaust the little world of her story people; nor is her understanding of any one diminished by her equal understanding of the others. The poor artist in *An April Masque* is not unworthy as a companion to the Artist; for life and ideals are greater than art —so exceedingly vaster that the difference between the best art and the worst becomes negligible in the sum of things. So, also, the difference between old and modern education is inconsiderable in the march of the years. *In New New England,* Captain Winthrop undertakes the education of Hannah Sherwin, aided thereto by a work entitled "The Universal Preceptor; being a General Grammar of Art, Science, and Useful Knowledge." "Up in our garret we have the very book he used," continues the narrator, "and modern research and science have proved that there is scarcely a true word in it. But don't waste any pity on Hannah for having such a mistaken teacher, for it is likely enough, don't you think, that research and science a hundred years from now will have proved that there is scarcely a word of truth in our school-books of to-day? It really doesn't seem to matter much."

Her sympathy for the boy or girl cribbed in by circumstance flashes out repeatedly, as in *The Bedquilt, The Deliverer,* and *As a Bird.* Aunt Mehetabel aged sixty-eight makes her initial appeal to the reader through the fact that she seems to be regarded a nonentity in the house of her brother. She must ask, even, for scraps to make the quilt. It is no ordinary quilt. Into its perfection go months of work laboriously materializing a design made possible through previous practice and the inspiration of a soul barred from other outlets of expression. When it is finished, her brother declares it must be sent to the fair; later, in an unwonted burst of generostity, he arranges for her to go. When she returns she has nothing to relate, except about the quilt, which has taken the first prize.

One sees her sitting there before the glass case, absorbed in rapt contemplation of her own handiwork, marveling that she has done it, deaf to the sounds of the fair, blind to all other sights. *The Deliverer* is a story of New England, in 1756, of the days when love of nature was held a sin, when the love of God was not greater than the fear of hell fire. Nathaniel Everett, son to the preacher, believes he is lost: "My heart is all full of carnal pleasures and desires. To look at the sun on the hillside—why I love it so that I forget my soul—hell—God—" His seizures do not avail to cure him. He says to Colonel Hall and M. LeMaury, who were to be his deliverers, "I—I would rather look at a haw-tree in blossom than meditate on the Almighty!" It is a turning point in Nathaniel's life when dying Colonel Hall goes calmly out with the final words to the Rev. Mr. Everett: "*I* don't believe in your damned little hell!" Nathaniel's final deliverance, the story suggests by the dénouement (placed first in the story order), is through Le Maury, whose name the boy took and by whose aid he became a great artist. *As a Bird Out of the Snare* shows triumph of spirit; but it is cause for tears to reflect that Jehiel Hawthorn was bound, year after year, to the farm while the pine tree grew high into heaven. He had vowed, "Before it's as tall as the ridge-pole of the house, I'll be on my way."

Not least of Mrs. Fisher's accomplishments is her faithful portrayal of the expressionless New England man and woman. Mehetabel is speechless when she tries to speak of the glories of her quilt; though she longs with her whole soul to convey the splendor of her vision, she falters. She dismisses recollections of hymn-book phraseology as not quite the thing. "Finally, 'I tell you it looked real well!' she assured them." So in *Petunias* (1912) Grandma Pritchard comes to the point in her rehearsal where the husband, who she had heard was killed at Gettysburg, returns. "I tell you—I tell you—*I was real glad to see him!*" So in *Flint and Fire* (1915) Emma Hulett "stopped short in the middle of the floor, looked at me silently, piteously, and found no word." And so Lem (*In Memory of L. H. W.*, entitled when originally published in 1912, *The Hillsboro Shepherd*) died, saying, "I'm—I'm real tired."

But such dumb-strickenness is a characteristic not only of New Englanders. *In Home Fires in France*, when Pierre *(The Permissionaire)* returns, he and his wife utter scream after scream of joy, "ringing up to the very heavens, frantic, incredulous, magnificent joy." But after the first wild cries had rocketed to the sky, "they had no words, no words at all." When André *(On the Edge,* in *The Day of Glory)* returns, Jeanne "knew nothing but that he was there, that she held him in her arms."

More than one critic has declared the stories in *Home Fires in France* to be the finest works of fiction produced by any American in the course of the war. Writ-

ten, it is reported, while Mrs. Fisher's little daughter
was convalescing from illness, they result from her
long familiarity with the French people and her "two
years intense experience in war work." Her passionate
sympathy for the oppressed nation thrills, vibrant,
throughout the collection. *The Real Motive* and *Hillsboro People* are but the peaceful expression of a heart
aflame in *Home Fires*. Dedicated to General Pershing,
whom Dorothy Canfield had known in Kansas when
she was a little girl, the book contains sketches, essays
and stories. Besides *The Permissionaire*, already mentioned, there are three other narratives, *A Little Kansas
Leaven, The First Time After,* and *La Pharmacienne.
Vignettes from Life at the Rear, The Refugee,* and
Eyes for the Blind lack the action that characterizes
those named first; but all, alike, are readable, and all
are designated as "fiction."

The theme of *The Permissionaire* is at once a con-
solation and a call to carry on. "What was in the
ground, alive, they could not kill," and so Pierre reclaimed his asparagus, Paulette her peonies, and the
man went back to the front after his furlough and the
rebuilding of his destroyed home with a memory of
the peas he had planted thrusting their green leaves
above the soil. *A Little Kansas Leaven* means that a
homely, ignorant girl roused by the call from France,
spent her small savings to reach Paris and to work
there so long as her few hundreds of dollars held out,
and that later she returned to Marshallton, Kansas,

with a straightforward story that speedily established
an ambulance.   This leaven worked before America
entered the war, and if the dénouement has in this
brief summary the suggestion of propaganda, it was
needed even when the story first appeared in *The Pictorial Review*, August, 1918. But the struggle of
Ellen Boardman is very real, and the absence of love
and beauty leaves a stark simplicity which is somehow
mightily convincing that it all happened.

The First Time After reveals Mrs. Fisher's ability
to put herself in another's place, from the stony despair
that succeeds blindness to the moment when the heart
is stirred by some natural touch to renewed feeling.
"He stooped and felt in his fingers the lace-like grace
of a fern-stalk. The sensation brought back to him
with shocking vividness all his boyhood, sun-flooded,
gone forever. . . . He flung himself down in the
midst of the ferns, the breaking-point come at last,
beating his forehead on the ground. . . . Dreadful
tears ran down from his blind eyes upon the ferns."
Later, he heard a thrush, "trying his voice wistfully."
And, later yet, he laughs, the first time since his
blindness.

La Pharmacienne pictures the sheltered life of
Madeleine, wife of the pharmacist; then, in contrast,
her heroic struggle to live and to keep her children
alive; and, finally, her successful effort to save the
pharmacy. Here, as in the other stories, the indomitable spirit of the French race interfuses itself through

pages written by an American woman. The self-effacement of the Directrice, in *Eyes for the Blind,* who had
found in the lists of the dead "two long years before,
the name which alone gave meaning to her life"; the
self-effacement of Amieux (in *Vignettes*), who refused the *croix de guerre* because its possession would
indicate to his mother that he had been in danger;
the self-effacement of the singing group described in
The Refugee—such effacement means national survival. The Marseillaisé has stirred its millions since
the time of Rouget de l'Isle, but never has it rung
more bravely than when the school children of Cousin
Jean sang it, sang the first stanza, the second stanza
and the chorus—and the elders joined in. Their singing might have meant death for all; but "There
were three hundred voices shouting it out, the tears
streaming down our cheeks." Never has it swelled
more triumphantly than in *The Day of Glory* (1919)
when the throngs of Paris swept to the Place de la
Concorde to salute the Statue of Strasbourg. And
Dorothy Canfield was there and rushed out into the
street and became a part of the spirit of thanksgiving
and shared her feelings with us across the sea:

> *"Allons, enfants de la patrie,*
> *Le Jour de Gloire est arrivé!*

The houses echoed to those words, repeated and
repeated by every band of jubilant men and women

and children who swept by, waving flags and shouting:

> *Come, children of our country,*
> *The Day of Glory is here!"*

Of this second and briefer volume, the opening piece, *On the Edge,* has been proclaimed the best story its author has written. This tribute is higher praise than it deserves and underestimates Mrs. Fisher's other narratives; but it is admirable in its restrained account of a brave Frenchwoman's struggle to protect and keep alive her family of six, children and foster-children, and for the convincing suggestion of her being 'on the edge,' hovering on the border of insanity. André, she dreamed, had come home. But there was the watch he had left for his oldest son! And the reader has a sudden revelation of the soldier heart: he had known she was driven almost past the bounds of sanity and that the gold case would remind her his visit had been not a dream but a throbbing reality. Or this is the interpretation that some of us like to make. But if there had not been the watch, there would have risen some other mute evidence of his presence to cheer her and restore her languishing courage.

Without crossing the border-line between sentiment and sentimentality, these stories pull constantly at the emotions. Has any man or woman read either volume without tears?

The struggles Mrs. Fisher finds of moment are between the individual and his environment *(The De-liverer)* ; between the individual and heredity *(A Good Fight and the Faith Kept,* first published as *The Con-queror,* 1916) ; between man and false standards of life *(A Sleep and a Forgetting,* first published under the title, *Gifts of Oblivion,* 1913) ; between man and eclipsed personality *(The First Time After);* the will to survive and the forces that make for destruction—almost all her French stories. The surprise ending has had small influence on her plots. Since she is primarily the novelist, avowedly interested in people, with story mechanics she concerns herself hardly at all. But *Flint and Fire* closes on a neat twist, dependent upon a trait of character; *A Sleep and a For-getting* startles by the disclosure that Warren recovered his memory eight years before he admitted the fact.

Vermont and its Green Mountains are the fit setting for a writer whose ideals are so high and whose living is so simple. If the vison of the Ideal Commonwealth ever is realized, perhaps the setting may be Hillsboro.

Mrs. Fisher's Short Stories:

Hillsboro People, 1915.
The Real Motive, 1916.
Home Fires in France, 1918.
The Day of Glory, 1919.

CHAPTER IV

ROBERT W. CHAMBERS

MR. ROBERT W. CHAMBERS is the author of some fifty volumes, including novels, short stories, nature books, poems, and one drama. Known to the majority of readers through his longer romances, he began his career as artist of the brush and gained his first literary triumph by a volume of short stories, *The King in Yellow*.

It is not possible in this résumé of Mr. Chambers's brief fiction even to take inventory of his novels, much less to voice a scientific or personal criticism or to venture upon consideration of their popularity. A complete account of so versatile and prolific a writer would discuss them as his significant accomplishment. If his admirers belong to a class of readers who seek sensation or revel in romance pushed to the utmost bounds of credibility, it is also true that his disclaimers belong to a class that objects, on principle and on hearsay, to reading him at all. The truth about his work lies not in extremes, but it is conceded that the extremist speaks with greater apparent force and picturesqueness.

Some years ago, Mr. Frederic Taber Cooper wrote an article on Mr. Chambers*, which was later attacked in part by Mr. John Curtis Underwood†. Mr. Underwood says, "If Mr. Chambers thoroughly deserves to be called the prince of wholesale and cheap illusion, of commercialized darkness and flippant immorality in American fiction, if he gets the highest current prices for literary lies and extravagant frivolity based on false social distinction and exclusively patrician ideals; if continually he assumes more than he proves, and alternately professes the most inconsequent triviality in his treatment of contemporary life and a pose of the social reformer of society from the inside, who satirizes what he exploits; then it is small wonder that a comparatively large and unsophisticated section of the reading public, who still buy and read his books, are at a loss just where and how to place him." Here is the expression of an extremist, obviously a thinker concerned about ethical values.

But the critic who is artist before he is social reformer will have a different word. Mr. Rupert Hughes, in writing of Mr. Chambers, spoke of his "unusual eye for color, and his delight in beauty of every sort," and he praised *The Fighting Chance:* "The book has a largeness of sympathy, a breadth of construction, and a finish of detail that give it a high place among American novels." Mr. Underwood

* See *Some American Story Tellers*, by Frederic Taber Cooper, Henry Holt and Co., 1911.
† In *Literature and Insurgency*, Mitchell Kennerley. 1914.

wrote: "Books like *The Fighting Chance* have more
to do with the tragedies of the divorce-court and the
stock exchange than either Mr. Chambers or critics
like Mr. Cooper are likely to imagine." Without al-
lowing the relation of art to morality to detain us,
we may assert that the critic who regards literature as
an artistic medium will see distinctive and distinguished
values in the narratives of Mr. Chambers; the critic
who regards literature as a vehicle for propaganda
may find in them definite forces for evil. There are,
of course, few moralist-critics who exclude from themselves the artist, as there are few artist-critics who
exclude from themselves the moralist. In any event,
it will be our pleasure to notice his marked characteristics in his briefer fiction.

Mr. Chambers reveals himself in his short stories a
man of the world, acquainted with states and kingdoms; a specialist in the art of the brush, in rugs, in
armor, in butterflies, in dogs; a historian with a fine
sense of historical perspective and a student who employs conscientious methods of research. He has written stories of Paris—the Latin quarter, in particular;
stories of artists at home and abroad; stories of game-
keepers and fire-wardens in the Adirondacks and of
millionaires on shooting preserves in Florida; many
stories of beautiful women and brave men; stories of
disordered brains; stories derived from French history, the Civil War in America and the World War;
stories of wild fancy and of the supernatural; stories

exploiting the back-to-nature cry and the simple life; stories that are humorous prophecies in the realm of wireless and mental telepathy. Nor is the list complete. He might say of himself with Bacon, "I have taken all knowledge to be my province."

His method, rooted in romance, has grown by what it fed on, so that the strongest criticism against his short stories is that they represent romance run mad. Yet, skilled technician that he is, Mr. Chambers knows how momentarily to compel belief. He throws the veil of mood upon the reader, rose color or blue; he employs the lure of realistic detail to clinch probability, while he subdues it to the spell of fantasy; he describes his settings with the consummate ease of one trained to appreciate color and form; and these scenes, which are true to nature, prevail upon the reader to accept the dramas acted in them.

His best stories, of rare beauty and spirituality, are those of the supernatural. They should live so long as theories of metempsychosis last—the subject is as old as Pythagoras—and so long as revenants return. His stories to be forgotten are those which impress upon the reader the physical charms of the bright-haired, blue-eyed heroine, approvedly through the eyes of the hero, and which would convince the reader that, within an hour or a day after meeting each other, the heroine is safely harbored in the hero's arms.

Robert W. Chambers was born in Brooklyn, May

26, 1865. He shares with his brother, Walter Boughton Chambers, the artistic gift: he was in Julian's Academy from 1886 to 1893; his brother, after taking a degree at Yale, studied architecture with Blondel in 1889. Before going to Paris, Robert was at the Art Students' League in New York, where he had as class-mate, Charles Dana Gibson. At the age of twenty-four he had painted pictures acceptable to the Salon. There is a legend that after returning to America in 1893 he and Gibson submitted sketches to *Life* and that his were taken but Gibson's returned. Urged by the writing instinct and by a desire to express himself more rapidly than the medium of the brush would allow, he produced his first novel, *In the Quarter* (1893). *The King in Yellow* (1895) made his reputation and determined his career.

His life as art student may be gleaned from certain stories in this first collection. *Rue Barrée,* which begins "one morning at Julian's," presents Kid Selby "drunk as a lord," a study of intoxication equalled only by Owen Wister's in *Philosophy Four,* and as indubitably drawn from life. In the *Street of Our Lady of the Fields,* Valentine names the artists whom she knows and who are more or less contemporaries of Mr. Chambers: Bouguereau, Henner, Constant, Laurens, Puvis de Chavannes, Dagnan and Courtois. One might also deduce from the book that while in France he had become interested in armor and falconry, and then or later in the elixir of life and metempsychosis as start-

ing points for adult fairy tales. *The Mask* and *The
Demoiselle D'Ys*, though the latter is somewhat over-
burdened with technical language, are both admirable
examples of the story-teller's art. Almost from the
first Mr. Chambers was sure of his manner. To know
one art is to know the principles of all art. Throughout this volume and all those succeeding it, the author's
training in drawing and painting serves for first aid
toward perfection of method. He might have been
thinking of himself when he wrote of Leeds in *The
Ghost of Chance* (in *The Tree of Heaven*): "The technique that sticks out like dry bones, the spineless lack
of construction, fads, pitiful eccentricities to cover in-
ability—nothing of these had ever, even in his student
days, threatened him with the pit-fall of common disaster." And if the tales here and there are already
the efflorescence of exaggerated romance, he justified
himself to himself. He said later, through the Countess in *A Journey to the Moon* (in *The Adventures of
a Modest Man*): "Romance is at least amusing; reality
alone is a sorry scarecrow clothed in the faded rags of
dreams."

In *The Yellow Sign*—to return to *The King in
Yellow*—which combines an artist and his model with
a supernatural theme, the author finds kinship with
Edgar Allan Poe. The horror achieved through the
coffin-worm watchman, the hearse and the yellow sign
is unforgettable; and the mysterious book, *The King in
Yellow*, so dire in its effects here and elsewhere, stands

for the power of suggestion which Mr. Chambers grasped at the outset. Outside of the stories mentioned, the collection sows the seed for the more regrettable harvest-portions of the author's later achievement. One striking exception should be noted. The beginning of the first story, *The Repairer of Reputations,* must draw a gasp from every reader who reads with awareness that it was written a quarter of a century before the year 1920 had dawned: "Towards the end of the year 1920 . . .The end of the war with Germany had left no visible scars upon the republic. . . . And even in New York a sudden craving for decency had swept away a great portion of the existing horrors. . . . In the following winter (1911-1912) began that agitation for the repeal of the laws prohibiting suicide, which bore its final fruit in the month of April, 1920, when the first Government Lethal Chamber was opened on Washington Square." With all due allowance for failure to foresee every detail accurately, no one will hesitate after reading the first three pages of this tale, to add to Mr. Chambers's other qualifications that of seer. For what he lacks in exactness is more than counterbalanced by the comprehensiveness of his vision. . . . It is to be hoped, however, that the Lethal Chamber never will be established!

Mr. Arthur Bartlett Maurice has pointed out, in *The New York of the Novelists,* that Mr. Chambers was living at 60 Washington Square South when he wrote *The King* and that not only the Square but its environs are used in a number of his early stories. But "The Robert W. Chambers of the later books, so far as the Borough of Manhattan is concerned, is essentially associated with the vast expanse of city which comes under the head of Tea, Tango, and Toper Land—in a word, the great hotels, clubs, and theatres; the sweep of Fifth Avenue from Murray Hill to the Plaza, and beyond along the east side of the Park, the Park itself, and the structures that line the Riverside Drive."

The Maker of Moons appeared the same year as *The King in Yellow.* Of the eight stories bound in its covers, the title narrative of some fifteen thousand words illustrates the author's progress in the unreal and the horrible. It has to do with the alleged discovery that gold may be synthesized, with the repulsive creature that accompanies the manufactured metal— "something soft and yellow with crab-like legs, all covered with coarse yellow hair," with Yue-Laou, who lived in the moon and perverted the Xin or good genii of China, with Yeth-hounds, or spirits of murdered children, passing through the woods at night, with the members of the Kuen-Yin, or sorcerers of China, and with Ysonde, the daughter of her who was created from a white lotus bud. Unreal, undoubtedly. But even the most fantastic of these motives are not without parallel: Eden Phillpotts's *Another Little Heath Hound* is the counterpart of the Yeth hound; James Branch Cabell's *The Hour of Freydis** recalls the

* *McClure's*, June, 1920.

origin of Ysonde. Mr. Chambers makes immediately
credible all these marvels by a device as old as DeFoe.
Tiffany's, the Metropolitan Museum, and the Cana-
dian woods are real, and they are the factual scenes
of the tale; Cockney-speaking Howlett and Game-
keeper David contribute to reality through person and
dialect; the narrator Cardenhe aids conviction through
his matter-of-fact style—notwithstanding the fantastic
passages, which are integrated through contrast; his
friends, Pierrepont and Barris, by their worldly pursuits, increase it.

Mr. Chambers is a necromancer here, as elsewhere.
The moons Yue-Lauo conjured up rise about you like
golden bubbles; later horror overwhelms you: "Up out
of the black lake reared a shadow, a nameless, shape-
less mass, headless, sightless, gigantic, gaping from end
to end." This power of magician he displays most
beautifully in *An Ideal Idol,* which is Chapter IV of
The Green Mouse, and part of the first story. He pursues his uncanny description of the horrible in *A Matter of Interest* (in *The Mystery of Choice,* 1896).
The thermosaurus in *A Matter of Interest* is a close
relative of the sea-monster in Kipling's *A Matter of
Fact,* copyright in 1892. It is interesting to compare
the tales, to notice the American writer's inventive
facility and his riot of imagination in contrast to the
economy and greater convincingness of Kipling.

In this volume, *The Mystery of Choice,* the author
continues his stories of the supernatural. *The Mes-*

senger, a ghost tale, covers the gap from 1760 to 1896; it uses thirty-nine skulls, a death's head moth (the messenger) and the gruesome incident of the Black Priest by way of steps to the climax: "We were looking into the eye-sockets of a skull." In conjunction with the modern Breton setting, with the simple minor characters of the action and with the lives of Lys and her husband, they produce sufficient plausibility for entertainment. At the other extreme from this longish story is *"Passeur!"* a brief *conte,* after the French models. The ghost returns, through a voice, to one who wished to be ferried over the stream, answering as in life to his "Passeur!", "V'la Monsieur!" He marvels, "and when he raised his eyes he saw that the Ferryman was Death."

The Haunts of Men (1898) is characterized by four stories of the Civil War, not one of which, however, is so satisfying as *In the Name of the Most High* (in *The Maker of Moons*). The best story in the volume is *The Whisper.* One of the first fruits of the Chinaman in New York, it furnished seed to succeeding writers; to-day the harvest is profuse. That the whisper itself effects surprise in the dénouement is noteworthy because Mr. Chambers so infrequently employs a terminal shock. The poignant drama is presented with the economy of an etching.

The Latin Quarter, too, continues to find representation, and the familiar figures of Elliott, Clifford *et al* reappear. *Enter the Queen,* with its substitute cornet-player who did *not* play was probably funny when it was written—as it is not now. Humor is largely a matter of fashion and successive eras must produce their own styles. The rattlesnake in *Yo Espero* and the shark that was the Collector of the Port are proof that their creator was still pursuing, with an eye to the reading public, tragic signs and symbols. He subdues them here to a happy end.

Mr. Chambers has a genius for titles. Occasionally he adapts a well-worn phrase, again he chooses an exotic feminine name, frequently he uses colors— green, yellow, red and blue—and he drew from the following stanza for this volume:

"How shall we seem each to the other, when,
  On that glad day, immortal, we shall meet—
Thou who, long since, didst pass with hastening feet—
  I, who still wait here, in the haunts of men?"

A Young Man in a Hurry (1903) consists largely of society stories of the superficial variety. The title story illustrates adequately the setting, the character types, and the method of the author throughout. A young man, the hero of the narrative, rushes from his office to a cab in which he expects to find his waiting sister. After a little, he discovers that the lady, who is not his sister, has expected her brother to join her. She and her brother were to hasten to Florida to rescue a younger sister from a hurried marriage. It develops that the hero and his sister were in a hurry

to reach St. Augustine, where a younger brother was
about to marry precipitately. The rest is easy, including the mating of the two who meet at the beginning.
We leave them looking for the benevolent clergyman
whom they saw immediately as they entered the diner
on the Eden Limited pulling out from the station.
The Pilgrim and *One Man in a Million* introduce lovers somewhat less headlong; *Pasque Florida* varies
the young love theme in reuniting a divorced couple.
Mr. Chambers has acquired the facility of moving
about with the idle rich, from town house to country
estate—an ease he has used to great gathering of
shekels these many years.

Having followed in summary Mr. Chambers's course
in writing brief fiction, and always remembering that
a number of his novels must be examined for his complete progress, we approach a sharp apex in *The Tree
of Heaven* (1907). He has extended his chain of
stories; but he has not since projected a climactic peak
so far into the ether. In this volume he expressed in
narrative form better than he will ever express again
his speculations on life and death and his envisioning
of the high possibilities of spirit. It should be remembered to his credit that he used the title a dozen
years before the English author. Miss Sinclair's Tree
of Heaven is the living ailanthus, however, whereas
that of Mr. Chambers is one woven in an ancient rug.
Ghosts, metempsychosis, separation of soul and body
and allied themes underlie most of the dramas here

enacted. Singly or in combination, they are at the basis of *The Carpet of Belshazzar, The Sign of Venus, The Case of Mr. Helmer, The Bridal Pair,* and *Out of the Depths.* Loss of memory and its restoration he was one of the first to handle, in *The Golden Pool.* Many changes have been rung on this *motif,* down to Wilbur Daniel Steele's *God's Mercy (Pictorial Review,* July, 1920) and all manifestations of amnesia and aphasia possible to handle in the shorter story. *The Swastika* humorously pits the power of the swastika against that of the crystal, and half-seriously, half-humorously reflects the spirit of the early twentieth century in its resurrection of rabbit feet, clover leaves, horseshoes and other luck symbols. *The Carpet* and *The Bridal Pair* are the pick of the volume; the first, for glowing imagination and conviction; the second, for spiritual beauty. *The Carpet* is a powerful orchestration of the *motif* first sounded in *The Demoiselle D'Ys.* It is, by and large, the finest short story Mr. Chambers ever wrote.

He was reflecting the spirit of the age in other ways. By the year 1908 the use of the wireless telegraph was well established, and the fictionists were following the trail of the scientists. Kipling's *Wireless (Traffics and Discoveries,* 1904) suggested that a wireless operating plant caught a message from the air and transmitted it to a drugstore clerk. Lines from the *Ode to a Nightingale* came to the counterpart of Keats in such a way as to hint that the spirit of Keats, or the same controlling force which impelled him to compose the Ode, was in contact with the sending apparatus, and was disturbing the transmission between the two experimental stations.   Mr. Chambers surpassed the British author in fancy and daring, as may be observed from a survey of *The Green Mouse* (1910).   Destyn has invented a machine which, taking advantage of the fact that the earth is circumscribed by wireless currents of electricity, is able to intercept the subconscious personalities of two people of opposite sex and to connect them.   The result is union which, though inevitable in the course of the ages, the machine has accelerated.   It aids destiny in pairing off and, incidentally, helps the author to achieve a story about each mating.   The work may be regarded as so many of its companion books are to be regarded: humorously prophetic of a distant fact or gently satirical of those persons quick to catch up fads, from mental telepathy to Ouija.

The business of thought transference he had just satirized in the same fashion in *Some Ladies in Haste* (1908).   The link that binds the numbers in this volume is Manners, with his uncanny gift of suggestion, the power to effect radical change in the lives of men and women, and to provide for them suitable mates.   Five couples, paired off, are the actors in the several dramas.   Under cover of his larger satirical purpose, he strikes a few playful blows at the back-to-nature cult and the ideal of the brotherhood of man;

at the same time, he seizes the opportunity for exploiting his very real interest in butterflies. He might well have used for his title *Some Ladies in Trees:* the volume opens with a pursuit that ends in the umbrageous foliage of an oak and closes with one that allows the hero to rescue the heroine from the crotch of a maple.

In *The Adventures of a Modest Man* (1911), the author returns to Paris. The thinnest of envelopes serves to hold the unrelated stories, produced ostensibly as fiction, by Williams, a character in the outer action. These pseudo-efforts of Williams include lovely artist models in New York, Vassar girls on the Caranay, and French countesses on the Seine, with the right gentleman properly directed by Fate, Chance and Destiny. Grotesque, if readable, some of these Destiny driven conclusions. The author remarks somewhere in the book, "Everybody's lives are full of grotesque episodes. The trouble is that the world is too serious to discover any absurdity in itself. We writers have to do that for it." Apology or justification, this statement explains the position of the author which apparently shifts from running with the hare to hunting with the hounds. He loves nature, for example; but he recognizes the absurdity in a fashion of the hour which equips young women with green nets and three-cornered envelopes and sends them in pursuit of butterflies along the Bronx River, or which commands them to discard the garments of the modern world and, dressed in cheese-cloth, armed with bow and arrow, to roam Dianas on well-conducted estates. . . . "Eccentricity is the full-blown blossom of mediocrity," he also permits one of his heroes to confess.

The Better Man, technically among the best of the author's works, represents in their maturity his exaggerations of type and his wizard-like realization of the improbable. The first five stories are set in forest preserves of New York State; *The Better Man* has its climax in Florida, as have five or six others of the fifteen stories in the volume. The ladies, if found in rustic setting, are not native to it; exotics by some chance transplanted to the backwoods they retain amid primitive conditions their hot-house attributes, as though cherished by all the safeguards known to civilization. In real life they would wither or freeze or become toughened to endure. The villain is, usually, some native who is lawless, though supposedly a representative of order, and who has the fragile lady in his power. The hero is, according to formula, an agent of the Forest Conservation Commissioner, every inch a man, polished of English and manner and dress. The outcome might be fraught with considerable anxiety in real life, granted existence of previous conditions. But there is never a doubt over the dénouement of these ruffian and gentleman contests. The brave hero, without undue damage to scenery or villain, bears the fair lady back to her proper setting of culture and refinement.

Barbarians (1917) rises above the preceding collection by virtue of its theme—the Great War—the author's interest in the subject and his proximity to it. Spite of his interest, he was too remote from the Civil and the Franco-Prussian Wars to succeed with them as short-story material. Here he combines his knowledge of France, his sympathy with the character of the French girl and his antagonism to the "barbarians" in a series of appealing and sometimes thrilling dramatic pictures. His butterfly flits, too, through a story or so. It has become his symbol, as it was Whistler's. A thing beautiful in form, color, and motion; tenuous, fragile, the thing of a season; and yet emblematic of the soul. Perhaps it would have no place in a Gradgrindian scheme of the universe. . . .

Mr. Chambers once asserted that he has no hard and fast rule of composition. "Sometimes I begin with the last chapter, sometimes in the middle, and sometimes I lay out an elaborate skeleton." He also indicates that he is under no delusion as to the status of authors. At best, he says, they "are not held in excessive esteem by really busy people, the general idea being—which is usually true—that literature is a godsend to those unfitted for real work. But very few authors comprehend what is their status in a brutal, practical and humorous world." So he wrote in *Number Seven (The Better Man)*. The hero of the same story, a man of literary aspirations, probably voices the author's thoughts when he admits in a note to the heroine: "You are quite right: art is work: never idleness."

Volumes of short stories by Mr. Chambers:

The King in Yellow, 1895.
The Maker of Moons, 1895.
The Mystery of Choice, 1896.
The Haunts of Men, 1898.
A Young Man in a Hurry, 1903.
The Tracer of Lost Persons, 1906.
The Tree of Heaven, 1907.
Some Ladies in Haste, 1908.
The Green Mouse, 1910.
Adventures of a Modest Man, 1911.
The Better Man, 1916.
Barbarians, 1917.

CHAPTER V

IRVIN S. COBB

IRVIN S. COBB, of whom I have the honor to be whom, was born, successfully, in Paducah, Kentucky, almost exactly one hundred years after the signing of the Declaration of Independence in your own city, thus making it possible for future generations to celebrate both centennials simultaneously in 1976. He is a member of an old, or Southern, family, his family being fully as old as any Southern family known. It extends back without a break to the Garden of Eden."

So wrote Irvin Shrewsbury Cobb to the editor of *The Saturday Evening Post* for the issue of October 6, 1917. As Ellis Parker Butler, his fellow humorist, puts it: "He came along as a sort of Centennial Souvenir, with the miniature liberty bells that the Paducahns keep on their what-nots." As a matter of fact, his birthday is June 23rd.

His school days passed uneventfully enough, their monotony broken by much reading of Cap Collier's dime novels in a corner of the barn loft. At the age of sixteen he drove an ice-wagon; at sixteen and a

half he became contributor to the local paper. He
wrote because he wished to illustrate; but later—he
declares it was in a spirit of pure unselfishness—he
decided to give up illustrating for writing. At the
age of nineteen, in the year 1895, he became editor
of *The News* and was advertised as the youngest managing editor of a daily paper in the United States. He
wrote a column headed "Sour Mash" and, according
to Robert H. Davis, stacked up more libel suits than a
newspaper of limited capital and with a staff of local
attorneys could handle before he moved to Louisville.
He was attached to the staff of the Louisville *Evening
Post* in 1898, and remained there until his marriage
to Laura Spencer Baker, of Savannah, Georgia, June
12, 1900. Mr. Cobb then returned to Paducah, where
he was managing editor of the *News-Democrat* until
1904.

He had easily become one of the best known reporters throughout the South and determined to seek
a cosmopolitan field for the exercise of his talent. He
arrived in New York in 1904. Having made a systematic tour of the newspaper offices without success, he was fired to show what he could do through
correspondence. He sat down in his boarding house
room and wrote every city editor. By return mail he
received offers of five positions, out of which he elected
that from *The Evening Sun*.

When the Portsmouth Peace Conference met, Mr.
Cobb was sent to help report it. Finding there were

enough men to cover the proceedings, he wrote on subjects not at all related to the Conference and mailed them to his paper. The distinction of these articles gave Mr. Cobb choice of work on any paper in New York. He went over to *The World* in 1905 and remained there as staff humorist and special writer, supplying *The Evening World* and the Sunday *World* with a humorous feature until 1911.

In Louisville he had extended his local reputation through reporting the Goebel murder case; in New York, through his report of the Thaw trial, he achieved a high-water mark in journalism.

In 1907, he tried his hand at musical comedy and wrote to order in a week's time *Funabashi*. Mr. Davis has said about this effort: "The absence of a guillotine in New York State accounts for his escape from this offense." William Johnston, of *The World,* placed it one of three mistakes made by Mr. Cobb in New York. The others were his purchase of a house in Park Hill, and leaving *The World*. The author himself probably felt no deep stirrings of remorse since he repeated his offense the next year in the musical skit, *Mr. Busybody*. Mr. Davis, who was on the staff of the Sunday *World* in 1903, tells of Mr. Cobb's popularity at *The World:* "He held levee daily, in the city room—a conclave that abroad would have been a salon. The cubs and the bosses, the stars and the stalk-horses, the best and the worst of the staff attended. . . . His running-fire of conversation is like the rattle of musketry. In New York Cobb found his voice. He got the chill of the ice-wagon out of his veins; he forgot his art and came to look upon managing editors as mere casuals." *

While he was on *The World*, then, Irvin Cobb rose to first rank as reporter. And if there is a subject he is sure he understands, it is that of reporting. "I know how to go out and get a news story and how to assemble the stuff afterward," he wrote in *The American Magazine*, August, 1919. "I know how to play on a news story as though it were a concertina or a crush hat; which is to say, I know how to stretch a small story out to the length of a column, and by the same token how to pack down a big story into the compass of a paragraph." He numbers among his assets an excellent memory, the ability to photograph a scene mentally and stow it away for use, and above all, a nose for news, or sense of news values. He has also learned by long training to produce an article in the briefest time of any desired number of words. Experience gave him this gauge, and brought him to ripened reporterhood. At the age of forty-three he stated that he had been a reporter for nearly twenty-seven years. He has reported for daily papers, trade papers, weekly papers, and Sunday papers; for syndicates, press associations, periodicals and magazines.

Lingering on Mr. Cobb's newspaper work is necessary for two reasons. First of all, he is primarily the

* *The American Magazine*, May, 1911.

journalist; second, his journalism has a direct relation to and bearing upon his work in fiction. His stories, like those of Richard Harding Davis, own the style-marks of the reporter; his material in fiction is drawn from the scenes of his reportorial exploits. When he was writing *The County Trot* (*Back Home*), his wife marveled at his life-like pictures of the Kentucky characters, all of whom he had really known. She asked him how it was possible for him to remember their faces after the lapse of so many years. He said, "Why, I can close my eyes and see the knot-holes that were in the fence around that fair-ground!" This small anecdote discloses observation and memory, as the story itself illustrates his fine sense of proportion. No insignificant phase of his artistry is this of writing to scale.

November, 1910, *The Saturday Evening Post* published Mr. Cobb's first short-story, *The Escape of Mr. Trimm*. It was followed by a number of other tales; among them *An Occurrence up a Side Street,* which brought Chaucer's *Pardoner's Tale* to date, and *The Belled Buzzard,* which lifted Mr. Cobb into popular fame. To the newspaper world the name of Irvin Cobb had long been familiar when, in 1913, the volume of nine stories under the title *The Escape of Mr. Trimm* appeared. But the book extended his popularity to the layman. On January 25, 1914, *The New York Times* published a list of best stories representing the opinions of current story writers. Montague

Glass, who designed *Potash and Perlmutter,* placed first O. Henry's *A Municipal Report,* and second Irvin Cobb's *The Belled Buzzard.* Mary Stewart Cutting mentioned it one of four "among the finest." Readers who had overlooked it searched back files of the *Post* or bought the book which contains it. A number of critics to-day regard it a superlatively wrought-out and dramatically presented study in conscience. The author's processes in developing fiction may be illustrated further by its inception and germination. Mr. and Mrs. Cobb were walking in the forest near her old home when, noticing the birds of carrion circling in the sky, he remarked, "I believe I'll write a story about a buzzard." He jotted down a word or two in his note-book, thrust the book back into his pocket —and a year later wrote out the narrative.

Since 1911 he has been staff contributor to *The Saturday Evening Post.* Among his non-fictive volumes embodying *Post* contributions are: *Cobb's Anatomy,* 1912; *Cobb's Bill of Fare,* 1913; *Europe Revised,* 1914; *Roughing It De Luxe,* 1914; *"Speaking of Operations——",* 1916, and *Eating in Two or Three Languages,* 1919. The chief characteristic of all these volumes is their Cobbesque brand of humor. Whether he offers a humorous guide to dentist or waist-line, laughs at the fakirs in the realm of "vittles" and music, tells what the average American has long felt about English bath-tubs and Venetian ruins, what the tourist of the Grand Canyon thinks of the California brag and pseudo-wild young men, or takes you confidentially and frankly with him into the operating room—it matters not. He effectively combines fact and fun.

In 1914, when War was declared, Mr. Cobb made preparations for the scene of action. After a vacation at North Hatley, Canada, he sailed for Europe. In 1915 appeared *Paths of Glory,* reprinted from *The Post,* a series of first-hand impressions from his visit to the Western Front. In 1918 was published *The Glory of the Coming,* a volume of articles written abroad in the spring and summer of 1918 and cabled or mailed back for publication at home.

On April 25, 1915, after Mr. Cobb's return from his first trip to the scene of war, several hundred of his friends gave him a dinner at the Waldorf Hotel. The toasts and telegrams to him were gathered into a small volume, *Irvin Cobb, His Book,* illustrated by his friends, the cartoonists. J. E. Hodder-Williams's tribute asserts that in Europe *Paths of Glory* was being proclaimed the most vivid, most moving, most convincing of all books on the Great War.

But, meantime, what of Mr. Cobb's fiction? In 1912, as it chanced, *Back Home* antedated the book in which his first story appeared. He had discovered that the real Southerner was unknown in New York, both on the stage and in magazines. Either he was a feudal aristocrat or a poor white. Much as O. Henry in *The Four Million* broke away from the New York type and created a new, Irvin Cobb broke from the traditional Southern type and introduced the actual. He wrote of the men and women in the South as he had known them in an average community. For most of his characters he had real models and for some of the stories he had substantial basis in fact. Judge Priest, of *Back Home* and succeeding volumes, is the best representative Southerner ever found in literature. We who know the South of Tennessee, Kentucky, Mississippi and Alabama know him well. We have heard his high, whiny voice, and noticed that he speaks dialect in every-day conversation but pure English when he sits in judgment; we have seen his pinky-red face, bald head and fringe of whiskers, his baggy trousers, bunchy umbrella and palm-leaf fan. We have marveled at the keenness of his mind, albeit he will not again see sixty-five. We know his room in the court house, his cluttered desk and the drawer into which he surreptitiously thrusts his latest dime novel. We are familiar with his friends, acquaintances and helpers: Dr. Lake, Sergeant Jimmy Bagby, Comrade Pressley Harper, Deputy jailer Dink Bynum, his cook Dilsey, and his body-servant Jeff. If the author who has created Judge Priest had written nothing but the tales in which the old Judge appears he would have the right to a tablet in the Hall of Fame.

In *Back Home* the stories architecturally fittest and by their matter best calculated to evoke tears or laughter are *Words and Music,* reminiscent of the Civil

War; *The County Trot,* touching the state sport; *The Mob from Massac,* interpreting mob behavior; *Up Clay Street,* describing a circus that will rouse the most blasé reader and lead him on to the saddest climax ever combined with a circus; *When the Fighting Was Good,* telling how Pressley Harper was given a chance to redeem an error and escape two years in the penitentiary; and *Strategem and Spoils,* recounting the Judge's adventures in New York with a certain company of shearers. The presence of the Judge in each holds together the ten stories.

Old Judge Priest (1916) continues the chronicles of the Judge and his people. The general level of excellence meets that of the former series, the worthiest instances being: *The Lord Provides,* which recounts the Christian burial of a girl who had gone wrong; *A Blending of the Parables,* which describes a reunion of Company B; *Judge Priest Comes Back,* and *A Chapter from the Life of an Ant,* in which the old man respectively takes a ruling hand in a political situation and turns detective.

Local Color also appeared in 1916. The stories collected under this title were written for *The Post* in 1914, 1915 and 1916, as were those in *Old Judge Priest.* But Mr. Cobb's matter here finds diversification. An old New York theater is the setting for *The Great Auk,* Fourteenth Street and Third Avenue and the Jefferson Market court-house for *The Field of Honor;* the city and Sing Sing for *Local Color.*

First Corinthians, The Eyes of the World and *Enter the Villain* are, also, New York stories. *Enter the Villain* is reminiscent of the author's newspaper experience as surely as *The Great Auk* resulted from his incursions into drama. *Blacker Than Sin* and *The Smart Aleck* have Southern settings and characters. The only mordaciously humorous story in the whole lot is *The Smart Aleck*. The first-mentioned three of New York locale are the best, and they are tragic.

Those Times and These (1917) continues the diversity of local color and points up, here and there, the difference between past and present. In technic and interest the volume falls below the high average set by its predecessors. Judge Priest is the hero of *Ex-Fightin' Billy;* a doctor, of the rather poetical and allegorical *And There Was Light* (a new note for Mr. Cobb) ; young French warriors are the pathetic heroes of *The Garb of Men*.

Fibble, D.D. (1916), and *The Life of the Party* (1919), the first a novelette, the second a longish short-story, are inconsequential from a literary point of view. Their chief asset for Mr. Cobb lies in their extension of his humor. Fibble, D.D., a burlesque of a clerical type all too familiar, suffers from following Mr. Tarkington's Kinosling of the *Penrod* stories. *The Life of the Party*, a mad extravaganza, is a motion-picture produced on the printed page.

From Place to Place (1920) contains stories published in 1918 and 1919 in *The Post, The Red Book* and *All Story* magazines. From whatever cause or explanation, the author returns in this volume to his best accomplishment. *The Gallowsmith, Boys Will Be Boys, The Luck Piece, Hoodwinked,* and *The Bull Called Emily* run the scale from the horrifics of the hangman through the pathos of Peep O'Day's belated boyhood to the laugh in *Emily.* South and North meet: Mr. Cobb is now equally at home in each.

So far, this author's greatest services to fiction have lain in the interpretation of South to North and of generation to generation. He once wrote an article in which he summed up his relation to temporal affairs, saying he was on the spot "when the audible celluloid cuff, E. P. Roe, the pug dog, the Congress gaiter, the hammer-gun, the safety bicycle, the mustache cup, parchesi, the catcher who took 'em off the bat with his bare hands, the peach-kernel watch charm, the pousse café, the operation for dehorning the human appendix, and the Dowie movement gave way, inch by inch, to the spit-ball, the automatic ejector, the rest-cure, the cold-storage egg, Henry Ford, the cabaret, Orville and Wilbur Wright, Eat-and-Grow Thin, Pay-and-grow thinner, rural free delivery, the imported Scotch niblick, Eleanor Glyn, middling-meat at forty-two cents a pound and stewed prunes at four bits a portion in any first-class restaurant." * Small wonder that with an appreciation, even meticulous, of the foibles of human beings as he sees them "looking both ways

* *The American Magazine,* May, 1917.

at forty" he should infuse into his fiction the human quality which distinguishes it from the work of others equally good in technic.

In workmanship he has been compared to Poe and Maupassant and Kipling; in his sense of humor to Mark Twain. But these comparisons are inept. His Southern origin, his heritage from a most American father and mother, and his training in journalism offer points of contact in one way or another with each of the objects of comparison. But the same forces conspired to bestow upon him an unapproachable individuality.

Mr. Cobb's short-story volumes:

Back Home, 1912.
The Escape of Mr. Trimm, 1913.
Old Judge Priest, 1916.
Local Color, 1916.
Those Times and These, 1917.
The Life of the Party, 1919.
From Place to Place, 1920.
Sundry Accounts, 1922.

CHAPTER VI

JAMES BRENDAN CONNOLLY

THOSE who respond to the call of the sea find in the stories of James Brendan Connolly a peculiar satisfaction and delight to be encountered nowhere else in modern fiction. The sea story inevitably suggests the name of Joseph Conrad but comparison between his romances and Mr. Connolly's simple accounts of the daring and reckless deeds of brave men, of the sea and plunging boats, would be inept. In this American writer's work there is none of the strangeness, the exoticism which mark the Conrad line, nor is there any of the self-consciousness which for many readers mars the later stories of Joseph Conrad.

Mr. Connolly writes chiefly of the sea and of the men who follow it, reproducing with gripping realism the actual life of New England deep-sea fishermen. Vividly he pictures the life on board of the hardy Gloucestermen, at the same time revealing the spirit of romance and adventure which lends glamour to their humble occupation. Mr. Connolly is occupied in all of his stories with elementary passions and emotions

—courage, fear, joy and sorrow, love and hate—hence their universality of appeal. He is local, it is true, as Thomas Hardy and Kipling are, in the sense that he has chosen to write chiefly of a certain area which he knows and loves; but he is not provincial. Whether he tells of a bull-fight in Lima, a Christmas Handicap in Manchester, or a smuggling episode in St. Pierre Miquelon, his men preserve their traditions and sense of race—they are Americans beyond doubt, Americans hailing from "that abode of modern vikings, the fishing port of Gloucester." In every tale these men move as living beings imbued with a spirit of kinship with the sea, men who daily look death in the face confronting it steadily, unafraid.

So well does Mr. Connolly know the sea and sailors that the conviction is forced upon us that he has experienced many of the adventures he describes with such wealth of realistic detail. Not such a writer is he as the " 'n' author" ironically described in his *Hiker Joy*: "At nine-thirty every morning he'd take a seat in front of the fire-place, in velvet slippers and a corduroy coat an' dope out about places 'n' people he never saw nor nobody else."

James B. Connolly has written no autobiographical sketches for publication as have many of our writers, nor has he revealed himself in lengthy paragraphs in his work. Nevertheless the reader gains a definite impression of personality from his stories; and we know that all art is partly autobiographical. A glance at the outline of James Brendan Connolly's life, given in *Who's Who,* stimulates the imagination; a background of varied experiences indeed lies behind his stirring tales. He was born, as we should expect of the delineator of New England seafaring men, in a great sea port, South Boston, Mass., in 1868, son of John and Ann (O'Donnell). He tells that his "earliest memories are of loafing days along the harbor front and the husky-voiced, roaring fellows coming ashore in the pulling boats from the men-o'-war". Some of his education he received in the public and parochial schools of Boston, and he spent also a few months in the scientific school of Harvard.

From 1892-1895 he was clerk, inspector and surveyor with the U. S. Engineers' Corps at Savannah, Georgia. That he himself possessed the attributes of physical strength and endurance characteristic of his heroes is evidenced by the fact that in 1896 he won the first Olympic championship of modern times at Athens. This feat later enabled him to create with marvelous realism the atmosphere in his soul-stirring *An Olympic Victor* (1908), an expanded short story in which he draws upon his knowledge of the incidents of the race. In 1898 he served with the 9th Massachusetts Infantry U. S. V., and was at the siege of Santiago.

On September 28, 1904, he was married to Elizabeth Frances Hurley of South Boston. In 1907-1908 he served in the United States navy, gaining experience and knowledge of men later reflected in his work. **Mr.**

Connolly had the privilege from President Roosevelt of cruising on United States war-ships, gunboats, destroyers, cruisers, battleships. Later, through the good offices of Secretary Daniels he became acquainted with submarines and navy air-planes. In interesting story-like articles such as *The Young Draft to the Front, The Fleet Stands By,* and others written in 1914 for Collier's Weekly, the results of these experiences are pictured. At the outbreak of the Great War Mr. Connolly learned aboard a troopship the game of escorting ships and hunting U-boats. *The U-Boat Hunters* (1918) and his latest book *Hiker Joy* (1920) present in different fashions his observation of some of the perils of the late war.

Such in brief is the life of James Brendan Connolly, a life replete with activity and adventure with the sea playing always the dominant rôle. Surely it may be said of him, as of Conrad, "Life has taught him many things, and the great charge of those that travel the seas has taught him one thing mainly, that fidelity to a trust is the supreme triumph and its betrayal the supreme dishonour of a man's life. Honour, loyalty, faith crown his conceptions, and he involves in them whatever beauty and strength is discernible in man's desire and achievement."

Mr. Connolly has been a frequent contributor to magazines, his contributions comprising short stories and songs of the sea, and narrative-descriptive-critical articles published in *Scribner's, Harper's, The Satur-*

*day Evening Post, Collier's, Everybody's, Metropol-
itan, Outlook, American, Hampton, Hearst's, Sunset,
Outing, Harper's Weekly,* and *Current Literature.* The
best of this work has been collected and published in
several volumes by Charles Scribner's Sons.

The first published book of Mr. Connolly's, *Jeb
Hutton* (1902), a story for boys of the life of a
Georgia boy, is wholesome, spirited and full of the
adventure dear to the heart of youth. Reviewers have
likened it in tone and spirit to *Captains Courageous,*
and in popularity with juvenile readers it undoubtedly
ranks with Kipling's classic.

But it is with the short stories of Mr. Connolly that
the present writer is concerned. The first volume of
these, *Out of Gloucester,* published in 1902, consists
of six "ripping good stories" of ocean adventure. As
a whole the group gives a graphic account of life on
board a fisherman and testifies to the author's
familiarity with the hard-driving Gloucester skipper
and his struggles with the sea. That Mr. Connolly's
sympathy is not limited to the Gloucestermen is shown
in *A Fisherman of Costla,* a moving little tale in which
the writer reveals his intimate knowledge of the
racial characteristics of the Irish fisherman. Tender-
hearted, unselfish Gerald Donohue who risks "making
a widder of Mora and orphans of the childer," not
for money but for the sake of an old friend's children
is a fine ideal portrait, one which lingers in the memory.
In the delightful extravagance of *Clancy* we see Mr.

Connolly's gay humor at its height. He has created in Tommy Clancy a character rivaling Kipling's *Mulvaney* in interest and suggestiveness. Like Mulvaney, Clancy has been "rejuced"; "I've been three times disrated—three times I've been skipper and three times back to the forehold. That's pretty near the record for a man of thirty-six. That's all, thirty-six. A little gray around the temples and a little strained in the heart but only thirty-six, Old Man."

The Deep Sea's Toll (1905), consists of eight stories of the Gloucester fishermen, their very titles proving them similar in spirit to those of the first collection— *The Sail-carriers, Dory-mates, On Georges Shoals,* and others—stories of deep-sea adventure which suggest that the fisherman's is the hardest life a man can choose. In these tales the author reveals a knowledge of seafaring men and their lives born of close association.

The thirteen tales in *The Crested Seas* (1907), also present the courageous, reckless exploits of the Gloucestermen with many of the old characters reappearing in new roles—Wesley Marrs and Tommy Clancy the sail-carriers, Dan Coleman the soft-hearted, Martin Carr the good natured, and others of the brave crew that Mr. Connolly loves to write about. Not alone does the writer sound the note of adventure in these stories; in *The Blasphemer, The Illimitable Senses,* and *The Drawn Shutter* he discloses his understanding of the psychology of the men of the sea, and his belief in the sea's mysterious influences. *The Illimitable Senses,* the most powerful of the collection, piques the imagination like a tale of Poe's. Mr. Connolly tells of a strange experience befalling "the most blasphemous crew that ever sailed out of Gloucester", men who invoked the devil, defied the Almighty, and profaned sacred things. A conversation touching on telepathy, psychic force, wireless telegraphy, and the limited senses of people of narrow vision, lifts the story, despite its lack of structural coherence, to a high plane of interest. Its length makes quoting impossible; to appreciate the largeness of Mr. Connolly's attitude toward the mysteries of suggestion, telepathy and things psychical one must read the conversation in its entirety. The man of the sea, he says in closing, "is never a sceptic; and so to him nothing is impossible." The story ends in a way somewhat reminiscent of Fitz James O'Brien's *What Was It? A Mystery.* "What was it? Was it—A hundred hypotheses took shape in the passenger's brain. But no, for thirty years the fleet had passed up that question, and in the fleet were those who dwelt ever on the brink of the Great Crossing and who dwelt there had thoughts beyond the measure of the roof-bound peoples."

Sea stories of the same type as those in his earlier books appear in *Open Water* (1910), but in *The Emigrants, Gree Gree Bush,* and *The Christmas Handicap,* Mr. Connolly demonstrates his ability to handle effectively the situations which arise on shore. Two of the sea stories charge liner captains with incompetency in time of danger; reading them one is left with the uncomfortable sense that the writer has not drawn upon his fancy alone for these tales. The pathos of the "old mother's" love for little Michel, her grandson, and old Joseph's sad and patient devotion to Sarah make *The Emigrants* a poignantly appealing sketch. Strikingly different in emotional effect is *Gree Gree Bush,* a story which shows the black heart of a white man on Africa's west coast. It is a tale of horror, ghastly throughout. The brutal realism of the conclusion lingers unpleasantly in the memory even though ethically we rejoice in the retribution which overtakes the unspeakable Bowles. " 'Stand up, you!' I said to Bowles, and took him and set him on his feet. And he stood there—as well as he could. And I brought the war club down—as if I was driving a stake. He went a foot deep into the mud. And his head was spread out like a red cauliflower.' "

In this collection some of the stories are not pleasant, but the book ends happily with *The Christmas Handicap.* The master touch is revealed in this tale of a professional runner, Ned King. The climactic point is reached in the champion's dramatic recital of the suspense of the contest, the final burst of speed which won the 'cap. And, as in many of the stories, the dénouement has to do with what Mr. Connolly calls humble, human, eternal love—"the greatest sprinter that ever laced a shoe" is reunited at last with his wife and child. There is stark human interest in the simple conclusion.

The eight stories in the volume entitled *Wide Courses* (1911), possess the interest and fascination of the earlier stories, some in the delightful humorous vein of Mr. Connolly, others in the dramatic key he most often touches, "the key of man in his indomitable courage doing battle with storm and wave, with the hardships of life that have hardened him." *The Seizure of the Aurora Borealis* and *Don Quixote Kieran, Pump-Man* relate in amusing fashion tales of sailors' fights; in the first a thirty-pound turkey figures as a weapon, in the latter we meet "a twentieth century Don Quixote with a wallop in each hand" and a "bruising bosun". Obviously, this is humor of a rough-and-tumble variety, but in *Laying the Hose-Pipe Ghost,* with its sixty-eight endorsements on a document, Mr. Connolly's mastery of the finer shades of humor is evident in the ironical treatment of naval red-tape. *Light-Ship 67*, in which Bud Harty goes to death in order to save the husband of the woman he loved, is the strongest story in the collection, dramatic in construction and intensely interesting throughout.

Although *Sonnie-Boy's People* (1913), does not bear a title suggestive of the sea, seven of the nine dashing tales nevertheless recount the adventures of seafaring men and ships. The story from which the collection takes its title etches an ideal portrait of an engineer, a man of genius, who in days of materialism was strong enough to set aside the allurements of money and fame, enduring exile and hardship that his country might be served. Mr. Connolly handles with supreme delicacy the subsidiary line of interest in the story, the exquisite romance of Andie Balfe and Marie Welkie, the idealist's sister. The best of the collection, *The Last Passenger,* recalls the loss of the *Titanic.* The interest lies in the author's convincing portrayal of the spiritual reactions of those on board the doomed ship. Nowhere is Mr. Connolly's keen insight into human nature more fully revealed. The characters assume an actuality almost startling : Lavis, the man of mystery, Linnell, the engineer, Cadogan whose struggle holds the centre of interest, and the pathetic Polish mother with her babe, all are imbued with the very breath of life. The sheer dramatic force of the dénouement alone marks the story as one of the strongest Mr. Connolly has written.

Undoubtedly the high water mark of Mr. Connolly's achievement in fictive writing is represented by *The Trawler,* a story which won first prize in Collier's $2,500 Short Story Contest in 1914. The judges, Ida M. Tarbell, the late Theodore Roosevelt, and Mark Sullivan were agreed not only in according it first place in the competition, but also in estimating it as worthy of a permanent place in our literature; Mr. Roosevelt because of its "elevation of sentiment, rugged knowledge of rugged men, strength and finish of writing"; Mark Sullivan because of its "excellence as a picture of life on the sea at the beginning of the twentieth century" and also because of the author's "length of reach into the depths of human nature, a sort of second sight about the springs of human emotion and human action."

The Trawler is a powerfully dramatic story with a big theme—the story of a man who died that another might live. Many tales of sacrifice have been written, the very device used by Mr. Connolly, that of a man's divesting himself of his garments for the sake of his friend, has been used before; but in no story does the "greater love" shine forth with so pure a brightness. The tale is told with characteristic simplicity; the movement is direct, swift, and inevitable as in a short story of De Maupassant. The note of pathos is struck at the very beginning when Hugh Glynn comes to the sorrowing parents to give the details of the death of their boy Arthur at sea. Mr. Connolly has created a strong emotional effect by the use of suggestion and restraint. Who can fail to be moved by the quiet grief so simply described? "John Snow at the kitchen table, I remember, one finger still in the pages of the black-lettered Bible he had been reading when Hugh Glynn stepped in, dropped his head on his chest and there let it rest. Mrs. Snow was crying out loud. Mary Snow said nothing, nor made a move except to sit in her chair and look to where in the light of the kitchen lamp, Hugh Glynn stood."

As the story progresses inexorably toward its climax

a vivid description of the stormy sea grips the reader with its realism and holds him in suspense. "The full gale was on us now—a living gale—and before the gale the sea ran higher than ever, and before the high seas the flying dory. Mountains of slate-blue water rolled down into valleys, and the valleys rolled up into mountains again, and all shifting so fast that no man might point a finger and say 'Here's one, there's one!'—quick and wild as that they were.

"From one great hill we would tumble only to fall into the next great hollow; and never did she make one of her wild plunges but the spume blew wide and high over her, and never did she check herself for even the quickest of breaths, striving the while to breast up the side of a mountain of water, but the sea would roll over her, and I'd say to myself again 'Now at last we're gone!' "

Mr. Connolly has conceived and wrought out the heroic character of Hugh Glynn so superbly that one feels certain the story embodying his glorious, albeit tragic, fate will hold a secure place in literature. Much longer—as are nearly all of Mr. Connolly's stories—than the average modern short story, consisting as it does of almost 12,000 words, *The Trawler* compels the reader's attention from beginning to end, playing upon the emotions like a *Sonata Pathétique*.

Published separately in book form in 1914, *The Trawler* lends distinction to the volume called *Head Winds* (1916), in which it is included. This collection is remarkable for the variety of stories which it contains: Gloucester fishermen, Continental immigrants, American blue-jackets, newspaper correspondents, soldiery of Central America, and Mississippi River steamboat people lend to its pages a greatly diversified interest. *Chavero* and *Colors!* two stories with a bearing on United States intervention in Mexico, *The Camera Man,* a tale of adventure, and *Quilten* have a touch of melodrama and suggest the screen. Easily one can imagine an audience of youthful devotees of the silent drama following with breathless interest and vociferous applause the exploits of the gallant marines in conflict with the Jenaguans, or Chiliano Joe's long quest for revenge. *Down River,* a story of Mississippi roustabouts combines humor with the undercurrent of tragedy inevitably connected with the consideration of a mingling of the black race and the white.

With the notable exception of *The Trawler, Mother Machree* is the best story in the collection. Like *The Fisherman of Costla,* it is a sympathetic study of racial characteristics, a story of the heritage an Irish family brought to America. The sorrows of Ann and John Lacy, their devotion to family ties, their love and loyalty are depicted with a passion and intensity truly Celtic. Reviewers have ranked *The Trawler* and *Mother Machree* with the most dramatic of modern sea stories.

Like the stories in *Head Winds,* the ten in *Running*

Free (1917), are diverse in content and treatment.
The Strategists is another story with Central American
locale and a touch of opera bouffe; wholly humorous
are *The Weeping Annie, The Bull Fight,* and *Dan
Magee: White Hope* in their lively presentation of adventure at sea and ashore; *A Bale of Blankets* with its
diverting satire on official red tape; *Breath o' Dawn,* in
which the engaging Killorin reappears; *Peter Stops
Ashore,* with its simple love interest and the luring
call of the sea; the delightfully extravagant absurdity
of Bill Green's tale in *The Medicine Ship*—all these are
in Mr. Connolly's lighter vein. Not one reaches the
level of the best in the other collections; not one fails
to satisfy a reader seeking diversion and entertainment.

Mr. Connolly's most recent book *Hiker Joy* (1920)
is likewise in light vein. It consists of a series of
sketches retailing the marvelous adventures of Hiker
Joy, a street urchin with the charm and shrewdness
of Richard Harding Davis's Gallegher, and the inimitable Old Bill Green. While youthful readers may
find most delight in following the thrilling experiences
in *Aboard the Horse-Boat, The Flying Sailor* and *The
North Sea Men,* others will prefer the passages in
which Hiker, who tells it all, expounds his literary
theories.

Reading Mr. Connolly's books leaves one with the
conviction that he is an author who has certain ideas
of his own concerning the technique of story-writing.
Some of his stories are told so impersonally that they

appear to have no point of view—they are merely
yarns spun for the entertainment of a group of
listeners. The story itself is everything—the spirited
action, the adventure, the humor hold the reader's interest and there is no thought of the author. In the
sketch *Dan Magee: White Hope* Mr. Connolly expresses his belief that the story, not the author or his
views of life, is the prime consideration: "And the
first thing in telling a story is to tell it, not to stop to
preach a sermon." And again in *Hiker Joy* we find
"The Yastor Libry is crowded with four 'n' five 'n'
six-hundred-page best sellers that coulda been told in
twenty pages and the tired reader not miss anything.
From the Yarabian Nights to old Homer and all the
way down the good story-tellers never loafed too much
once they started to tell a story, so lay off too much
talky-talky an' don't try to make yuhself out too wise
a guy in tellin' your story." Undoubtedly in his own
work Mr. Connolly has done just this. In differentiat-
ing between the novel and the story in *Hiker Joy* he
definitely formulates his theory: " 'A novel is mostly
talky-talky and a story's mostly doing, isn't it?'

" 'But how does a man go about writing a story?' I
ask him.

" 'I don't know's he goes about it at all,' he says.
'Aren't stories all the time bouncing up in front of
you?' "

One feels that Mr. Connolly has put these theories
into practice; certainly his stories are "mostly doing",

and the indirectness of their telling often suggests a
fine disregard for the mechanics of plot construction.
Frequently we find a story within a story; unlike Kipling Mr. Connolly does not break off with "but that's
another story" when a second tale injects itself into
his plot.

The debatable question of style is also disposed of
characteristically by Old Bill Green.   " 'What's that
style stuff?' I says.

" 'The litry umpires 've written many books on what
style is but no two of 'em 're yet agreed on what it is,'
says Bill. 'But if yuh force me I'd say a n'author's
style is his way of putting his story over an' if he's
got any way a tall of his own it's maybe better for him
to use that way than copy somebody else's that don't
come nachral to him. You write like you talk an'
sometimes your talk is fierce but it's your own way an'
don't let me or any body else kid you out of it.' "

Mr. Connolly has aptly described his own method of
putting his story over. His way is undoubtedly his
own; no hint is there anywhere that Mr. Connolly has
played the sedulous ape to other writers. H. W.
Boynton, in reviewing one of Mr. Connolly's books,
says of the stories, "They are told with great technical skill yet dare have a character of their own, instead
of following slavishly that O. Henry formula which
now threatens to stultify American short-story
writing."

Mr. Connolly's style is virile, clear, and simple; his

prose rarely fails in vividness, is never inflated, and is marked always by vigor and robustness of thought and emotion. The rugged simplicity of his style is its distinctive charm. His stories abound in striking pictures painted in impressionistic fashion; stormy seas and peaceful waters, rocky shores, fishing boats and the men who man them are graphically described with a few broad strokes. In these descriptions the writer's sensitiveness to the appeal of color is a dominant characteristic.

With its nautical flavor Mr. Connolly's style is vigorous, its effect refreshing as a salt-laden breeze. Only in *An Olympic Victor* does he depart from the rugged simplicity characteristic of his sea-stories. In creating the Greek atmosphere he has permitted the "purple light of youth" and young love to lend a different tone—a tone languorous, poetic.

In the conception and portrayal of character Mr. Connolly is, beyond doubt, an artist. The sublimity, the pathos, the charm, the power of human character are brought out in every tale. Rather, these traits reveal themselves since Mr. Connolly's method is dramatic, not analytic. Hugh Glynn, Tommy Clancy, Gerald Donohue, John and Jerome Lacy, Cadogan, Chick Mangan and the rest reveal their strength and their weakness in action and speech.

It is interesting to note that though women play but minor rôles in these stories, the strongest motivating force in the lives of the men depicted is the love of

woman, of home and children. Men drive their ships
and recklessly carry sail in the endeavor to reach home
in time for a birthday or Christmas with the little ones,
or to be with a beloved wife in her hour of need. Mr.
Connolly knows not only the outward lives of these
men but their inner lives also; he has talked with them
aboard ship in the night-watches when men become
holy as little children, revealing their souls simply.
And he knows good women as thoroughly. Hugh
Glynn, in *The Trawler* tells of this knowledge in words
not easily to be forgotten. " 'Because she's too strong
a soul to be spoiled of her life by any one man;
because no matter what man she marries, in her heart
will be the image, not of the man her husband is, but
of the man she'd wish him to be, and in the image of
that man of her fancy will her children be born.
Women moulded of God to be the mothers of great
men are fashioned that way, Simon. They dream
great dreams for their children's sake to come, and
their hearts go out to the man who helps to make
their dreams come true. If I've learned anything of
good women in life, Simon, it is that. And no saying,
I may be wrong in that too, Simon, but so far I've
met no man who knows more of it than I to gainsay
me.' "

Mr. Connolly has presented in his stories no erotic
emotions, no hectic, morbid persons; his men and
women are normal, well-balanced human beings. His
is a healthy art and he has written of the action in

which healthy life issues. The decadent strain which marks some of the fiction of our day is noticeably absent from his work. His appeal is to the best that is in us; like the sea of which he writes Mr. Connolly's stories are big, wholesome, clean. From the best of his work we carry away a feeling of respect and admiration for men who lead hard lives cheerfully, men who brave danger and death without thought of complaint for the sake of the eternal verities. In every story Mr. Connolly has pictured life effectively, if sometimes sketchily, and in every story there is the stamp of individuality, the individuality born of the writer's passion for the sea. Like that early American master of the sea tale, James Fenimore Cooper, Mr. Connolly handles action supremely well, but unlike Cooper's extravagant fabrications of salt water adventure his stories are almost invariably direct and convincing. It is safe to say that just as Mary Wilkins Freeman, Alice Brown, and Sarah Orne Jewett have spoken for humble life in New England villages, so James Brendan Connolly has found in the lives of New England deep sea fishermen an inspiration that has permanently enriched the American short story.

Mr. Connolly's short stories:

Out of Gloucester, 1902.
The Deep Sea's Toll, 1905.
The Crested Seas, 1907.
An Olympic Victor, 1908.

Open Water, 1910.
Wide Courses, 1911.
Sonnie-Boy's People, 1913.
The Trawler, 1914.
Head Winds, 1916.
Running Free, 1917.
Hiker Joy, 1920.
Tide Rips, 1922.

E. K. T.

CHAPTER VII

R ICHARD HARDING DAVIS was born in
Philadelphia, April 18, 1864. He died at Crossroads Farm, near Mt. Kisco, New York,
within seven days of his fifty-second birthday, April
11, 1916.

Successful in journalism and in fiction, known best
for his *Soldiers of Fortune, The Princess Aline, Ranson's Folly* and *Captain Macklin,* he has yet to receive
just praise for his work in the short story. This
fact is the more remarkable if one considers his many
volumes of these briefer forms, their entertaining quality, their sound technic and their romantic reflection
of life. More, perhaps, than the accomplishment of
any other author in this collection, they represent the
production of one who learned through journalism
how to use his tools in fiction and of one whose early
determination to write never wavered. At the time
of his death, R. H. D. had signed a contract to write
six stories at a figure which, according to his brother,
Charles Belmont Davis, or so far as this brother
knew, was the highest ever offered an American au-

thor. Perhaps the tradition that Mr. Davis is novelist
rather than short story writer depends somewhat upon
the length of his narratives. *In the Fog,* for example,
really a "long-short" of not more than 35,000 words
is commonly thought of as a novel. Similar state-
ments might be made of *Ranson's Folly. The King's
Jackal, Vera, the Medium, The Scarlet Car,* and other
works on the border line between short story and
novelette.

It is not easy to pigeon-hole Mr. Davis. Arthur
Bartlett Maurice wrote some years ago (*Bookman,*
April, 1906) that his one dominant note is the social
note, possibly the superficially social note. And he
was a sort of matinée hero among fictionists. Handsome, debonair, a touch of the supercilious in his
manner, of affectation in his speech, and of nice regard for his dress, he was a perfect gentleman in the
social sense. Small wonder that he was the admiration and the despair of gilded youth. But he was
much more than the conventional gentleman, one devoted to a fixed code of personal conduct. He was
the essential noble man who hates wrong and injustice,
who does his individual best to uphold standards of
truth and honor. And this real manhood underlies
the smooth savoir faire of his art. His brother, in
Adventures and Letters of Richard Harding Davis—
a work no less authoritative than entertaining—says
that even in the days of his schooling at the Episcopal
Academy, when his reports filled the house with gloom

and ever-increasing fears as to the possibilities of his future, he stood morally so very high. To do an unworthy act was quite beyond his understanding. According to this brother, to others who knew him well and to those who knew him through his literary expression, R. H. D. lived a life of a chevalier without reproach.

His father's greatest pride in him was the recognition that something of the divine element had been given him, that his voice always rang out sweet and pure, and that he taught humanity. Yet by no means must it be forgotten that he was a red-blood writer.

The changing world of his last years set its mark upon him; but the camera shows that his beauty of face remained, even though his expression had deepened to a warrior sternness. His friend, Gouverneur Morris, wrote that at fifty he might have posed to some Praxiteles and, copied in marble, gone down the ages as a "statue of a young athlete."

He numbered among his friends and acquaintances at various times Ethel Barrymore, Augustus Thomas, Joseph Jefferson, John Drew, E. H. Sothern, Frances Hodgson Burnett, Horace Howard Furness, Arthur Brisbane, The Clevelands, The Gilders, Charles Dana Gibson, Maude Adams, Gouverneur Morris, Somers Somerset, Lloyd C. Griscom, Frederic Remington, Stephen Crane, Anthony Hope, Harold Frederic, John Fox, Jr., Sir James Barrie, Henry Irving, Ellen Terry, Theodore Roosevelt—but the list grows over-long before it is nearly complete. Accept Mr. Dunne's statement that he probably knew "more waiters, generals, actors and princes" than any man who ever lived.

His experience as reporter and the list of his international acquaintances explain in part the stories of Mr. Davis. His stage of action may be New York —city or suburb—London, Cairo, Valencia, Tangier, Cuba, Monte Carlo, or an ocean vessel. Ships figure with remarkable frequency: *The Amateur, The Spy, The Consul, The Fever Ship* at once come to mind. He wrote about Van Bibber, society man; but also about Rags Raegen and Hefty Burke of the East Side. He wrote one of the best dog stories in *The Bar Sinister,* two of the best newspaper stories in *Gallegher* and *A Derelict;* many first-rate stories for boys —*The Reporter Who Made Himself King, The Great Tri-Club Tennis Tournament,* and *The Boy Scout,* for instance; the best story about a consul yet written (*The Consul*) ; some capital love stories—*A Charmed Life* and *The Red Cross Girl,* for example; one of the best spy stories in *Somewhere in France.* He touched the psychic in *Vera, the Medium, The Messengers* and elsewhere; he produced a new reaction over hidden spoils in *My Buried Treasure,* and a wild extravaganza thrill from dreams in *The Man Who Could Not Lose.*

Nor is his type of conflict less varied. The struggle of Gallegher's wits precedes his race against time; A Leander of the East River tests his endurance in swimming; Austin Ford, of *The Amateur* (detective tale of joyous departure from formula), tries to follow up and bring home a criminal; "Rags, My Disreputable Friend," debates between his own life and that of the baby; the hero of *A Walk up the Avenue* battles between meanness and manhood.

Constant in all his stories is a liveliness or buoyancy of tone, and inseparably woven throughout all a thread of humor. This humor runs the circuit of cynicism, satire, irony, and mere fun-making; it lies in character and grows out of character, bringing about humor of situation rather than emerging from it. It flashes in an apparent chance clause, as in this sentence from *Her First Appearance:* "Every member of the Lester Comic Opera Company—down to the wardrobe woman's son, who would have had to work if his mother lost her place, was sick with anxiety." And it tosses the reader like a cork on its uproarious flood in *The Man Who Could Not Lose.*

His freshness and buoyancy are explained by his wide travels. He needed change to stimulate his creative powers, and he wrote directly out of his experience.

In his early years, Richard Harding Davis owed much to his mother, and so long as she lived—until 1910, when he was away from her he wrote her a daily letter. "That was the only habit he had," wrote Gouverneur Morris shortly after his death. "He was a slave to it." Rebecca Harding Davis, in *The Iron Mills* and other works, did as much for her time as any woman had done for her generation, as R. H. D. himself wrote her on her birthday in 1901. From her he received the instinct and the desire to write; from her and his father, the sense of logical and ethical values which characterizes his work and his career.

In 1880, "Dick" Davis left the Episcopal Academy and went to Swarthmore College, where, no more successful than he had been at the first school, he remained only one year. In fact, he seems never to have distinguished himself in the academic ranks, and so drew upon himself the criticism that he must have acquired ignorance since no one could possibly have been born with quite so large a stock of it. In 1881, he went to live with an Uncle, a Professor at Lehigh, and continued his studies at a preparatory school. In February, 1882, he saw his first skit in print; in 1884 he published—through the financial aid of his family —his first book.

In 1885 he left Lehigh for Johns Hopkins, where he took a special course in subjects that would best fit him for his chosen profession. Desirous of steady newspaper work, he left Hopkins in the spring of 1886, ready for the first journalistic position he could find. It chanced, however, that he first went to Cuba, with the President of the Bethlehem Steel Company, and there secured material which came to light ten years

later in *Soldiers of Fortune.* On his return, he
worked a short time on *The Record,* but left it in three
months. The editor did not like him, he wrote his
mother, because he wore gloves on cold days. On
The Press, to which he advanced after his first experience, he remained for three years. His ability was
first tested by the Johnstown flood disaster and revealed in the stories he sent his paper from the Cone-
maugh Valley.

In 1888, Richard Harding Davis, now twenty-four
years of age, was a national figure. He was star
reporter on *The Press,* and was acquiring fame as
interviewer and news gatherer. Tricks of the journalist's trade he drops here and there in his stories,
whether in the first two or three pages of one so early
as *The Reporter Who Made Himself King,* or in
one so recent as *The Red Cross Girl:* "Reporters
become star reporters because they observe things that
other people miss and because they do not let it appear that they have observed them. When the great
man who is being interviewed blurts out that which is
indiscreet but most important, the cub reporter says:
'That's most interesting, sir. I'll make a note of that.'
And so warns the great man into silence. But the
star reporter receives the indiscreet utterance as though
it bored him; and the great man does not know he
has blundered until he reads of it the next morning
under screaming headlines."

He was not only writing fiction, but was selling it,

as checks for various sums, as high as one for $50 from *St. Nicholas,* indicate. If he owes to the swift strokes of the reporter his spontaneity and enthusiasm, he owes to his own pains the sharp lines of the etcher which fix his writing into whatever it will have of permanence. It is as though in his work he took wholly to heart and practice the advice he received in a letter from Robert Louis Stevenson: "—the cheap finish and ready made methods to which journalism leads you must try to counteract in private writing with the most considerate slowness and on the most ambitious models." Obviously, from his stories he learned much about writing from both Stevenson and Kipling.

In 1889 R. H. D. accompanied a team of cricketers from Philadelphia to Ireland and England and reported the matches for the Philadelphia *Telegraph.* It was on this trip to London that he first met Charles Dana Gibson, afterwards associated with him as illustrator. "Dick was twenty-four years old when he came into the smoking-room of the Victoria Hotel after midnight one July night—he was dressed as a Thames boatman . . . He had adventure written all over him . . . His life was filled with just the sort of adventure he liked best." So Mr. Gibson recalled at the time of Mr. Davis's death.

On his return he visited New York in the hope of finding a berth on a newspaper, but tried several offices without success. There are several legends as to what happened ultimately: one is to the effect that he put himself into the clutches of a green-goods man, trapped him with marked money, and went to *The Evening Sun* with the story. But his brother's account is as follows: On his way to the station after his unsuccessful search, he sat down on a park bench. Presently along came Arthur Brisbane, whom young Davis had lately met in London. Now the editor of the *Sun*, he offered Davis a position on the staff.

Coincidence handled in many fashions is one of the striking peculiarities of R. H. D.'s work. Such experiences as the one just recorded probably lay at the bottom of his repeated use of apparent accident—another name for Fate. In *A Charmed Life*, he develops a series of coincidences which compel the reader's belief through his love charm *motif;* in *The God of Coincidence* he tells such an amazing instance of coincidence that he must induce belief through the title —which otherwise might have been *The Man in the Green Hat*—and through a number of easily acceptable examples, given at the outset. That he knew how to secure belief is proof of his skill. In *The Long Arm* he uses the coincidence at the climax and gains credulity by a seriousness of manner, as though he staked his word on the amazing circumstances he recounts. *The Long Arm*, it may be noted in passing, illustrated the Stevenson influence, even to diction. Swanson reflects: "If life be an ill thing, I can lay it down," a conclusion reached by the older writer's

Markheim in the story bearing his name. In *The Boy Scout* a slight but kindly act of the scout—"Do a good turn every day"—sets in motion a ripple whose widening circles touch the shores of far-off lands.

In New York, then, Dick Davis continued his work in journalism and fiction. He reported news events, and wrote articles and special features, with emphasis on theatrical people. He loved the theater, "painty and gassy and dusty," as he loved the country. Van Bibber, a frequenter of the green room, is the first of many heroes belonging to the same race: "a race of kindly, generous souled bounders, gentlemen at heart," Mr. Maurice dubs them. He instances as an example of the "breaks" of these heroes of Mr. Davis the visit of Van Bibber to Carruthers (in *Her First Appearance,* afterwards dramatized as *The Littlest Girl*). With the child in his arms, he reads that gentleman, the child's father, "a solemn lesson on the duties of paternity."

In 1890 R. H. D. became a star of the first magnitude when he burst forth in *Scribner's Magazine,* with *Gallegher. The Other Woman* and *My Disreputable Friend, Mr. Raegen,* appeared shortly after and with a number of Van Bibber stories were published in 1891, in a volume dedicated to "My Mother." *Gallegher* must have been a work of long inception; for his father wrote, in 1888, "Have you done anything on Gallegher? That is by far the best work you have done—oh, by far . . ." In 1890, he thought

A Walk up the Avenue superior to it; but the verdict
of critics has maintained, rather, the superiority of
the newspaper story. *My Disreputable Friend* was
afterwards dramatized, as a curtain raiser, with E. H.
Sothern in the rôle of Rags.

Combining journalism and fiction meant that one
incident frequently served for both. About one of
the tales written in these early years, he wrote his
mother, "The ladies in the Tombs were the Shippens
. . . and Mamie Blake is a real girl, and the story is
true from start to finish." Five or six years later,
in London, he and Ethel Barrymore were lost one
evening, for the reason that one is usually lost in
London. He wrote an account of the incident to
some one of his family and used his first-hand experience in the story, *In the Fog.* And his very last tale,
The Deserter, reads like fiction, yet is at the same time
a matter of fact.

Yet, to revert to the year 1890, he was cautioning
his father not to believe that "a man must have an
intimate acquaintance with whatever he writes of in-
timately." And he cites another story of the same
era, *Mr. Travers' First Hunt,* as proof. A lot of
people, he said, would not believe he had written it,
because they knew he did not hunt. No contrasting
examples could better show the writer's twofold ability—an ability demanded by fiction, always: that of
making a fact in life appear a fact in fiction and that
of making a fiction appear a fact.

In these years he learned to keep to his ideals: he rejected numerous offers that promised momentarily greater money. He asked and received criticism on his stories, frequently from his father and mother, whose guidance he trusted. "Do only your best work if you starve doing it," they both enjoined him. His father wrote him in 1890, "It is good work, with brain, bone, nerve, muscle in it. It is human, with healthy pulse and heartsome glow in it."

In 1890 Mr. Davis left the *Sun* to become managing Editor of *Harper's Weekly*, under the editorship of George William Curtis. This step advanced him in fame and gave opportunity for wider recognition through his arrangement to edit the *Weekly* part of every year and to travel the remainder.

His *Stories for Boys*, copyright by Charles Scribner's Sons, 1891, reveal his continued interest in youth and its adventures, first manifested in *Gallegher*.

In 1892, January, he took a trip which resulted in *The West from a Car Window*. And just here may be listed a number of his factual works growing out of his reporter's life from this time to the end of his life. *Rulers of the Mediterranean* (1894); *Our English Cousins* (1894); *About Paris* (1895); *Three Gringos in Venezuela and Central America* (1896); *A Year from a Reporter's Note Book* (1897), including *Cuba in War Time*, *The Millennial Celebration at Buda-Pest*, *With the Greek Soldiers*, and other articles; *With Both Armies in South Africa* (1900);

Notes of a War Correspondent (1910); *With the Allies* (1914); *With the Allies in Salonika* (1916). All these reveal his descriptive power, his ability to narrate facts and to interpret the life he observed, as his fictive stories, paralleling the settings and characters of his actual experiences, reveal his skill in the construction of artistic narrative.

In 1892 he visited London (May to August) and fraternized at Oxford with the undergraduates. In August he returned, visited his father's family at Marion on Cape Cod, and early in the autumn was fulfilling the editorial half of his contract. He reported certain events in connection with the World's Fair at Chicago, worked at his desk in Franklin Square, and in February (1893) was off for a tour of the Mediterranean. On April 16, he wrote: "I have been in Spain, France, Italy, Germany, Austria, Hungary, Serbia, Bulgaria, Turkey, Greece, Egypt, and Morocco. I have sat on the rock of Gibraltar sailed on the Nile and the Suez Canal and crossed through the Dardanelles, over the Balkans, the Steppes of Hungary and the Danube and the Rhine." After Paris and London, he returned to Marion, where he finished his novel, *Soldiers of Fortune*. (He sold it, 1895, to Scribner's Sons for $5,000. It was published in volume form, 1897, with a dedication to Charles Dana and Irene Gibson.) We hear of him in the fall, at his desk and in the social life of the city. In February, 1894, he wrote the novel, *The Princess Aline,* the heroine of which was the future ill-starred Empress of Russia. This same year he was again in London on a social visit, and in Paris, whither he hastened at the news of President Carnot's assassination. January, 1895, he set out for South and Central America (*The Three Gringos* chiefly resulting from this trip). By April he back working on his articles and stories.

Even so congested a summary must make clear that Mr. Davis's life from 1892 to 1895 was suggestive of the old saw, "Off again, on again, gone again." But the years 1896 and 1897 were climactic in activity. "In the space of twelve months," his brother Charles Belmont has summed up, "he reported the Coronation at Moscow, the Millennial Celebration, The Spanish-Cuban War, the McKinley Inauguration, the Greek-Turkish War and the Queen's Jubilee." At the same time, or in this time, he was writing *Captain Macklin,* a novel in the earlier part of which he displayed, according to friendly critics, a power truly Thackerayan. Also, in 1896, appeared *Cinderella and Other Stories,* containing the popular favorites, *The Editor's Story,* and *The Reporter Who Made Himself King.*

April, 1897, he spent with his brother, for the most part, in Florence, Italy. In the late summer he returned to Cape Cod, but was back in London in December. There he remained until war between the United States and Spain seemed inevitable, when he came back to New York and started to Key West.

During that war he acted as correspondent for the London *Times,* for the New York *Herald* and for *Scribner's Magazine.* The war over, he stopped for a brief time in New York and a visit to Marion. That was in 1898, the year of the publication of *The King's Jackal.* Early in 1899 he was in London.

Now follows one of the most spectacular and romantic episodes connected with Mr. Davis's romantic life, one that became famous over all the world. In the spring of 1899 he proposed by cable to Miss Cecil Clark, of Chicago. On her acceptance of his heart and hand, Mr. Davis found himself unable to leave London and so sent the engagement ring by William Thomas Jaggers, No. 757 in the London District Messenger Service. Young Jaggers made the trip between March 11 and March 29, obtained receipts for letters sent by Mr. Davis, and was back in London a week before the time set as that of his expected return.

On May 4, 1899, Mr. Davis and Miss Clark were married, at Marion. After some weeks at home, they spent the summer in London and at Aix-les-Bains. Early in 1900 they set out for the Boer War. Cape Town, Ladysmith, and Pretoria figure in Mr. Davis's letters and articles written at this time. When they returned to America in the fall of 1900 they lived in East 58th Street, but in the spring they went to the summer home on Cape Cod, where they remained for a year, May, 1901, to the spring of 1902. They left then for Madrid, where Mr. Davis reported the Coronation ceremonies consequent upon Alfonso's ascending the throne. They continued to London, to be present at Edward's coronation, but learned, while they were visiting the Kiplings, that it had been postponed on account of the king's illness.

Meantime, of Mr. Davis's fictive works, had appeared *The Lion and the Unicorn* (copyright, 1899), *In the Fog* (1901), and *Ranson's Folly* (1902). The last named contains, in addition to the title story, *La Lettre d'Amour*, *A Derelict* and *The Bar Sinister* with *In the Fog* repeated. It is the best collection up to the time of its publication.

Once more, after a sojourn at Marion and New York City, during which time he bought Crossroads Farm, the Davis's sailed away, this time for the Orient. The Russo-Japanese War was on. On his arrival in Japan, R. H. D. found, as Jack London before him had found, that he could not get within two or three miles of the firing line. He met London, by the way, of whom he records "a tremendous impression of vitality and power." John Fox, Jr., was there, too; and he and Davis, led by promises of seeing some fighting, wasted six months in a vain endeavor to get near the scene of action. He came back, hastening from Vancouver to Philadelphia because of his father's fatal illness.

In July, 1905, Mr. Davis and his wife moved to Crossroads. Thereafter he resided for the most part

at this country home in the warmer months; but in
the colder seasons he turned to the tropics. Even
so early as the Cuban War he suffered from neuralgia
of the hip. "I saw him writhing on the ground with
sciatica, during that campaign, like a snake," John
Fox wrote of him, "but pulling his twisted figure
straight and his tortured face into a smile if a soldier
or a stranger passed."

He published, 1906, *The Scarlet Car,* a novelette
with a Broadway and road-to-New Haven setting.

At the request of Robert J. Collier, R. H. D. went
to the Congo in 1907 to investigate the situation there.
By May he was again in Mount Kisco. Shortly afterward, he converted his drama, *The Galloper,* into a
musical comedy, *The Yankee Tourist,* with Raymond
Hitchcock as star. Until the fall of 1908 he was in
New York, Mt. Kisco, Marion, and Cuba. In December he and Mrs. Davis were in Cheyne Walk, London, living in Turner's house, hard by Carlyle's.
August, 1909, he was back at Crossroads, where he
spent the greater part of the following three years.

Personal unhappiness, one might judge from the
stories of Richard Harding Davis, never assailed him.
Nor did he permit the sorrows of his own life to
find expression in his fiction. But they came, and
when they came, he played "Let's Pretend" and made
believe they were imaginary. For some years he and
his wife had been estranged, so that neither their
separation nor their divorce came as a surprise to their

close friends. To this domestic upheaval in 1910 was added the grief of his mother's loss: Rebecca Harding Davis died in September of the same year.

At this time the friendship of the Gouverneur Morrises meant much to him. He visited them at Aiken in 1910, dedicated *Once upon a Time* (1910) to Gouverneur; and after two journeys to London in 1911— one to the coronation of George and the other to his sister, Nora Davis Farrar—he again turned to Aiken in January, 1912.

In June, 1912, he reported the Republican Convention at Chicago. On July 8 he married Miss Elizabeth Genevieve McEvoy, known better by her stage name, Bessie McCoy. His collection of stories, *The Red Cross Girl* (1912), is dedicated to her, as is also the following volume, *The Lost Road* (1913).

In the autumn of 1913 he and Augustus Thomas spent a month in Cuba, producing a film version of *Soldiers of Fortune*. It was one of the first big motion picture productions, one in which the government war vessels participated by permission of the United States. His experience in "movie" circles undoubtedly influenced his subsequent short-stories; but it is to be questioned whether it would have brought about, ever, a conscious or unconscious catering to demands of the screen. He wrote his story, leaving the picture to take care of itself.

Late in April, 1914, R. H. D. left the Crossroads

and started for Vera Cruz, to report what seemed an imminent clash between Mexico and the United States. He went on the first transport that landed troops; and again fell in with Jack London, who was aboard. He came back to New York in June and sailed on August 4, with his wife, on the *Lusitania*. Once on the other side, he started for Brussels, where he arrived in time to see the entry of the German troops. His article on this subject is one of his best pieces of descriptive writing, and to those who read his *Tribune* letters from day to day he brought home the first full meaning of the World War.

He returned, October, 1914, to write his first book on the great conflict. He and Mrs. Davis spent the winter in the city, where January 4, 1915, his daughter, Hope, was born. In April they went out to Cross-roads, as it chanced, a year from the day that was to mark his death. He took the course in military training at Plattsburg, where the sham battles must have recalled earlier days, such as had produced his *Peace Maneuvers* (in *Once upon a Time*). In the same month *Somewhere in France* was published, the last of his collections.

By November he was visiting the trenches outside Rheims, having returned to Europe in October. A few days later he was in Athens, off for Salonica. November 30 he wrote his brother, "It ought to be a place for great stories." And there it was that he found the setting for his last narrative, *The Deserter.**

Mr. Davis sailed for home, by way of London, February, 1916. March 21, 1916, he fell ill, and on April 11 he died. He was buried at Philadelphia.

The amazing quality of Mr. Davis's work lies in one word—youth. "He was youth incarnate," John Fox, Jr., wrote of him. "He not only refused to grow old himself, he refused to write about old age." Finley Peter Dunne confirmed this statement in words to the same purport. And John T. McCutcheon: "In his writing he was the interpreter of chivalrous, well-bred youth, and his heroes were young, clean-thinking college men, heroic big game hunters, war correspondents and idealized men about town, who always did the noble thing, disdaining the unworthy in act or motive."

That Robert Clay, in *Soldiers of Fortune,* would have needed one hundred and fifty years to achieve the various feats of diplomacy and engineering ascribed to him is an example of his idealistic concept of man.

He succeeds best with his men; for if ever a writer put himself into his stories, Richard Harding Davis did. Whether the reporter in *Gallegher* or the one

* In it Jimmie Hare, McCutcheon, Bass and W. G. Shepherd all have part, and to it Mr. Shepherd wrote a moving sequel, *The Scar That Tripled.*

who made himself king or the "I" of *The Deserter;*
whether the hero of the Van Bibber stories, or young
Stuart who sits opposite the understudy of Miss Dela-
mar or Chesterton on his night ride to the sea-coast;
whether Sam Ward of *The Red Cross Girl*, Lowell
of *The God of Coincidence,* or Billy Barlow of *Billy
and the Big Stick;* whether the husband in *Playing
Dead*—whether he masquerades convincingly as any
one of these, he is none the less Richard Harding
Davis. Not that he is obtrusively so to the reader.
For the different facets, lights, settings and varied
action mean a constancy of novelty.

In his earlier efforts he did not succeed with his
women. The critic was right who said that they give
the impression one gets upon catching sight of a beautiful face in a passing carriage. But in his later stories,
say beginning with those now grouped in *The Red
Cross Girl,* he is more successful. Even though the
hero is still the hero, the women are warm and breathing. Greater space would permit analysis of his later
success; its explanation to be found in his life. If
he had lived, his daughter Hope—to whom yet a baby,
his last book was dedicated—would have provided a
new stimulus and given a new slant to his fiction, as
Bessie McCoy Davis, her mother, had done. One
may say this; for of all lovely love letters given the
world, the few which the public are privileged to read
are unsurpassed. And it is said, with truth, so far

as the evidence reveals, that he wrote letters more easily than he wrote any other kind of composition.

The professional cynic, cited by Mr. Maurice, may assert that the beginnings of Mr. Davis's stories are positive triumphs, because a composite of them would run something as follows: "Miss Van Knickerbocker was seriously annoyed. The unexpected departure of the butler was most inopportune. The second man was obviously incompetent; the illness of the chef and of the coachman had already complicated her household arrangements, and the affair of the third footman and the fifth and sixth chambermaids, etc., etc."

But no cynic may detract from the endings of his stories. Better than any other American writer of his generation—barring questionably the surprise dénouements of O. Henry—he knew how to hold interest to the last and to make his close the strongest part of his narrative. Read *The Spy* and when you come to the final page read it, if you can, without tears. It is one of the few superb endings in fiction, a dénouement tragically moving, yet satisfying. Or take *The Consul.* You will thrill to admiration and satisfaction that one incorruptible victim of politics received his reward. Or exult over *The Bar Sinister,* which drops the curtain on the Wyndham Kid "taking blue ribbons away from father." Or chortle aloud in glee over the final hundred words of *The Naked Man.* The truth is that R. H. D. rarely failed in his wind-up, whether in tragedy or comedy.

The Deserter closes:

" 'You can all go to hell!' said Mr. Hamlin. "We heard the door slam and his hobnailed boots pounding down the stairs. No one spoke. Instead, in unhappy silence we stood staring at the floor. Where the uniform had lain was a pool of mud and melted snow and the darker stains of stale blood."

He meant to make you joyful over Mr. Hamlin's farewell remark; and sober over the closing paragraph. He was a master of contrast and sudden, yet effective, transition.

His mastery of description he achieved by hard labor. "He worked upon a principle of elimination," his friend Gouverneur Morris wrote. "If he wished to describe an automobile turning in at a gate, he made first a long and elaborate description from which there was omitted no detail which the most observant pair of eyes in Christendom had ever noted with respect to just such a turning. Thereupon he would begin a process of omitting one by one those details which he had been at such pains to recall; and after each omission he would ask himself: 'Does the picture remain?' " And so he experimented "until after Herculean labor there remained for the reader one of those swiftly flashed, ice-clear pictures (complete in every detail) with which his tales and romances are so delightfully and continuously adorned." Thus it was he achieved that picturesque effect, which as his friend McCutcheon said, "was photographic even to the sounds and smells."

To his ultimate swift and vivid pictures he added novelty of situation and a fine feeling for the dramatic moment. Therein lies his success as a writer of brief fiction.

Volumes containing Mr. Davis's short stories:

Gallegher and Other Stories, 1891.
Stories for Boys, 1891.
Van Bibber and Others, 1892.
The Exiles, 1894.
Cinderella and Other Stories, 1896.
Episodes in Van Bibber's Life, 1899.
The Lion and the Unicorn, 1899.
In the Fog, 1901.
Ranson's Folly, 1902.
The Bar Sinister, 1903.
Once upon a Time, 1910.
The Man Who Could Not Lose, 1911.
The Red Cross Girl, 1912.
The Lost Road, 1913.
The Boy Scout, 1914.
Somewhere in France, 1915.
The Deserter, 1917.
The Boy Scout and Other Stories, 1917.

CHAPTER VIII

MARGARET DELAND

I N one important particular the work of Margaret
Deland resembles that of William Cowper. As
the poet of the eighteenth century consciously
integrated religion and verse, so the fiction writer a
hundred years later has made it the essence of her short
stories and novels. If success be measured by vast
numbers of the common folk who have enjoyed him
through several generations, success crowns the efforts
of the man who wrote *The Olney Hymns* and *The
Task;* if its gauge is present popularity, then success
attends the author of *Where the Laborers Are Few*
and *The Awakening of Helena Ritchie.*

This dominant theme is most powerfully evident
in her novels. *John Ward, Preacher,* with its problems of faith and doubt established the place of Mrs.
Deland alongside the author of *Robert Elsmere. The
Awakening,* which in the hands of a less gifted writer
might have deliquesced into a mere tract, became
under her molding a great religious drama of the
nineteenth century. Whether apprehended through
the printed page or observed in the person of Miss

Margaret Anglin, who acted the title rôle, Helena is a human being who sins and struggles and repents and finds peace. At no time is she a puppet obviously propelled by the didactic showman behind the scenes. The achievement of Mrs. Deland is the dramatization of theological, religious and moral problems. It has been held that no intensely thematic fiction can be dramatic; but there are exceptions, among which are her novels and stories. The former by their greater magnitude and weight are more impressive; the latter by their concentration, their exclusion of ancillary material, are more poignant.

Margaret Wade Campbell was born in Allegheny, Pennsylvania, February 23, 1857. Because her parents died in her infancy, she lived for fifteen or sixteen years with her mother's sister, also a Mrs. Campbell, in Manchester. Although her childhood was happy in events of an everyday and practical nature, it found the added joy of illusion in "make-believe" and entered the land of fancy through stories read and invented. It is recorded by Donald McDonald, in an article published some years ago, that she and her young friend Betty set up a hospital for bugs and beetles, and finding the patients loath to stay put, tacked them to their board couches. In spite of brickdust tea and tender ministrations, the mortality was considerable. Margaret's browsing about a well-stocked family library of English classics undoubtedly gave her a relish for good books. Her aunt's censorship of her fiction reading permitted *Robinson Crusoe:* it is the "immortal" work Dr. Lavendar had read more times than he remembered.

Situated near Allegheny and Pittsburgh ("Mercer," in the stories), Manchester ("Old Chester") was in those days a village of comfortable houses, old fashioned gardens and green hills that sloped to the Ohio River. In *The Promises of Dorothea,* the author says it looked down upon the outside world, kindly but pityingly; in *The Story of a Child* it lay folded in a green silence a hundred years behind the times. Every house was like the other: a broad porch opened into a wide hall bordered by square rooms in which open fireplaces were surmounted by tall wooden mantel-pieces. The flower beds were surrounded by box hedges; the orchards were laid out in straight lines.

In the works which have come to be synonymous with Mrs. Deland and Old Chester, she has portrayed with large comprehension and loving detail the men and women who lived, or might have lived, in Manchester. It is immaterial whether she draws from life or imagination, whether she creates composites or re-creates individuals. She has created Old Chester, which will endure as the reflection of a conservative, West Pennsylvania town of pure British inhabitants, akin to their New England compeers, and not unlike the folk of English provinces. Old Chester can scarcely be named without a thought of Tiverton, Our Village, or Cranford. Refinement was characteristic of its females, to paraphrase Miss Ferris, and the protection of its youth was a religion.

If the "we" of her stories be proof, Margaret Campbell received her early education in a school like Miss Bailey's, described in *The Apotheosis of the Reverend Mr. Spangler,* and mentioned many times elsewhere. "For accomplishments, there was fine sewing every Wednesday afternoon; and on Mondays, with sharply pointed pencils, we copied trees and houses from neat little prints; also we had lessons upon the piano-forte, so there was not one of us, who when she left Miss Ellen's, could not play at least three pieces." She went for a time to a boarding school at Pelham Priory, near New York, whence she shortly set out to Cooper Union, in the City. There she took a course in drawing and design, graduating at the head of her class, and subsequently winning in a competitive examination the appointment of instructor in design at the Girls' Normal College (now Hunter College of the City of New York). Here she remained until 1880, when she was married to Lorin Deland, and went to live in Boston.

The story of Mrs. Deland's first ventures in literature has become a tradition, and like an old ballad is found in more than one version. Doubtless on inquiry, she would vouchsafe the simple facts; but it is pleasant to read, here, that her first verses were written on the wrapper of a bulky package she was carrying home from the butcher's; there, that they were jotted down in an account book; elsewhere, that they were scrawled on the brown paper she used in her college work. We prefer to keep all the legends at the cost of a single fact. In 1886, these first verses and others were collected under the title, *The Old Garden,* fit title for the initial accomplishment of one who has been, always, surrounded by flowers. In *Good for the Soul,* Mrs. Deland describes an ideal garden : . . . . "a great two hundred foot square, sunk between four green terraces; it was packed with all sorts of flowers, and overflowing with fragrance; all the beds were bordered with sweet alyssum and mignonette, and within them the flowers stood, pressing their glowing faces together in masses of riotous color— the glittering satin yellow California poppies; the heavenly blue of nemophila; crimson mallow, snow-white shining phlox; sweet peas and carnations, gilly flowers and bachelor's buttons, and everywhere the golden sparks of coreopsis; there were blots of burning scarlet, sheets of orange and lilac and dazzling white." Harriet Prescott Spofford once said that Mrs. Deland's home on Beacon Hill was all windows and flowers; and according to Lucy Purdy, a fig tree had been coaxed into bearing fruit under her roof. In 1915 Kathleen Norris, who visited her at Dedham, recorded as the most interesting detail a garden in the midst of which a fire-bell, inverted in a stone wheel, held the water that was the lily-pond. For many summers

Mrs. Deland has gone to her home at Kennebunkport, Maine, and there worked out of doors.

After the success of *John Ward, Preacher* (1888) Mrs. Deland wrote *The Story of a Child* (1892). In this novelette of 35,000 words she evinces that sympathy for and understanding of children which later softened *The Awakening of Helena Ritchie* and through small David contributed to its popularity. Since the early nineties the child has come to be an integral part of fiction and the subject of innumerable stories; but he had not been exploited when Mrs. Deland wrote her book about Ellen Dale. A revelatory passage of her insight into the mind operation of a little girl is that wherein Ellen sits in twilight preoccupation, dreaming. Suppose Grandmother's head and Mrs. Wright's head were to roll off and down the steps beside her! She flees for comfort to Betsey, still perturbed by the fear of a dead, dead world; but she reflects that if everybody were dead she could walk into the queen's palace and try on a crown. By the time she reaches Betsey she has no desire to throw herself into that friend's arms.

This expression of interest in child life is not a transitory "sport"; it is a permanent part of the characteristic fibre and structure of her fiction. She touches, for example, the pathos of lonely childhood in Theophilus Bell *(Justice and the Judge,* in *Old Chester Tales)* and realizes it through the little boy's cherishing his father's old pipe—sole possession that connected him with the days when he had known that father's love. She presents a pleasing objective study of childhood in Anna (*The Child's Mother,* of *Old Chester Tales*) and in such a way as to make convincing Rachel King's affection for her.

Following *The Story of a Child,* appeared a volume of five tales, more or less about Old Chester, *Mr. Tommy Dove* (1893). The fact that the work is long out of print does not debar the reader from a glimpse of the apothecary hero of the titular piece; for he recurs here and there in subsequent stories. *A Fourth Class Apopintment,* first published in *Harper's,* January, 1892, with a Penniville, Pennsylvania, setting, may be found as of Purham, Vermont, under the new title *Partners* (1913). The characters are certainly those of Western Pennsylvania; the dénouement, in its solution of the problem to save mother is similar to that of *The Unexpectedness of Mr. Horace Shields,* whose hero marries Lucy that she may have a home, or that of *The House of Rimmon,* wherein William West similarly rescues Lydia Blair. *The Face on the Wall,* which so far as we know has not been reprinted since its appearance in *Mr. Tommy Dove,* is a sympathetic study of the artistic temperament, in its conflict between the base and the noble, as manifested in Paul Calkins.

In *The Wisdom of Fools* (1897) Mrs. Deland presents problems social and ethical which, or so she seems to say, not all the wisdom of fools can answer.

Where Ignorance Is Bliss, 'Tis Folly to Be Wise, the
first story, is typical of the lot, three of which have
their action in Western Pennsylvania. William West
is to be married to Amy Townsend. He is a good
man. But when he confesses to her that in the remote
past he committed forgery he meets with a revulsion
so great as to forbid all hope of marriage. (Amy
is a blood relation of Hergesheimer's Hester Stanes,
in *The Dark Fleece*). The story closes with a discussion over his step: Was he fool or saint for confess-
ing? In his own meditation he had decided that "if
his love for Amy was deep enough and unselfish
enough, he would hold his tongue"; but he had, inconsequentially enough, failed to hold it. Oddly, in a
companion piece, *Good for the Soul (Old Chester
Tales)* Mrs. Deland solves the same problem from the
woman's point of view. Elizabeth Day is, like
William West of the other story, good. But before
her marriage she has sinned. Her husband does not
know. Shall she tell him? Unable to decide for herself, she calls upon Dr. Lavendar. "I charge you
bear the burden of silence," he counsels her, "because
you love your husband." As before, the end expresses
doubt of the legitimacy of the advice for all cases.
But Elizabeth bravely held her tongue. . . .

The second story in the volume, *The House of
Rimmon* (Reprinted in *R. J.'s Mother and Some
Other People*, 1908) forecasts incidentally the litera-
ture of labor problems. But its chief concern is the

soul struggle of Lydia Blair, whose guiding principle of Duty is in conflict with her brother's ideals. She solves her painful riddle by leaving her brother's house and entering a shop. But the author cannot consent to leave her there and allows William West (of the first story) to burn his tokens of the past and rescue her for his wife.

The Law, or the Gospel presents a young philanthropist, Sarah Wharton, in the endeavor to save Nellie Sherman, weak, devoid of physical or mental or moral health. Sarah keeps the girl alive, and is repaid by Nellie's wreckage of two or three souls. Sarah has no money for further aid, and has to reject a real opportunity for benevolence. Has one a right to interfere with the laws of nature, to the extent Sarah Wharton interfered? To battle for the life of the degenerate? Who knows? The story is significant in that a second large interest of Mrs. Deland is for unfortunate women. Their redemption has been one of her solicitudes; to them her home has been a refuge. *The Child's Mother (Old Chester Tales)* portrays in Mary Dean another Nellie Sherman, but directs the action to a more hopeful conclusion.

Old Chester Tales (1898), in spite of the fact that the town has already appeared as the locale of previous stories, focuses Mrs. Deland's rays of interest on Old Chester, which concentrates them and becomes thereby the first burning glass of her short fiction.

Old Chester means Dales, Wrights, Lavendars, the Doves (through Mrs. Dove, who was Jane Temple), the Jay girls, the Barkleys, the Kings, the two Miss Ferrises, the Steeles, the John Smiths— so the author asserts in the first story of the volume. And they are the families that reappear in *Dr. Lavendar's People* (1903) and *Around Old Chester* (1915). A reader comes to take incidental pleasure in recognizing old friends and in reflecting on family history and relations as he pursues his way through these and later chronicles. There is Mr. Ezra Blakeley, conveyer and statistician, hero of *Miss Maria (Old Chester Tales)*, minor character of *The Note (Dr. Lavendar's People)* and other episodes, who paradoxically enlivens the pages with his dead facts. There is his uncompromisingly plain spoken sister-in-law of the deep bass voice, who is particularly delightful— because so right—in the story of the Reverend Mr. Spangler: "They are all fools, in their different way; but one must be kind to them." There is William King, who married his wife Martha for her commonsense and who, as village doctor, turns up only not quite so often as the beloved rector. There is poorrich Miss Lydia Sampson, of *The Grasshopper and the Ant (Dr. Lavendar's People)*, who is again the heroine of a story, *An Old Chester Secret*, in *Harper's*, 1920. Above all, there is Dr. Lavendar, whose cohesive, but not ubiquitous, presence welds the tales. Dr. Lavendar is probably a composite character; he may draw from the Rev. Phillips Brooks, whom Mrs. Deland knew long before she wrote the Lavendar narratives; from her Uncle, the Rev. Dr. William Campbell, once President of Rutgers College; and from Dr. Francis Harrington, to whom *Dr. Lavendar's People* is dedicated.

A number of her characters while retaining their own individuality recall those from earlier or contemporary literature. Lydia Sampson, the seamstress who found Sunday so tedious that she employed it in embroidering her shroud, is own sister to Louisa Ellis, Mrs. Freeman's New England Nun, who often sewed a seam for the pure pleasure of sewing. Amelia, the stupid kindly wife of Thomas Dilworth, is reminiscent of Thackeray's Amelia and Mrs. Freeman's Amelia Lamkin. Outside the main figures, the characters "run to types": inept, good-natured men, such as David Bailey, one of the "fools" in the Spangler story, George Gale (of *Turn About,* in *Around Old Chester);* insane or subnormal women, like Mrs. King (of *The Child's Mother)* and Annie (of *At the Stuffed Animal House);* the mean weakling exemplified in Tom Hastings of *The Thief (Around Old Chester),* the weakling who boasts a streak of good, vitalized in the person of Algy Keen (*The Note,* in *Dr. Lavendar's People);* the mean giant, represented in Lewis Halsey (*The Harvest of Fear).*

Mrs. Deland's skill in characterization is that of the biographer. Her fictive people no less than her

Cleopatra, Queen Elizabeth, Joan of Arc and other figures in *Studies of Great Women* (*Harper's Bazar,* 1900) proclaim her the analyst of mankind, particularly of womankind. For in spite of her greatest character, Dr. Lavendar, her men are otherwise less life-like than her women.

Her sense of humor, a possession which she never cheapens by overuse, with which she just leavens the seriousness of her work, emerges through the peccadilloes of her men and women, or in her own comments on life. Miss Mary Ferris had taken to her bed thirty years ago and had never risen ("except on Saturday, when the sheets are changed, my dear!"). Charles Welwood might have had a memoir written about him had he died young; "for in those days the anaemic child was a great part of spiritual literature". To Mr. Ezra was attached the "awful interest of the free-thinker" because he believed the world had been created not in six days but in six periods. Miss Bailey did not find it necessary to teach that rubbing a cat's fur the wrong way would produce sparks. "But it was very interesting, and as Mrs. Barkley said if such things did not go too far and lead to scepticism they would do not harm." William Rives's petty disposition is hit off perfectly when he asks Dr. Lavendar for the return of a postage stamp.

From *Old Chester Tales* have been reprinted *Where the Laborers Are Few* and *Good for the Soul. An Encore* (1907) and *A Voice* (1912) were subsequently reprinted in *Around Old Chester.* *A Voice* recalls Sir Arthur Quiller-Couch's *Love of Naomi,* as its hero John Fenn is reminiscent of William Geake. Each young preacher, in love with the lady, believes he is troubled about her soul. Mrs. Deland's story is diverting in its use of a love potion and the all but tragic consequences of John Fenn's imbibing it. *An Encore,* one of her best stories for plot, recounts the failure of Alfred Price to bear off Letty Morris in the springtime of their lives; and their triumphant elopement, forty-eight years later, when she is sixty-six and he seventy. Not the least of its charm lies in the avoidance of the ridiculous, except as it is provided through the son and daughter who are absurd in their efforts to prevent what they regard as ridiculous. *Sally (Old Chester Tales)* presents a situation which finds a parallel in Thomas Hardy's *A Waiting Supper;* but Mrs. Deland is optimistic, the English writer fatalistic.

One scene of *The Third Volume (Around Old Chester)* reaches the highest dramatic peak in the chain of Mrs. Deland's short stories. Peter Walton and his wife Eunice loved each other with more than absorbing and enduring love. When she died he would have taken his life, in the insanity of his grief, but for his brother Paul. Casting about for some means to delay his imminent suicide, Paul prevailed upon him to decide whether he should do so through a game of backgammon. At the critical point in the game, played in the room where Eunice lay dead, Peter seized his wife's hand and forced it to drop the die for him. She should determine whether he would follow her or stay behind. The die fell, a double five. Paul threw, he declared, a double six. He lied. He had thrown a five and two. Shortly, he fell into a decline, the lie heavy on his soul. But when he confessed just before he died, his brother Peter had a satisfactory interpretation. Eunice, he thought, had suggested the lie to Paul that he, Peter, might not sin in taking his own life. Thomas Hardy's dice throwing, in *The Return of the Native,* has been much praised. This scene is its equal.

Around Old Chester came after *R. J.'s Mother and Some Other People* (1908). *Many Waters,* of the latter volume, which had received a prize in a *Collier's* competition, is admired in some quarters more than others of the author's tales. The struggle is emphasized, rather than the problem, for after the wife discovers that her husband is a thief she battles with him, and successfully, to make restitution. This volume touches the Old Chester locale only here and there. *The Mormon* and *R. J.'s Mother,* for example, lead the reader into more cosmopolitan settings.

It should be remembered that Mrs. Deland's novels were also appearing: *The Awakening of Helena Ritchie* (1906), *The Iron Woman* (1911) and *The Rising Tide* (1916). Articles and informal essays on the war, originally contributed to various periodicals, were gathered up and published in 1919 under the title, *Small Things*. These essays are beyond the present discussion but not one of her books better reveals her acceptance of the age in which she lives. As Edith Wharton and Dorothy Canfield had done, she fared gallantly forth overseas when she felt the time had come for her to serve. It is illuminating to compare her girls of the earlier stories with the flesh and blood youngsters who were her protegées abroad. Dorothea, of the first story in *Old Chester Tales,* is a true specimen of the timid, shrinking, colorless girl whose actions are predetermined ordinarily, by her elders. It is a long call from her and her brave "promises" to the girls crossing the ocean, parents regardless, for work in France. "You never could tell where the damned thing was going to hit," remarks one of the young ladies, apropos of a shell. Mrs. Drayton in an Old Chester tale says, "I once heard him use a profane word myself. I should not be willing to repeat it. It was—not the worst one, but the one with 'r' in it, you know."

Mrs. Deland inscribes most of her works to her husband. *The Promises of Alice* (1919), a long short story, bears the dedication date May, 1917, and conveys the year of his death: "To Lorin/ This/ The Book He Helped Me Write/ In Our Last Winter Together." The setting of this tale is New England, and the chief character is the daughter of a preacher who has been dedicated to missionary service. Her development is not in the direction planned. The presentation and solution of her problem form the ganglion of the story.

In a letter to the present writer, Mrs. Deland once expressed certain preferences for her own work, though she confessed she found it hard to make up her own mind about them. "I think that the first story in 'R. J.'s Mother,' the one that gives the title to the book, is, perhaps, technically more satisfactory to me, or perhaps I ought to say less unsatisfactory to me than any of the others. At the same time, I do not think that it is as *real* a piece of work as some of the Old Chester Tales. I object to 'Many Waters,' because it is not simple enough. It verges once or twice, I am afraid, upon 'fine writing,' which I detest. I suppose I fell into the temptation of 'fine writing,' because the theme was so emotional that it tempted one into adjectives. It would have been a good deal better story, I think, if it had been condensed by at least one quarter of its present length, and almost every other adjective cut out. The Old Chester stories have the defect of their qualities. They are supposed to be memories, and as memory wanders constantly into side tracks, so these stories are longer than is desirable."

Mrs. Deland speaks, then, of her feeling about the writing of stories as contained in her essay *The Girl Who Writes* (in *The Common Way*, 1904) and says that by her own tests some of her stories would fall short of what they ought to be. "I fancy if I had to choose any of them, I would take 'Good for the Soul,' because though technically it is not as compact a piece of work as 'R. J.'s Mother,' it is, I think, humanly truer. And on the whole, it is humanity that counts, rather than art."

Mrs. Deland's Short Stories:

Mr. Tommy Dove, and Other Stories, 1893.
The Wisdom of Fools, 1897.
Old Chester Tales, 1898.
Dr. Lavendar's People, 1903.
R. J.'s Mother and Some Other People, 1908.
Around Old Chester, 1915.

CHAPTER IX

FEW critics have accused Miss Edna Ferber of preaching a doctrine. "Me'n George Cohan," she wrote in 1912, "we jest aims to amuse." But few would deny that her stories possess qualities sane and wholesome. And the philosophy on which they are built is Work, with a capital W—Carlylean Work.

It is not remarkable that the joy of work illuminated throughout her scintillant pages has been forgotten in the display itself, as the great cause of a Fifth Avenue night-parade may be a matter of indifference to the observer who "just loves pageants and processions, anyway." The flying flags, the drum-beat of the march, the staccato tread, the calcium reds and yellows may obscure the slogan bearing banner. It is remarkable that the inciting force of Miss Ferber's triumphant march has been neglected by the student of underlying causes. There are those of us who believe it to be the significant word she has chanted to the sisters of her generation.

To one who has followed her stories from the beginning, Miss Ferber would seem to have undergone a silent communion with herself, and after asking, "What shall my writing stand for?" answered un-hesitatingly, "Work!" In the Emma McChesney stories, which require three volumes—with one or two overflowing into succeeding collections, she emphasizes the beauty and joy and satisfaction that are the need of labor. And her second published story was an Emma story: *Representing T. A. Buck* (*American,* March, 1911). It succeeded *The Homely Heroine,* her first, published in *Everybody's,* November, 1910. This fact, again, may escape the reader of her first volume, *Buttered Side Down* (March, 1912), which although it groups a number of her representative "working" characters in *The Leading Lady, A Bush League Hero,* and *The Kitchen Side of the Door* yet presents variations of the main theme. As for ex-ample, the last-named cries aloud that the busy-folk on the kitchen side are more respectable than the tip-pling ladies and gentlemen (by courtesy) in front. But *Roast Beef Medium* (1913), including stories written and published before some of those in the first volume, essays to sound what becomes a trumpet call in *Emma McChesney and Co.* (1915).

Hortense of *Blue Serge* thinks:

"If you're not busy, you can't be happy very long."

"No," said Emma, "idleness, when you're not used to it, is misery."

And Miss Smalley of the same story:

"I've found out that work is a kind of self-oiler. If you're used to it, the minute you stop you begin to get rusty, and your hinges creak and you clog up, and the next thing you know you break down. Work that you like to do is a blessing. It keeps you young."

And the author herself (in *Sisters Under Their Skin*):

"In the face of the girl who works, whether she be a spindle-legged errand-girl or a ten thousand dollar a year foreign buyer, you will find both vivacity and depth of expression." . . . She begins this story by asserting: "Women who know the joys and sorrows of a pay envelope do not speak of girls who work as working girls." The whole story hangs on this thesis.

When Emma visited her son, Jock, and her daughter-in-law, Grace, and her grand-daughter, Emma McChesney, charming elderly women came to call.

They fell into two classes: " . . . the placid, black-silk, rather vague women of middle-age, whose face has the blank look of the sheltered woman and who wrinkles early from sheer lack of sufficient activity or vital interest in life; and the wiry, well-dressed, assertive type who talked about her club work and her charities." In their eyes was that distrust of Emma which lurks in the eyes of a woman as she looks at another woman of her own age who doesn't show it."

And the volume ends with this final statement (in *An Étude for Emma*): " . . . there's nothing equal to the soul-filling satisfaction that you get in solo-work."

Miss Ferber has expressed sincerely her own beliefs in these and other passages, and throughout the larger structural values of her stories: in Emma's continuous struggle with the game of life, exemplified in a series of individual conflicts; in her efforts to make of Jock a man, and in her great service to the T. A. Buck Featherloom Petticoat Company. In an article entitled *The Joy of the Job (American,* March, 1918), she says she is sorry for any woman who can play when she wishes. "Play is no treat for an idler." She works, according to her statement, three hundred and fifty mornings a year; she may play golf on the three hundred and fifty-first. It is not that she lacks desire to play, as the pink and green sweaters stream past her door. But the habit of work and the satisfaction that comes from having worked are such that she knows the eighteen holes of golf would be dull and flat once she deserted her typewriter for the links. "And that's the secret of the glory of the work habit. Once you've had to earn your play, you never again can relish it unearned."

From Kalamazoo, Michigan, where she was born August 15, 1887, Edna Ferber moved at an early age to Appleton, Wisconsin. There she went to "grade

school" and to "high school," and there at seventeen
years of age she began work on *The Daily Crescent,*
the youngest reporter of her time. "It was a harrow-
ing job," she admits, including as it did for her day's
work "everything from the Courthouse to the Chicken
Pie Supper at Odd Fellows' Hall, from St. Joseph's
Monastery to the crippled flagman at the railroad crossing up in the chute, from the dry goods store to Lawrence University." Small wonder she learned humanity. When a critic suggested that her tales possessed
an insight into human nature "which, if not genuine,
is very well stimulated," her retort was forthcoming:
"Humanity? Which of us really knows it? But take
a fairly intelligent girl of seventeen, put her on a country daily newspaper, and then keep her on one paper
or another, country and city, for six years, and—well,
she just naturally can't help learning some things about
some folks." . . . It is but logical that human interest
leads all other qualities of her fiction.

Miss Ferber has told how from a hammock on her
father's porch, where she spent much time at a season
when she required rest—or as she phrases it, when
the shop-sign read "Closed for Repairs"—she studied
the passing townspeople. Life became for her a great
storehouse in which at desire she may now enter, and
from the shelves of which she may take down whatever she needs.

She was correspondent for two Milwaukee papers
in these years of 'prenticeship and, later, for *The Chi-*

cago Tribune. And she finished before she was twenty-four her first novel, *Dawn O'Hara,* her experience with which speaks for her artistic and literary ideals. For she threw the script into the waste-basket, whence her mother rescued it. This work, to some extent autobiographic, was published in 1911 and brought its author immediate success. After its publication she found ready market for her short stories.

Many of these first tales depend for background upon Appleton, which becomes "our town" in *The Homely Heroine, The Leading Lady, Where the Car Turns at Eighteenth*—spite of its title—and *A Bush League Hero* (all in *Buttered Side Down*). *A Bush League Hero* was written after a summer of watching the Bush League team play in Appleton, as Miss Ferber wrote the *Bookman* critic who expressed amusement over her naïveté in connection with the sport of baseball. By and by, in succeeding volumes, Appleton, Beloit, and Slatersville gave way to Chicago and New York, and even to cities of other countries. But Chicago and New York are her preferred settings, as St. Louis and New York are Fannie Hurst's.

Her earlier stories, like her later ones, are about men clerks, women clerks, milliners, traveling salesmen and saleswomen, cooks, stenographers, leading ladies, household drudges, advertising specialists—the list is incomplete. No writer shows greater growth in story-making than Miss Ferber—one need only compare *Roast Beef Medium* with any of the later McChesney stories—but she has never been "strong on plot." As she herself admits she does not know—and presumably cares less—what a plot is, she can hardly feel her confessed ignorance to be a handicap. In fact, she goes so far now and then as to twit the critic who insists upon plot as the *sine qua non* of a story. In *The Eldest* (of *Cheerful—By Request,* 1918) she makes her critic, you will remember, a Self-Complacent Young Cub, who says: "Trouble with your stuff is that it lacks plot. Your characterization's all right, and your dialogue. But your stuff lacks *raison d'être*—if you know what I mean." To which she retorts: "But people's insides are often so much more interesting than their outsides. . . ." And it is with people she succeeds best. *The Eldest,* for instance, when it appeared some years ago in *McClure's,* was praised by Franklin P. Adams as the best short story of the year. Yet the plot is worn thin: a lover comes back after many years, only to marry the sister, the younger sister, of his former sweetheart. The interest lies in the character of Rose, the drudge, the slave, the living sacrifice, eternally new as eternally old. In the same volume, *The Gay Old Dog,* which has been reprinted at least twice, faithfully portrays a loop-hound, as he would be known in his Windy City, the young man grown old through sacrifice, the counterpart of *The Eldest.* Gallant Emma McChesney, cheerfully fighting to hold down a man-size job—knowing it requires six times as much work from a woman as from a man to draw for her the same salary—sprang into existence as the ideal of the modern business woman. She will reflect this particular age in her own particular so long as popular interest holds; after that time she will serve for the antiquarian. She is the heroine of *Roast Beef Medium*, of the five stories in *Personality Plus* (1914), of which her son is the hero, and of *Emma McChesney and Co.* (1915). From the number, or chapters, of the last-named, one may select diverting so-called stories. No reader will find fault with *Chickens,* displaying the strong mother hand of this charming saleswoman; nor with *Pink Tights and Ginghams,* "featuring"—as Emma would say—her sympathy for her sex; nor with *Broadway to Buenos Aires,* proving her business acumen, her boundless energy, and her zest for a fight; nor with *Thanks to Miss Morrissey,* wherein after all she reverts to an old-fashioned sort of woman. But the truth is that the author is a novelist in her method. She leaves the reader with memories of her people, as novels do and should do, not with memories of a story. The individual tales of Emma's prowess dwindle in comparison with the fabric he creates out of Miss Ferber's generous distribution of scraps and his own pleasurable tedium in piecing them together. They are ultimately forgotten in the whole pattern. Mrs. McChesney has become real to her creator. In addressing a class at Columbia University, Miss Ferber said quaintly, "When Emma walks in upon me, I *must* give her my attention!"

Even the early stories of Miss Ferber emphasize for the first time in fiction a motive as old as the stomach of man: food. Pearlie Schultz, the Homely Heroine, wins her first—and doubtless her last—kiss through her noodle soup, her fried chicken, and hot biscuits; Jennie of *Maymeys from Cuba* succumbs, in her hunger, to a Scotch scone, after mouth-watering descriptions, by the author, of a corner fruit-stand and the grocery department of a big store. If you would be made ravenous, O weary of palate one! read *Maymeys from Cuba*. And if you would recall the days of yore read the description (in *The Kitchen Side of the Door*) "of a little world fragrant with mint, breathing of orange and lemon peel, perfumed with pineapple, redolent of cinnamon and clove, reeking of things spirituous." Of a world where "the splutter of the broiler was replaced by the hiss of the siphon, and the pop-pop of corks and the tinkle and clink of ice against glass." Perhaps after this devastating passage, the point should be made that no better temperance story has ever been published; beside it, most others look like ready-made propaganda.

Nor does the author forget the negative aspect of this food business. Emma McChesney, who first appears in "our town," dying—in her travel-weariness —for something "cool, and green, and fresh," is informed by the waitress that the menu offers "ham'n aigs, mutton chops, cold veal, cold roast"—to which Emma hopelessly interrupts, "Two, fried." Spectators at the performance of *Our Mrs. McChesney* will not forget Ethel Barrymore's winning question about the prospect for supper, the desk clerk's "Hungarian goulash!" nor Ethel's "My God!" as she departed stairward.

Keats's feast in *The Eve of St. Agnes* has long been praised by epicures, in art, if not in food. The marvel is that no one between Keats and Edna Ferber so emphasized the gustatory appeal. She continues it, with subtle discrimination, in *The Gay Old Dog*. He was the kind of man who mixes his own salad dressing. "He liked to call for a bowl, some cracked ice, lemon, garlic, paprika, salt, pepper, vinegar, and oil, and make a rite of it."

So does Miss Ferber make a rite of food as her generation makes of it a ceremonial. Three titles out of six covering her stories suggest eating, the latest of which is humorously reflective, unconsciously so, perhaps, of reduced rations ensuing upon the war: *Half Portions* (1920). Or is it indicative that the author is losing her own zest in food? Some years ago she thought in terms of food comparisons. For example, to the Editor of *The New York Times*,* she wrote: "I'm the sort of person who, when asked point-blank her choice of ice-cream, says, 'Chocolate, I think —no, peach! No—chocolate! Oh, I don't know.' That being true, how can you expect me to name off-hand the story which I consider the best short story

* January 25, 1914.

in the English language?" It may be mentioned, in
passing, that she lists Maupassant's *The String* and
The Necklace, O. Henry's *An Unfinished Story*, Jesse
Lynch Williams's *Stolen Story*, and Neil Lyon's *Love
in a Mist* among those she has preferred—at various
times. In her article, *The Joy of the Job*, note the
conditions upon which the "chicken salad is a poem,
the coffee a dream, the French pastry a divine confec-
tion." Be it understood that all this is quoted in
admiration.

Miss Ferber compensates her reader for lack of plot
values by her character interest, as has been observed,
and also by interest in immediate detail. And this is
but another way of saying that she entertains by her
style. She probably worked like a young fury, through
newspaper training and through conscious study of
word composition, to achieve her brilliant pyrotech-
nics. In her first collection, she is guilty of the absurd,
" 'No, you don't!' hissed Gus." She had still to learn,
apparently, that hissing requires a sibilant sound. Or,
if she meant to burlesque faintly, her purpose is
not obvious. In her first book, again, she refers
too frequently to the trite, or the prevalent trick. "The
short November afternoon was drawing to its close
(as our best talent would put it)" . . . " 'Better bathe
your eyes in *eau de cologne* or whatever it is they're
always dabbing on 'em in books.' " . . . "As the novelists have it, their eyes met." . . . "As the story

writers put it, he hadn't even devoured her with his gaze." . . . Her later stories have hardly outgrown this habit of jerking and calling halt to the steady march of the narrative, or these interruptions for which no contrasting cleverness and originality can compensate.

This author, like Mr. Joseph Hergesheimer, probably grew up with The Duchess. But her sardonic references to the lady leave doubt as to her opinion. She knew her Martin Chuzzlewit, her Jane Eyre, her O. Henry, and her Bible. Her admiration for George Cohan is genuine. She depreciates, by implication, the "balled-up" style of Henry James. Dickens and O. Henry are her forbears in humor, as the Holy Scriptures back her philosophy. . . .

From a sort of cavil against New York, Miss Ferber finally came to New York—no, "came on" to New York, with her heroine in *Sun Dried*. Then, her first story in *Emma McChesney and Co.* gets away from Manhattan. Her love for travel and her journalistic ability to profit by new scenes are reflected in *Broadway to Buenos Aires* no less than in her own photographs and fact articles. *The Guiding Miss Gowd* (of *Cheerful—by Request*) testifies to an acquaintanceship with Rome, as the photograph of Miss Ferber stepping from the porch of a summer house in Hawaii is proof of her presence there. *"Ain't Nature Wonderful?"* (*McClure's,* August, 1920) creates the certainty, as well as her photograph facing an article

she wrote for *The American,* of December, 1916, that
she knows the Rockies.

All her stories belong to the O. Henry school, but
like her younger sister, Fannie Hurst, she has stolen
away and farther on, bearing with her from the modern
wizard only the trick of catching interest or the turn
of a phrase.   If O. Henry had never opened *Hearts
and Crosses* with "Baldy Woods reached for the bottle
and got it," perhaps she might not have begun *Cheerful—by Request* with "The editors paid for the lunch
(as editors do)."   But life has expanded in the decade
and more since O. Henry's passing; it swings in arcs
beyond the reach he needed to compass all of it he
would.   This one of his successors has widened the
sweep, as the lover of New Bagdad would have done
had he lived.

Half Portions is a varied assortment of new tales,
as *Cheerful—by Request* gathers up old and new.   The
best are, as one would anticipate, stories of character,
wherein the "story"—from a technical point of view—
is usually negligible.   *Old Lady Mandel* is but the
summing up of the career of a professional mother.
Yet *One Hundred Per Cent,* besides bringing Emma
back, happens to be one of the first-rank patriotic
stories published in the progress of the War.   *April
25th, as Usual* marks the height of her accomplishment for 1919.   After its appearance in *The Ladies'
Home Journal* it was voted by the Committee from
the Society of Arts and Sciences one of the best among

thirty-two stories of the year, and was reprinted in the Society's annual volume—*The O. Henry Memorial Award Prize Stories.*

Miss Ferber stretches a continually expanding canvas; she is prodigally wasteful of whole novels in stories like *The Gay Old Dog* and *Old Lady Mandel.* The novel, we venture to predict, is the field wherein she will ultimately "lay by" her most important work.

Miss Ferber's books of stories:

Buttered Side Down, 1912.
Roast Beef Medium, 1913.
Personality Plus, 1914.
Emma McChesney and Co., 1915.
Cheerful—by Request, 1918.
Half Portions, 1920.

CHAPTER X

MANY years have gone by since a writer in *Harper's Weekly* stated, "It seems a supererogation to say aught in praise of her work now, but we are apt to take our literary benefactors so much for granted that we fail to realize their greatness, and fall short of that lively sense of appreciation which we accord the fresh and unaccustomed writer new to his laurels. Since *A Humble Romance* was written, other authors have come and gone, some have stayed, and will stay with honorable excellence, but to none do we owe so much during these years for that distinction and honor which upholds our literary ideals as to the name of Mary Wilkins Freeman."

If this was true in 1903, it is superlatively so to-day: for Mrs. Freeman's succeeding books, her variety of subjects and the extension of her literary territory have strengthened her claim. A reviewer taking stock in 1900 of her short-story store might have put down to her credit: Item 1. Two containers of New England stories of contemporary life labeled, respectively, *A Humble Romance* (1887), and *A New England Nun*

(1891). Contents indigenous to Massachusetts and Vermont, and recommended in particular to buyers of herbs and tonics. Item 2. Two containers of an odd mixture, seemingly for children but agreeing better with adults, labeled *Young Lucretia* (1892), and *The Love of Parson Lord* (1900). Item 3. One vessel of cunningly distilled colonial essence, marked—for lack of more appropriate symbol—*Silence* (1898). Accompanying this, a sort of baby sample, which may be transferred later to a larger vessel: *In Colonial Times* (1899). And the reviewer might have referred to her novels: See shelves above and below for similar substances, done up in individual packets.

A reviewer a score of years later must add to Mrs. Freeman's short-story stock: *Understudies* (1901), *Six Trees* (1903), *The Wind in the Rosebush* (1903), *The Givers* (1904), *The Fair Lavinia* (1907), *The Winning Lady* (1909), and *The Copy Cat* (1914). In general, he will observe that the six animals, six flowers and six trees included under the first two of these titles are used allegorically, that *The Wind in the Rosebush* is a set of six ghost stories, that *The Givers, The Fair Lavinia* and *The Winning Lady* carry on the traditions of her first two volumes, with perhaps a diminution of New England and a heightening of America, and that *The Copy Cat* is the most delightful book about children, for adult reading, which the author has yet turned out. And the same reviewer would note that her best novel, *The Portion of Labor,* was published in 1901. He might recall that Conan Doyle said in 1894 that her *Pembroke* of that year was the greatest piece of American fiction since *The Scarlet Letter*.

Any criticism or appreciation of this writer of short stories should take account, as well, of her novels. To do so is not possible in these limits. But since she is novelist second and story-writer first, tentative conclusions will need less correction than if drawn from her novels alone.

Mary Eleanor Wilkins was born in the year of Edith Wharton and O. Henry, 1862, at Randolph, Massachusetts. When very young she went to Brattleboro, Vermont, where she passed her childhood and girlhood. In 1874 she spent a year at Mt. Holyoke Seminary. On her father's death she returned to Randolph. There, with her friend, Miss Mary Wales, she lived until 1902. On January first of that year she was married to Dr. Charles Freeman, of Metuchen, New Jersey. The years since then have meant for her literary work a loss of intensity in exchange for a corresponding breadth. Uprooting her plant from New England has slightly changed its flower; it blows more freely, though it lacks the distinctive perfume of its native soil.

One of the first considerations attendant upon even the slightest reflections over Mrs. Freeman's stories is their number; a second is their variety, within a given range. Yet it is still the fashion to think loosely that Mrs. Freeman has written books only of New England *genre* life. She has been compared falsely to Gerard Dow, the painter, with whom the connection is one of subject matter only—as another critic has stated— and with whom the comparison holds in only one direction. The popular concept, it is true, has in its favor that this author's most distinctive achievement is the interpretation of the New England folk life of the last quarter of the twentieth century. But this is by no means to say that the rest is inconsiderable or that it would be negligible if her tales treating of the humbler classes were lost forever.

Her prolificness and her variety are explainable in part by her system of work. She told Margaret Hamilton Welch, a number of years ago, that she used two machines, on which were two novels going simultaneously. Conceivably, for rest from either, the two would be of as different types as she could manage. She recently expressed herself to the present writer as being of the "sequential" order. She sits down to write, not knowing what will come, but she begins and continues, thought following thought. She composes, sometimes, seven thousand words a day, typing as she goes; but such a strain may result in enforced idleness for a proportionate period. It has been stated in articles on her work that she plans before composition. This method would be preferable for the arguments of those who advise construction before writing; but the truth is that by her own confession Mrs. Freeman is one of the rare and vanishing craftswomen who progress by inspiration. Mary Brecht Pulver is another. Mrs. Freeman, however, joins to her first inspirational draft a professional finish. She revises two and three times.

Miss Wilkins was in her twenties when she was emboldened to send to Miss Mary L. Booth, Editor of *Harper's Bazar* the manuscript entitled *Two Old Lovers*. It is an old story now, that Miss Booth was about to lay the script aside, thinking from the immature style that some child had written it—in the middle eighties Miss Wilkins was using her pen—when her attention was arrested. She read it three times in as many moods and accepted it. The payment was twenty-five dollars. This tale is somewhat more anecdotal in type than are its successors, though it is handled in the short-story manner, with accent on the period of waiting and suspense, rather than upon the snap at the close.

An Honest Soul appeared in *Harper's*, July, 1884, and is neither better nor worse than the average companion pieces of *A Humble Romance*. Its theme is unique, if apparently trivial—Martha Patch, over seventy, who weaves rag carpets, pieces quilts and braids rugs, has been engaged by two of her neighbors, "Mis' Bliss and Mis' Bennet," to piece a quilt for each, respectively. After Martha has finished the quilts, she decides she has confused the scraps, pain-

fully takes out her stitches, transfers the bits of cloth
—and then finds that she was right at first. In her
effort to do the right thing and in her battle with
pride and poverty, she very nearly dies. But "Mis'
Peters" finds her and restores her with a bit of toast,
a dropped egg, and the inevitable New England tea.
The tale is of representative length—four or five
thousand words—and it is further illustrative of the
characters brought for the first time in a democratic
way before American readers—old, poor old, women.

Old Lady Pingree's case is more pathetic than that
of Martha. She is lame in one hip, so old she has not
only taken thought of her burial clothes and money
but has directed "Mis' Holmes" where to look for
each in the event of her sudden demise. But one yet
poorer than she died first, to whom Old Lady Pingree
gave away her shroud and her eighty dollars of burial
money. The pathos of these worn-out bodies, aged
without having lived, is not emphasized by sob-getting
stuff; but he will be a wretched sort of reader whose
eyes will not burn at the final words of Old Lady Pingree. After she has received the gift of two hundred
dollars, she looks fondly after Benny and Jenny and
wonders whether "they are any happier thinkin' about
gettin' married than I am thinkin' about gettin' buried."

Her old women show, on occasion, a strength of
character, a kind of masculine determination, which
somewhat controverts the theory that they live in a

man-ruled world.   An Independent Thinker is one of
this type, and later Old Woman Magoun (in *The
Winning Lady*, 1909).   Mrs. Magoun has taken care
of her grandchild Lily since the mother's death. After
Lily is fourteen or so, still at heart a little girl carrying
about her doll, her father catches sight of her—and
her beauty.   Old Woman Magoun divines that he is
about to make an evil bargain with regard to Lily, and
she sets off with the child to Lawyer Mason's.   She
pleads vainly that the lawyer and his wife adopt the
little girl.   On the way home she permits Lily, who
has partaken of a sour apple and a glass of milk, to
eat night-shade berries.   The result is inevitable—as
the old woman had foreseen.

These aged ladies are frequently spinsters living
alone, like Betsey *(A Poetess,* of *A New England
Nun);* or in pairs, like Charlotte and Harriet Shattuck,
who ran away from the Old Ladies' Home *(A Mistaken Charity),* back to their poor hovel and its pump-
kin vines.   Nor are the old ladies always poor or
humble. In *The Willow Ware* (of *The Fair Lavinia*)
young Adeline Weaver lives with her stately and conventional Aunts Elizabeth and Jane; Caroline Munson
is the heroine of *A Symphony in Lavender (A Humble Romance),* the title alone being adequately descriptive.   Louisa Ellis, the New England Nun, is endowed
with a sufficiency of worldly goods.   Elizabeth and
Emily Babcock (of *A Gala Dress* in *A New England
Nun)* are poor, but distinctly of a class above that of

flat-footed Matilda Jennings; the Allerton sisters *(The Travelling Sister,* in *The Winning Lady),* though of dwindled possessions, are "college educated" and their very names—Helen, Camille, Susanne—point to a higher social stratum than that of A Poetess, An Old Arithmetician and the humble sisters of these.

The Three Sisters and the Old Beau (in *The Love of Parson Lord)* strikingly relates Mrs. Freeman to Hawthorne. Rachel, Nancy, and Camilla—of whom the youngest is nearly seventy—entertain the old man who is said to be as old as the oldest sister. After the death of the other two, he weds Camilla. The bridal procession cannot but recall that of *The Wedding Knell.* The kinship between the two writers emerges more strongly in *Silence,* a story for which the author has expressed a preference because of its dramatic nature. The time is that of colonial days, and besides this period-kinship with *The Scarlet Letter,* the mood and the diction of the two are similar. The story of the Hawthorne vein that we prefer, however, is *The Gold (The Fair Lavinia).* In no respect does it disappoint one who seeks a good story in character and action, a shock at the end—not at all calculated, in the mechanical sense—and a reflection of the period chosen. No reader will forget the substance of the dénouement: "She looked at the letter again, and called out its contents again in a voice shrill with hysteria: 'The andirons, the fire-set, the handles on the highboy, the handles on the desk, the trimmings of the clock, the pendulum, the trimmings on the best bed, the handles on the dresser, the key of the desk— Gold.' "

Of the stories in *Silence*, we have a weakness for *The Buckley Lady*. It takes one back to samplers, Watts's Hymns, and gravestones bearing crude cherubim heads and wings; but also to one of the loveliest ladies of fiction. Persis Buckley was, quite literally, made a lady by her own family, that she might be worthy of the gentleman who would return for her in a coach and four. Her heavy sister Submit offers a good foil for her beauty: "Her complexion, although she had lived so much within doors, was not sickly, but pale and fine as a white lily. Her eyes were like dark stars, and her hair was a braided cap of gold, with light curls falling from it around her face and her sweet neck." And Tabitha admitted that she could play, had a pretty voice for a song, and could dance —"though that's not to be spoken of in this godly town." Her loveliness was so poignant that when the ultimate hero came and looked upon her, "a tremor ran over him, his lips twitched, and all the color left his face." The Fair Lavinia is described as of such beauty that when Harry Fielding fails, time after time, to catch a glimpse of her, you become convinced she is another Marjorie Daw. But he eventually finds her —only to prefer the real heroine, Isabel Done. *Evelina's Garden,* of this same collection, is the story for which, out of all she has written, Mrs. Freeman has an expressed predilection.

Her young women of the modern era are too frail and negative for one always to sympathize with them. Levina (of *Brakes and White Vi'lets*) is a slender young girl, whose "fair colorless hair was combed smoothly straight back from her high, pale forehead; her serious blue eyes looked solemnly out from beneath it." Nanny Penn, of *The Revolt of "Mother,"* is blonde, heavy, and not very strong. Most of these girls, you know, will continue their non-complaining, laborious existence as wives of farmers or day laborers. But, occasionally, long repression breaks out, as with Narcissa Stone, past middle age. After her father's death, as may be recalled, she took her mother to New York with the intention of remaining one year on the fifteen hundred dollars insurance money. (See *One Good Time, in The Love of Parson Lord.*) There is no humor, only satisfaction, in Narcissa's account of her six days in New York, for her or her faithful William Crane; but there is for the reader. And there is a deep understanding of the rebellion that long had smoldered toward this flare. Repression may emerge as successful rebellion in the married woman's life; as with Mother of the famous *Revolt*. This story first appeared in *Harper's,* September, 1890. Theodore Roosevelt, then Governor of New York, in addressing a gathering of mothers recommended them to read it, for its strong moral lesson. Probably this reference accounts for its popularity. It has been reprinted in half a dozen collections of stories (outside of the author's *A New England Nun*) and lauded as a "model" by story technicians.

But it has been a *bête noire* to its author. She says in *The Saturday Evening Post*, December 8, 1917, as she has said many times in substance: "People go right on with almost Prussian dogmatism, insisting that the Revolt of Mother is my one and only work. It is most emphatically not. Were I not truthful, having been born so near Plymouth Rock, I would deny I ever wrote that story. I would foist it upon somebody else.

"In the first place, all fiction ought to be true, and the Revolt of Mother is not in the least true. When I wrote that little tale I threw my New England traditions to the wind and trampled on my New England conscience. I have had and still have retribution." She insists that the story is spineless. "There never was in New England a woman like Mother. If there had been she most certainly would not have moved into the palatial barn. . . . She simply would have lacked the nerve. She would also have lacked the imagination." And she adds that, as a rule, women in New England villages do hold the household reins, and with good reason. "They really can drive better."

"It is a dreadful confession, but that woman called 'Mother' in The Revolt of 'Mother' is impossible. I sacrificed truth when I wrote the story. . . . My literary career has been halted by the success of the big fib in that story. Too late I admit it. The harm is done. But I can at least warn other writers. When you write a short story stick to the truth. If there is not a story in the truth, knit until truth happens which does contain a story."

It is not amiss to parenthesize over that figure drawn from knitting. Mrs. Freeman knitted during the World War, though she has been taken to task by at least one critic for producing in its progress the child stuff of *The Copy-Cat!* The stories of *The Copy-Cat* had been produced before war was declared. . . .

But to revert to *The Revolt*. Mrs. Freeman is a story-maker, preëminently, and although she combines assurance with "merciless modesty," she does not always, we are inclined to believe, distinguish between her better and her inferior work. Stevenson knew that you can make a story true by finding the right key for it. *The Revolt* is pitched right; the characters are clear, like the people you see standing before you, or that you recall from last year through vibrant memory. The fact is that whether any New England woman ever has moved into a barn or ever will move, "Mother" did so. We know it. It is entirely useless for the author to repent and to try to convince us otherwise. The truth in fiction is stronger than the fact in life. It is lamentable that this narrative, as a coin held near the eyes will cut off the sun, has obscured many other good tales by this author. It is not superior to *A Gala Dress, A New England Nun,*

A Church Mouse, or *A Kitchen Colonel,* all of the same collection, not to mention four stories of as many other volumes: *The Gold, The Buckley Lady, The Givers,* and *The Shadows on the Wall.*

Mrs. Freeman has stated that she does not lift characters from life. "All in my books who are real, are dead," she once stated. But she also admitted that her making the characters do the things that individuals of the type they represent would do in similar environment is remarkably confirmed. One is perfectly convinced that energetic Sophia Lane (of *The Givers*) was capable of returning useless and undesirable wedding gifts sent her niece, and equally convinced that she was capable of securing desirable ones to take their places. And, again, one is equally sure that somewhere Sophia Lane has her counterpart in real life.

Her most successful heroine of the homely type is she of *A Humble Romance.* Critics have commented upon the indelibility of the events and the portrait of Sally. "Her finger joints and wrist bones were knotty and out of proportion, her elbows which her rolled-up sleeves displayed, were pointed and knobby, her shoulders bent, her feet spread beyond their natural bounds —from head to foot she was a little discordant note. She had a pale, peaked face, her scanty fair hair was strained tightly back and twisted into a tiny knot, and her expression was at once passive and eager."

A girl above her sisters in beauty is required for one type of heroine; but one below them, in fortune and looks, is more frequently preferred. And this is true, in particular, when she happens to be one of the numberless variants of the Cinderella heroine, who finally comes out ahead. If she possesses some master virtue, as Sally possessed loyalty, she will win. No reader can forget Sally, her marriage to the tin peddler, Jake's disappearance, her long waiting, her peddling the tins, and her child-like joy over Jake's return.

Her old men are complements of the female characters; they are either set like "Father" of *The Revolt*, and Alfred Tollet of *Gentian*, or ascetic, like Nicholas Gunn, The Solitary. Else, they are old men who are terribly in subjection to the females. Barney Swan, described in the title, *A Village Lear*, dies in the house of Sarah Arnold, with delirious visions of Ellen and Viny, his ungrateful daughters, coming to him across the fields. *A Kitchen Colonel* portrays Abel Lee, aged seventy-eight, as self-effacing, from the first picture wherein he cleans dandelions, to the last, wherein he hastens from the room of the wedding, missing the essential ceremony, to see that the milk does not burn. Within closer limits she differentiates her old men well. The kitchen colonel is handsome, though his face is spare; his features show gentle patience. Old Ephraim, his neighbor, has sharp features, "his old blue eyes took on a hard twinkle, like blue beads."

Mary Moss once estimated in an article for *The Bookman:* "In the census of a Mary Wilkins village the proportion of inhabitants would approximate sixty women upwards of seventy years old, five old men, fifteen middle-aged women, eight middle-aged men, seven girls, three eligible bachelors, two children." One may extend the principle: two of the three bachelors would live together, forty of the old women singly, and seventeen in various combinations with her own class or the other possible inhabitants; the eight middle-aged men and the seven girls would be shared in various relationships among the fifteen middle-aged women. The houses in which they lived would be dominated by the kitchen, with emphasis on the sink; in the living room a center table would boast a lamp mat and lamp, or else an array of albums; the mantel-piece would support an old-fashioned clock; and a bracket on the wall, wax flowers under a case of glass. A hair-cloth sofa, chairs and pictures might complete the list of remaining properties. The author introduces a typical family in *One Good Time:* "Richard Stone was nearly seventy-five years old when he died, his wife was over sixty, and his daughter Narcissa past middle-age."

You will observe that the season Mrs. Freeman favors is usually one of snow. Her country is cold and barren; but from it spring flowers clean and rare, like those on all high and stony places; over it is the bracing mountain air, and throughout its length and breadth a homely sympathy. And blue houstonias bloom in the cemeteries.

There are now more than two children in proportion

to the other members of the village. Chronologically, Young Lucretia—who placed Christmas presents for herself on the tree, because, as she told her aunts, "they said you was cross and stingy . . . an' I didn't want 'em to think you were"—is followed by *The Little Maid at the Door* (in *Silence*), a story of deserted childhood set in the days of the Salem witchcraft terror. Mrs. Freeman has a canny knowledge of childish mental processes: "She turned about and went back to the house, with tears rolling over her cheeks; but she did not sob aloud, as she would have done had her mother been near to hear." This Little Maid finds comfort in a corn-cob after her "poppet" had been thrown down the well, recalling Cosette, in *Les Misérables,* who crooned over her make-shift doll before Jean Valjean presented her with the beauty from the shop. Again, Love Lord's doll has been taken away from her. She finds it in the garret: "She gazed at its poor old rag face, its wide mouth painted grotesquely with pokeberry juice, its staring eyes outlined in circles of India ink. She stroked lovingly the scanty locks made from a ravelled brown silk stocking. She knew that the doll was miserably ugly, but, by a sort of under-knowledge of love, she also knew she was fair. . . . She kissed her as she had never kissed any living thing." So does this author reveal her understanding of one type of little girl. Lucy, of *The Givers,* is the sister of the Little Maid and of Love Lord. She illustrates, still further, the author's ability to get under the skins of her very young people. You are sure had you been in Little Lucy's place you would be uncertain whether you were Lucy Ames or Lucy Hooper and whether you had come from Brookfield, Massachusetts, or Cleveland, Ohio. Little Girl-Afraid-of-a-Dog (in *The Winning Lady*) is equally well psychologized, with respect to fear succeeded by fearlessness.

In *The Copy-Cat* (1914), the author has created types which become epitomes of living individuals we all know. The Cock of the Walk, Little Lucy Rose and Big Sister Solly are in the gallery with Penrod, William Sylvanus Baxter's sister Jane, and Randolph H. Dukes. Big Sister Solly represents the child who, out of her loneliness, invents, creates—nay, to whom comes—a Big Sister Solly. Perhaps your own lonely little sister, who came along after you grew up and went to college, was visited by one of these loving and lovely companions. "Little Hon" came to your small sister and "went away" when the vacation time took you to her again. If the being that Content Adams envisioned may be regarded as an evoked ghost, she represents only one of the numerous spirit types Mrs. Freeman has created. The Little Maid, we know, is dead and buried in her straight, white robe. But when sweet Ann Bailey came to the Proctor house she leaned eagerly from her pillion and smiled and kissed her hand.

"Why look you thus, Ann?" her husband asked, looking about at her.

"See you not the little maid in the door?" she whispered low, for fear of the goodly company. "I trow she looks better than she did. The roses are in her cheeks, and they have combed her yellow hair, and put a clean white gown on her. She holds a little doll, too."

This story seems to say at the close that we see only the ghosts we wish to see. Ann's husband had caught sight of others, when first he and she rode by. But in the atmosphere of witchcraft, the represented facts bring you a strange thrill.

The Wind in the Rosebush, including six tales of the supernatural, contains one remarkable vampire story—though no such word is used of Luella Miller —and one capital, real ghost tale—*The Shadows on the Wall.* This story, which successfully challenges the reader to believe in the shadow of a ghost makes use of a principle most modern technicians have seized. One believes in shadows sooner than realities because the shadow implies the reality; suggestion is stronger than statement. If, then, the shadow of a ghost falls upon the wall, the ghost, even though invisible, must be present. This story, one of Mrs. Freeman's very best, has been justly admired. Julian Hawthorne reprinted it in his *Library of Mystery and Detective Stories (American);* W. Patten included it in his first volume of *International Short Stories.*

Mrs. Freeman's work has been criticized as lacking color. The nature of her subject-matter would bar it —except in the tales of young love and her later stories about children—but her fondness for green looks out here and there from her earliest to her latest pages. It is well adapted to her slight and fair girls: Adeline (of *The Willow-Ware*) dresses in a cross-barred muslin, sprigged with green leaves, ties a green ribbon about her waist and puts on her necklace of emeralds before she descends to meet Elias Harwell. The Buckley Lady, in her green silk pelisse, green petticoat and green bonnet, sits "undistinguishable as a green plant against the trunk of the tree." *The Ring with the Green Stone (Harper's,* February, 1917) throws a green atmosphere over the reader, at the outset of the tale. No writer better understands, though it may be unconscious art with this author, the value of integrating her effects, in color and sound. If they are sparingly needed, these harmonies, she gets along without them.

She also manages well her story clues. If a little girl is to die of eating poisonous berries, she will not eat them too unexpectedly and fortuitously. She will notice them much earlier in the action and ask whether she may have them. If Barney Swan is to be taken in at the last by Sarah Arnold, then Sarah will appear in the opening of the story, not at the last moment by coincidence.

Emphasis has been laid upon Mrs. Freeman's characters, rather than her plot, for the purpose of suggesting her people and her locale who give significance to the plots. In stories however brief, these characters are struggling; sometimes they are involved in complications. It may be only a struggle to be honest in the matter of scraps; it may be a struggle between two strong wills, as between "Father" and "Mother" of *The Revolt;* it may be a struggle of a young girl to "bear up" and have faith until her husband returns, a struggle combined with another line of interest which brings about the complication in *A Humble Romance.* Mrs. Freeman seldom writes a "story" that is other than a story, resting on solid, if slight, groundwork of plot or fable. It will be observed that neither her *Understudies* nor her *Six Trees* has been drawn upon for illustration. The titles are accurate: these are studies, like those of *People in Our Neighborhood.* They were listed above because of the kinship they bear to the short story and because of their brevity. The author's object was to create pictures detached from action. Yet even here, her narrative often does the describing. When we think of Amanda Todd: the Friend of Cats (*People of Our Neighborhood*), we think rather of the ten saucers filled with milk, for the cat, one for each day of Amanda's absence. In recalling *Morning-Glory* (of *Understudies*), we remember that Alexander Bemis was a boy of promise, but that he had a love affair which, ending disastrously, may have had something to do with his ultimate failure. We may lose sight of the morning-glory comparison, that is, in following the actual incidents.

Mrs. Freeman's short-stories are always units.

Very occasionally a character of one story may reappear in another; but the stories themselves are separate and independent; there is no interlinking. Rather are some of her so-called novels a series of interlinking tales. Her best work will stand, a collection of stories of village and country life, reflecting a phase of society in an era that is passing.

Her style is marked by extreme clearness. It is the notable quality in her fiction as it is the quality she urges upon The Girl Who Wants to Write: "Above all things in the matter of style strive for clarity. . . . If you lack complete mastery of a language, use short sentences and simple words." Her own sentences, of French brevity, etch her clear pictures upon the reader's brain. And her contribution is American, as she urges Americanism upon the young writer: "If a writer is American, she should carry her patriotism into her work. Look upon the scene with American eyes, and from an American viewpoint."

Mrs. Freeman's volumes of short stories:

A Humble Romance, 1887.
A New England Nun, 1891.
Young Lucretia, 1892.
Silence, and Other Stories, 1898.
In Colonial Times, 1899.
The Love of Parson Lord, and Other Stories,
  1900.
Understudies, 1901.

Six Trees, 1903.
The Wind in the Rosebush, 1903.
The Givers, 1904.
The Fair Lavinia and Others, 1907.
The Winning Lady, 1909.
The Copy-Cat, 1914.

CHAPTER XI

THROUGHOUT the literature of English fiction there have been men and women of sufficient courage to write of life as it is—not as it might be or should be. Thomas Deloney, realist of the Elizabethan Age, mirrored the world of weavers and cobblers about the time Sir Philip Sidney was constructing the romantic kingdom of Arcadia; Jane Austen reflected the early nineteenth century in works which gently satirized such exaggerations as Mrs. Radcliffe's *The Mysteries of Udolpho;* Anthony Trollope, somewhat later, in his study of existing conditions, balanced the caricatures of Dickens. A similar process has operated in France, by which the realists have maintained the equilibrium of letters; in Russia the realists have dominated.

In America, the romance of Hawthorne and of Poe was succeeded by a hybrid romantic-realism in Bret Harte, after whom William Dean Howells, Mary Wilkins Freeman and Hamlin Garland contributed in their stories, pictures of things as they are. It might appear, as Mr. Cabell says, in effect, in *Beyond*

Life (we cite from memory), that the daily paper affords realism and that the essence of literature is away from fact. It is true, also, that the "real short story" is by its very conditioning a romantic composition. But these criteria do not prevent a lively flow of gratitude to those writers whose concept of art is photographic rather than creative.

Of the realists America has produced, Hamlin Garland is the most unsparing. This fact results from his literary ideals: that truth is a higher quality than beauty, "and that to spread the reign of justice should everywhere be the design and intent of the artist"; and, further, from the fact that the life he knew, upon which he depended for his expression, was severer than that reflected by Mr. Howells, Miss Wilkins, or any other realistic writer in America. For Mr. Garland writes of life as he knows and has known it. His *A Son of the Middle Border* (1917) is a great human document, covering a time and place attempted by no other factual work. In its description of the Middle West it is comparable to Parkman's *The California and Oregon Trail;* in its autobiographical nature, to *The Education of Henry Adams.* In this book Mr. Garland asserts that "childish impressions are the fundamentals upon which an author's fictional output is based." To read the volume and to read his stories is to know, past adventure, that his real life and his stories are of one and the same material. The identity is so marked that here and there the same incidents occur, the same characters, and the same criticisms of life.

Hamlin Garland was born at West Salem, Wisconsin, September 16, 1860. His earliest memories are of Greene's Coulé, or Coolly, where he and his mother and older sister and small brother Frank were living when his father, Richard Garland, returned from the Civil War. His grandfather Garland had gone West, from Maine; his mother's people, the McClintocks, were from Ohio. The elder Garland was a mystic and dreamer; Richard Garland was a concise story teller and lover of drama; Hamlin's mother and Uncle David played the violin. In these details one finds part explanation of the boy who was to become the most distinguished of the Garland family.

The population of Wisconsin in those days was almost pure American; Dudley, McKinley, Bailey, and similar names occur with frequency in Mr. Garland's biography, as Ripley, Gilman, and McLane occur in his stories. He has not omitted the Indian, fast vanishing before the march of the Caucasian, nor the Norse, the immigrant infusion. But, in general, his own history and that of his fictive men and women belong to communities settled by New Englanders.

Life on the farm in Wisconsin and later in Iowa, whither the family moved in 1868, was a mingled grind and joy to Hamlin; he rose at five o'clock to help with the milking of the cows and currying of the horses; in his eighth year he took part in haying and husking, at ten he drove a plow. He has never forgotten the straining of his tendons as his feet sank in the upturned loam, nor the rawness of his arms from binding grain, nor the callous of his hands from corn "shucking," nor the muck of the barnyard where he saw to the needs of the cattle. Neither has he forgotten the sunlight on the upland, the calls of the forest, the community life expressing itself in quilting bees and barn raisings, the groups around the fireside on winter evenings, the excitement of visitin' and goin' to the circus.

Appreciative of a bracing fall morning, he writes in *A Son of the Middle Border:* "The frost lay white on every surface, the frozen ground rang like iron under the steel-shod feet of the horses, and the breath of the men rose up in little white puffs of steam." Exemplifying a boy's hardships, he writes of milking: "We all hated it. We saw no poetry in it. We hated it in summer when the mosquitoes bit and the cows slashed us with their tails, and we hated it still more in the winter time when they stood in crowded malodorous stalls."

There were few books in Hamlin Garland's early home: the Bible and an agricultural report; later, *Mother Goose, Aladdin and His Wonderful Lamp,* and *Beauty and the Beast.* After the family moved to Mitchell County, where the boy knew the "poetry of the unplowed spaces," he started to school and got a taste of literature from McGuffey's Readers. Through these, he made the acquaintance of Scott, Byron, Southey and other poets; through their sonorous rhythm he was fired to be an orator. Like most other story writers of the present day, he found out also, around the age of ten or eleven, the joy to be extracted from Beadle's Dime Novels. And he was profoundly interested in *The Hoosier Schoolmaster* as it appeared serially. It was in school at Dry Run, not so far from the town of Osage, that young Garland made the friendship of Burton Babcock, a character continuing through several chapters of *A Son of the Middle Border,* as his counterpart, Milton Jennings, occurs in the fiction more than once.

The removal of the family, for a year, to Osage gave the boy an immediate environment better suited to his tastes. His reading expanded, for he took omnivorous pleasure in the medley of morsels chance provided. He found joy at the age of fifteen in *Paradise Lost,* though he implies it was largely in the cursing passages. In Osage it was that he heard a sermon which, because of a climactic passage on beauty, opened his eyes to the world of art.

All this time he was a day laborer for his father, harvesting and binding grain. With his wages he was able to enter the Cedar Valley Seminary, where he took the complete course despite the fact that his father's return to the farm meant a harder struggle for him to do so. He and a friend rented a room and did their own cooking. He was determined to get away from the farm, resenting "the dung fork, the smell of manure and greasy clothing." In these formative years he was influenced by the swing of Joaquin Miller's verse, and primarily by William Dean Howells's *The Undiscovered Country*. From that time, 1879 or 1880, the love of realism grew in his heart.

In 1880 Richard Garland's pioneer spirit urged him to the land of the Dakotas, where, at Ordway, he took up a homestead. Hamlin, having finished the Seminary course, set out to look for a school. But once on the road the boy was drawn, by the love of exploration and adventure, through the Middle Western States even to the spending of his last dollar. He took up carpentering as a means of livelihood; then lured by the call of the East he fared forth, this time with his brother Frank, to Boston. After seeing the homes of American authors in and around Cambridge, he continued to the White Mountains, then to New York and Washington. In the fall, he went back to the West and taught for one year in Grundy County, Illinois. Then, in the spring of 1883, he staked a claim in Dakota, which he held down through the succeeding winter of blizzards and cold at forty below. The next year, he mortgaged his claim and set his face again to the East.

In Boston he went about a systematic and comprehensive course of reading, possible through the facilities of the public library. He read English literature, he read the evolutionists, and he read the sociologists. He became interested in the theories of Henry George. He rejoiced to be in the vicinity of Holmes, Lowell and Howells. So greatly did the city exercise its fascination for him that after reading fourteen hours a day without proper physical nourishment and later standing in the balcony of the theater where Edwin Booth played, he crystallized the more solidly his determination to make a place for himself. Through the first work of his pen, lectures on American literature and Booth's acting, he obtained a place in Moses True Brown's School of Oratory. He was there until 1891, when he definitely gave up teaching. It is significant that Boston did not fire his imagination. His first writing of any moment was the description of an Iowa corn husking, inspired by hearing a coal shovel scraping outside his window. He put into *The Western Corn Husking* the feelings of the man who had been there and who reported faithfully what he saw and knew. With the twenty-five dollars *The New American Magazine* paid him for this story he bought his mother a silk dress and his father *The Memoirs of General Grant*.

His first visit home, in 1887, brought back poignantly to him the "pungent realities of the streamless plain." "Each moment was a revelation of new ugliness as well as of remembered beauties." But he did not know then that he had found his theme. He returned to farm work and saw new meaning in the details forced upon his attention: the calloused hands, the swollen muscles, the grimy sweat. Perhaps he dimly apprehended that no exaltation of such toil, no romantic poetizings about the dignity of such labor could serve beauty; he knew it could not serve truth. His feelings at this epoch find parallel in those of Edwin Markham, who looked at *The Man with the Hoe* and flung the famous challenge to the world: "Whose breath blew out the light within his brain?" He wrote to his friend Joseph Kirkland, whose reply set him thinking. "You're the first actual farmer in American fiction,—now tell the truth about it."

He found himself again in Boston, with his literary concepts taking shape, and as soon as he was established he wrote fast and incessantly. At first, the stories all came back; then, as now, the editors wanted something charming and humorous and uplifting. But he had made up his mind to tell the truth about the farm. "I have lived the life and I know that farming is not entirely made up of berrying, tossing the new-mown hay and singing *The Old Oaken Bucket* on the porch in the moonlight." . . . "The grime and the mud and the sweat and the dust exist. They still form a large part of life on the farm, and I intend that they shall go into my stories in their proper proportions." Trying seriously to understand the realistic school of fiction—knowing it to be his own— he read Howells, who was now his friend, and Henry James and the European realists. He met Alice

Brown, Louise Imogene Guiney, Mary Wilkins; he came under the spell of James Herne, who wrote *Shore Acres,* and in whose company Frank Garland was acting.

After a second visit to his old home he was confirmed in his "sorrowful notions" of life on the plain and resumed his writing with the full intention of telling the truth about the western farm. *A Prairie Heroine* sent to *The Arena* drew a check for one hundred dollars and a statement from the editor, B. O. Flower, that he wanted more of the same sort of thing. *A Spring Romance* was bought by *The Century* and other stories found acceptance. His first volume, *Main-Travelled Roads,* was published in 1891, followed by *Prairie Folks* (1892) and *Other Main-Travelled Roads,* 1892. It is to be remembered, however, that in *Main-Travelled Roads* and *Other Main-Travelled Roads* (definitive edition) the reader will find—according to the author's own statement—all the short stories which came from his pen between 1887 and 1889. In the definitive edition he says, "Though conditions have changed since that time, yet for the hired man and the renter farm life in the West is still a stern round of drudgery." He presents that life not as the summer boarder sees it, but as the farmer endures it. And in another place he has stated that in answer to criticism on his portrayal of farm life, he said, "A proper proportion of the sweat, flies, heat, dirt and drudgery of it all shall go in." And it is there. He discovered, however from the criticism of Howells, Matthews and Stedman that to find acceptance he must balance Significance and Beauty. Hence, the æsthetic came to assume a greater part than the didactic; the artist to correct the preacher.

These three volumes are, by general verdict, the best of Mr. Garland's books. His first long novel, *A Spoil of Office* (1892), he wrote after revisiting the West for renewed observation; the most popular of his long stories, *Rose of Dutchers Coolly*, appeared in 1895. A steady stream has poured from his pen, including reminiscence *(Boy Life on the Prairie)*, poems *(Prairie Songs)*, essays *(Crumbling Idols)*, and realistic novels, among which are *Cavanagh, Forest Ranger* and *Money Magic*.

In 1892 Mr. Garland left Boston for New York. In 1893 he visited Chicago and the World's Fair in company with his parents and in the same fall bought a home at West Salem. Later he returned to New York, where he now lives. He was married in 1899 to Miss Zulima Taft, sister of Lorado Taft, the sculptor.

Main-Travelled Roads includes two stories which had gone from publisher to publisher without finding acceptance: *Up the Coulé* and *A Branch Road*. The first of these is the best example of unflinching realism produced in its decade. It also illustrates, as may be seen by comparison with the actual life reflected, the approved method of the realist artist. Howard Mc-

Lane visits his old home after he has found success
as an actor (Howard is patently a composite of Hamlin and Frank, as they appear in *A Son of the Middle
Border*); Howard takes a silk dress to his mother and
a book of memoirs to his brother. (So did Mr. Garland take the dress to his mother and the book to his
father); Howard worked with the farm hands (so
did Mr. Garland, on his first return); Howard loathed
the barnyard (so did Mr. Garland). See the scene
from Howard's angle: "How wretchedly familiar it
all was! The miry cow-yard, with the hollow trampled out around the horse-trough, the disconsolate hens
standing under the wagons and sheds, a pig wal-
lowing across the sty, and for atmosphere the deso-
late, falling rain." Making his way around the periph-
ery of the yard, clinging to the fence, he comes upon
the barn, where Grant is mending a harness.
"The old man was holding the trace in his hard brown
hands; the boy was lying on a wisp of hay. It was
a small barn, and poor at that. There was a bad
smell, as of dead rats, about it, and the rain fell
through the shingles here and there"—(*Up the Coulé*).
See it from Mr. Garland's angle: "Clearing out from
behind the animals was one of our never ending jobs,
and hauling the compost out on the fields was one of
the tasks which, as my father grimly said, 'We always
put off till it rains so hard we can't work out of
doors.' This was no joke to us, for not only did we
work out of doors, we worked while standing ankle-

deep in the slime of the yard, getting full benefit of the drizzle." And on his return (the return comparable to Howard Grant's), he says, "there is no escape even on a modern 'model farm' from the odor of the barn"—*(A Son of the Middle Border)*.

Further parallels might be cited, but it is needless to continue checking off details: any one may do so by comparing Mr. Garland's visit with that of Howard. By way of a further comment on the realistic method, however, it will be observed that as Howard is a composite of Hamlin and Frank, so Grant in the fictive story represents the father, Richard Garland, of real life. This deduction is not to be misconstrued that the characters or personalities are copies; it is drawn to illustrate the selective and combining operations of the realist—the methods in the main allowed to him as an artist.

Take another story, *A Day of Grace (Other Main-Travelled Roads)*, and compare Milton Jennings with Mr. Garland's friend Burton. In *A Son of the Middle Border* Hamlin meets Burton one afternoon and inquires about the bulbous contents of Burton's pockets. He receives this reply: " 'I went over to see Nettie. I intended to give her these apples,' he indicated the fruit by a touch on each pocket, 'but when I got there I found old Bill Watson, dressed to kill and large as life, sitting in the parlor. I was so afraid of his finding out what I had in my pockets that I didn't go in.' " In *A Day of Grace*, Milton says: " 'Well, when I got

over there I found young Conley's sorrel hitched to
one post and Walt Brown's gray hitched to the other.
I went in but I didn't stay long; in fact, I didn't sit
down. I was afraid those infernal apples would roll
out of my pockets.' "

Young men, many of them, are among Mr. Garland's chief characters; they are those, with the girls,
whom the wing of romance brushes. But even in
his stories of youth, the setting of real life is never
lost; in his most successful love stories, the nagging,
the irritation of everyday life, is never omitted.
When Lyman Gilman asks for Marietta Bacon *(William Bacon's Hired Man,* of *Prairie Folks,* later
William Bacon's Man, in the revised edition of *Other
Main-Travelled Roads),* he meets such savage response
that, to save himself, he knocks Bacon down. Then
he flees with Marietta. But, in spite of the fact that
they are ultimately forgiven and that Mr. Garland,
in learning to emphasize the æsthetic at the cost of
the didactic, ends on the "happy" note, the reader
knows that love and youth have conquered for only
a brief space. The grind of farm life will bend and
crush Marietta, coarsen Lyman, and in the long run
stamp them, as it has placed its die on Lucretia Burns
and Sim Burns. *Sim Burns's Wife* (so entitled in
Prairie Folks; Lucretia Burns, in *Other Main-
Travelled Roads)* is a dirge of life in death, the story
of a woman of the farm, cowed, broken, cast down
to the dust of despair by the harshness of her hus-

band and the ugly toil of her daily routine. Sim is a brute because his share of existence has developed his brute nature. *Before the Low Green Door* (of *Wayside Courtships* (1897), reprinted in *Other Main-Travelled Roads*) is a black diamond that flashes somberly the life, through one death bed scene, of an older and more pathetic figure. Her "poor, faithful hands, hacked and knotted and worn by thirty years of ceaseless daily toil . . . lay there motionless upon the coverlet." Martha, the visitor, asks her if she has found no compensation; if she is sorry she has had children. "I ain't glad," she replies. "They'll haf to grow old jest as I have—git bent and die. They ain't be'n much comfort to me . . . "

Hands have a powerful meaning for Mr. Garland. Again, the passage just cited, has a parallel more than once in his autobiography. "A twinge of pain went through my heart as I looked into their dim eyes and studied their heavy knuckles. I thought of the hand of Edwin Booth, of the flower-like palm of Helena Modjeska, of the subtle touch of Inness, and I said, 'Is it not time that the human hand ceased to be primarily a bludgeon for hammering a bare living out of the earth?' "

The author portrays not only the anguish and pathos of the women's lives, the crassness and the enforced brutality of the young men, the ugly struggle of the older men to survive—relieved insufficiently by the graces of love and compassion and gallantry; he

touches with the same vivifying effect of reality—
here synonymous with realism—the country settings,
sports and pastimes. *Saturday Night on the Farm*
(*Prairie Folks*) treats the reader to the *New Magdalen,* the drama by Wilkie Collins, as it was presented
at the town hall; then transfers him in the company
of the farm boys to the village saloon, and finally
regales him with a fight. In *The Sociable at Dudley's*
the young people move through the mazes of Weevily
Wheat; *Daddy Deering* has for hero the violinist who
rasps out directions for the dance.

Frequently the author sets the action of his tales in
the church, "meeting house." In *Elder Pill, Preacher*
(*Prairie Folks*) he presents the fighting parson admir-
ably, then having gained the reader's sympathy for
Elder Pill, he allows the reader to see that exhorter in
most insincere wind-bag flights of oratory; but he
justifies his first impression, for the Elder meets with
enlightenment, turns right about face and humbly goes
after education. The effect of exhorters upon sensitive souls is set forth by Mr. Garland without mincing
words. The women cry out, fall down, roll on the
ground, stiffen, and gasp as they suffer catalepsy
induced by the preacher's explosive ranting and mad
cavorting among the moaning audience.

In his brighter moments, Mr. Garland is optimistic.
"I admit," he closes his preface to the definitive edition of *Other Main-Travelled Roads* (1913), "youth
and love are able to transform a bleak prairie into a

poem, and to make of a barbed wire lane a highway of romance." He does not, however, emphasize the romance.

"What are you going to do about it?" is a question this author sometimes discusses through the dialogue of his characters. Man's laws are to blame rather than nature's laws. Radbourn, who talks to Lily *(Sim Burns's Wife)*, would abolish all indirect taxes, have state control of privileges when private ownership would interfere with equal rights, and would destroy speculative holdings. But it is more than conceivable that Mr. Garland's contribution to solving the problem lies in painting the picture. That the solution has not come is evidenced by the latest census report which states that sixty towns hold one fourth of the American population. The farmer has learned, as Mr. Garland learned, that the life is hard and lacks compensation; he has returned, therefore, to the city. But this is not "the right answer"; for the farm cannot be neglected. The wise man will be the one who directs an exodus to it which will be, somehow, at whatever cost, unattended by the discomforts, indecencies and suffering that have attended the necessary struggles of all pioneers.

The salubrious effect of such realism as Mr. Garland's is the correction of false romantic ideals, which obscure the vision of the reader and blind him to existing and unhappy conditions. The unhealthful reaction

to such realism is pessimism and, ultimately, despair.
If men of long past cycles had not fought and conquered, we their descendants would be sitting to-day in
trees. The conquering spirit is the weapon. Meantime, men must work—and women; for they have
not time to weep.

Mr. Garland's works:

Main-Travelled Roads, 1890-8.
Jason Edwards, 1891-7.
A Little Norsk, 1891.
Prairie Folks, 1892-8.
A Spoil of Office, 1892-7.
A Member of the 3d House, 1892-7.
Crumbling Idols, 1893.
Rose of Dutchers Coolly, 1895-8.
Wayside Courtships, 1897.
Ulysses Grant (biog.), 1898.
Prairie Songs, 1894.
The Spirit of Sweetwater, 1898.
The Eagle's Heart, 1900.
Her Mountain Lover, 1901.
The Captain of the Gray Horse Troop, 1902.
Hesper, 1903.
Light of the Star, 1904.
The Tyranny of the Dark, 1905.
The Long Trail, 1907.
Money Magic, 1907.
Boy Life on the Prairie, 1907.

The Shadow World, 1908.
Cavanagh, Forest Ranger, 1909.
Victor Olnee's Discipline, 1911.
Other Main-Travelled Roads, 1913.
A Son of the Middle Border, 1917.
A Daughter of the Middle Border, 1921.

CHAPTER XII

"O. HENRY"

ON December 2, 1897, the S. S. McClure Company wrote acceptance of a story, *The Miracle of Lava Cañon.* The letter addressed to W. S. Porter, Austin, Texas, is the first record of a short-story accepted from the pen of the man now known as O. Henry.

From April 25, 1898, to July 24, 1901, William Sydney Porter was in prison, whence he emerged a craftsman in the art of narrative. In the decade before his death, June 5, 1910, he wrote two hundred and fifty short-stories, ten volumes of which were published in the year 1904 to 1910.

The name of O. Henry is indissolubly associated with the short-story. He is the most popular of American story writers; more than two million sets of his works have been sold and there is no diminution in the sales. His books have appeared in London in shilling editions and de luxe editions; in New York, for fifty cents the volume and five hundred dollars the set. He has been translated into a number of European languages; it is only a matter of time until he will be translated into all. To his memory rise tablets, a hotel bearing his name, and a prize for the best short-story annually produced in America.* If he knows, he must delight in the assortment. He was suggested for the Hall of Fame just as the necessary ten years since his death had rounded to completion.

What are the open secrets of his success and his popularity? The successful story writer—emphasis on story—will be popular. For narrative is of all literary types the most entertaining to the greatest number. O. Henry conveyed the greatest enjoyment in a given space. This ability means that he infused into every sentence the spirit of life. No dead matter cumbers his pages. His narrative is neither bare, unadorned plot, nor plot padded with flabbiness of faded philosophy, lumpy cushions of exposition or fatty flesh of description. His native ability in selection and suggestion and his sense of proportion he brought to efficiency through mastery of technique. Out of his discriminating selection comes novelty of subject and treatment; out of his sense of proportion comes perfect adjustment of parts. His power of suggestion enabled him to choose words and to join them in sentences which carry electric currents. His stories shock through their combination of currents, another way of affirming that he mastered the art of surprise.

In so far as the artist touches the heart of one person, so far he is an artist. He succeeds in direct ratio

* Founded by the Society of Arts and Sciences.

to the number emotionally moved.   O. Henry swept
with sure resonance the master chords; for he knew
what makes men happy and what makes men sad.   He
used over and again, in varying combinations, the
common denominator of the greatest appeal.   Wholesome laughter and tears were his objectives.   He refrained from attacking subtle shades of emotion or literary shadows of passion, as he refrained from gross
melodrama.   He was endowed with a unique sense of
humor.   "I am the only original dispenser of sun-
shine," he whimsically wrote.   And he acquired,
through attrition, something of the power of divine
sympathy.

The artist must know life and reflect it as best he
may through the peculiarly tinged lens of his temperament.   Within a certain area of middle-class life, O.
Henry was on familiar terms with many types of humanity.   This area is bounded on the West by his
cowboys and ranches, on the East by his shop-girls
and Bagdad-by-the-Subway, on the South by his col-
onels and the domain of the Gentle Grafter.   He kept
close to the scenes and lives with which he had first-
hand acquaintance.   His work, therefore, has continuity as his own life had it.   Stephen Leacock has reminded us, "It is an error of the grossest kind to say
that O. Henry's work is not sustained.   In reality his
canvas is vast.   His New York stories, like those of
Central America or of the West, form one great picture as gloriously comprehensive in its scope as the

lengthiest novel of a Dickens or the canvas of a Da Vinci."

Of his stories, fifteen have settings in Central and South America, which he had visited; twenty-one have for various backgrounds southern states he knew; forty are set on the wide stage of Texas, where he lived a number of years; fifty or more in New York, his adopted home and the one that held for him the greatest attraction. He was never in England, and only his earliest story preserved, the slap-stick burlesque, *Lord Oakhurst's Curse,* pretends to an English setting. He was never in France, and (besides the farcical *Tracked to Doom,* which parodies Le Cocq) only *Roads of Destiny,* influenced by Stevenson's *Sire de Malétroit's Door,* has there its *mise en scene.*

All great artists have been democratic. O. Henry was the first of short-story fabricants never to condescend by word or feeling to any of his characters. His shop-girl is an entity, not less than the grafter, the grafter not less than the aristocrat colonel." "Most literary men," said Francis Hackett of *The Chicago Evening Post,* "discuss those who are not 'élite' as a physician would discuss a case—scientifically, often humanly, interested, but always with a strong sense of the case's defects and deficiencies. To O. Henry, on the contrary, the clerk is neither abnormal nor subnormal. He writes of him without patronizing him." With Maupassant, he treats his characters objectively; and if his own cynicism intrudes, it is softened with the kindliest humor, not sharpened by the French author's sneer.

His life has been called drab. Drab it was, placed alongside the blue and purple thrills of Jack London's vivid career or the symphonic colors of R. H. D.'s orchestrated experiences. But he rounded many western islands and traveled far in the realms of gold.

His work was determined by his incursions into the land of fancy as it was by his outward contacts. From his boyhood love for the dime novel and from his acquaintance with Jimmie Connors emerged the *Retrieved Reformation* of Jimmy Valentine. From the later exorcism of ghost stories, he conjured out of the fourth dimension *The Furnished Room*, redolent of mignonette. From the treasure of the *Arabian Nights* he drew titles—*The Caliph and the Cad, the Bird of Bagdad*—and his favorite names for New York, The City of too Many Caliphs and Bagdad-by-the-Subway, as well as an atmosphere through which he viewed its passing show. In the days of his pharmacal researches he probably came across the name of the French chemist, Etienne-Ossian Henry, and later borrowed its abbreviated form (perhaps by unconscious trick of memory) for his pen-name. Certainly he introduced his pharmaceutical knowledge into a number of tales, up to the final, *Let Me Feel Your Pulse.* Upon his services as draftsman depended *Georgia's Ruling, Witches' Loaves,* and *Buried Treasure.*

Friends in San Rosario, alone, would testify that he had been teller or bookkeeper in a bank.

In O. Henry existed the nice balance of conditions essential to success. His father gave up doctoring to become an inventor; his mother painted pictures and wrote verse. He practised story-telling at school; his ears and eyes were wide open; he read with avidity. Out of various environments he gathered much; he suffered, and then he wrote.

William Sidney Porter (Sydney, later) was born in Greensboro, North Carolina, September 11, 1862. There in a town of 2,500 people he lived to the age of nineteen. His early memories were those of lying on the floor of the barn where his father worked at the problem of perpetual motion; of playing at Ku-Klux and Indian with his friend, Tom Tate; of roaming about, fishing and hunting, leaving usually to the other fellow the angling and the shooting. He learned to box, fence and play chess; he dreamed and read. According to his friend Tom, the boys owned at the age of seven or eight a collection of George Munro's dime novels second only to the array on a cigar stand.

The only schooling Will Porter had was at the hands of his Aunt Evelina. She seems to have been a rare teacher, one who loved literature and fostered its spirit among her charges. Between 1874 and 1883, Willie Porter read more than in all the years afterward, and he read—he said—nothing but the classics.

On Friday nights Miss Lina gathered the students about her fire, where they roasted chestnuts and told stories on the collaborative plan. He was her best story-teller, as he was her best all-round pupil and artist. His drawings, even then bearing evidence of his kinship to Worth, the cartoonist, she used for models.

About 1877 Will Porter began working in his Uncle Clark Porter's drugstore, and there he remained until 1882. The chief assets to his career from that experience were, first, much reading from the novelists— Dickens, Thackeray, Reade, Lytton, Collins, Hugo, and Dumas; second, a practical knowledge of pharmacy, which made endurable the after years in Columbus and which he also used in his stories. "A short examination of his work would show that he knew the names of about seventeen drugs," sums up Stephen Leacock, "and was able to describe the rolling of pills with the life-like accuracy of one who has rolled them." But whatever his knowledge compassed, it served him at need. Third, he improved his skill in drawing, by sketching the customers and characters who visited the store. Dr. C. Alphonso Smith, O. Henry's friend and biographer, says: "The skill of the story-teller that was to be is seen to better advantage in his pictures of groups than in his pictures of individuals. . . . They gave room for a sort of collective interpretation which seems to me very closely related to the plots of his short stories. There is the same selection of a central theme, the same saturation with a controlling idea, the same careful choice of contributory details, the same rejection of non-essentials, and the same ability to fuse both theme and details into a single totality of effect."

Because of close confinement and the fear of tuberculosis—his mother had died at the age of thirty-two, when he was only three years old—he began to rebel at the prospect of life spent further in the store. In March, 1882, he left for Texas with Dr. and Mrs. Hall, who were going out to visit their son, "Red," or Jesse Lee Hall. So closed the first epoch of Will Porter's life.

In 1882, on the ranch superintended by Lee Hall, and in his excursions from it, the boy from Carolina saw something of the struggle between legitimate owners and cattle thieves. Texas and Hall opened to him the world of romance. His first story, mentioned above and afterwards revised as *An Afternoon Miracle,* reveals that the possibilities of the ranch paved the way for his success in fiction. Reminiscent of this period are *The Higher Abdication, Hygeia at the Solito, The Missing Chord, The Last of the Troubadours, Madame Bo-Peep of the Ranches,* and other tales, all flavored with what he himself once called "the elusive tincture of affairs," as he knew them in La Salle County. It is a matter of record that he was writing in 1882 and 1883 stories which in the opinion of his friend, Mrs. Hall, equalled those of Rider Haggard; but these he destroyed. He continued his reading, branching out into history, biography and science. Tennyson was his favorite poet and Webster's Unabridged Dictionary his constant, if not pocket, companion. He studied French and German, it is to be suspected to their ultimate sole availability for humorous effect. " 'Tiens!' shouts the Gray Wolf, now maddened to desperation, and drawing his gleaming knife, 'Voilà! Canaille! Tout le monde, carte blanche enbonpoint sauve qui peut entre nous révenez nous a nous moutons!' " (Tracked to Doom). He probably achieved proficiency in Spanish.

In March, 1884, he went to Austin, where he lived with the ex-Carolinian, Joe Harrell, and became as one of the family. Arthur W. Page observes that it was his ironical fate to be a dreamer and yet to be harnessed to tasks that brought his head from the clouds to the commonplaces of the store and the street. But if his successive occupations are responsible in part for his breadth of sympathy, therein lies compensation. He was clerk in a tobacco store, he was bookkeeper, draftsman, singer in church choirs, member of a military company, and cartoonist during the years in Austin. And all the while he lived in an atmosphere of adventure that was the product of his own imagination.

In 1884 he worked for a real estate firm. From January, 1887, to January, 1891, he held the position in the General Land Office as Assistant Compiling Draftsman. On July 5, 1887, he married Athol Roach,

and it is significant that this is the year he began to
rely upon his pen as an additional source of income.
According to R. H. Davis of *Munsey's Magazine,* who
met him years later, O. Henry was "buoyant and lazy
in prosperity, depressed and productive in adversity."
It is probable at this time in Austin—years on which
he looked back afterward as the happiest of his life—
that he was driven to write by the mere need for more
money.   He was happy in his home and wife and, after
she came, his daughter Margaret.   *Georgia's Ruling,*
written in prison and published in *The Outlook,* June
30, 1900, may be viewed as the effort of one suffering
from nostalgia to comfort himself with pictures of the
past.   *Witches' Loaves (Argosy,* March, 1904), *Buried Treasure (Ainslee's,* July, 1908), *Bexar Script
2692* (written in 1894, but published first in *Rolling
Stones)*—all witness the "copy" value of the Land
Office.

January 21, 1891, Mr. Porter resigned his position
as draftsman and entered the First National Bank of
Austin as teller.   This position he held until December, 1894, when, having bought the printing outfit of
Brann's *Iconoclast,* he projected *The Rolling Stone.*
This weekly was a forerunner of his methods as humorist and caricaturist in his later work; it revealed
to him, moreover, that he was fitted to take up writing
seriously.   When the paper failed—April 27, 1895—
he went to Houston.   There he held a position on *The*

Daily Post. His first column appeared October 18, his last on June 22, 1896.

What his biographer terms the shadowed years were close upon him. Indictments against Mr. Porter summoned him from Houston in 1896; he was charged with embezzling funds from the Bank of Austin. One item read, "On November 12, 1895, $299.60." Dr. Smith has pointed out, "Nothing in O. Henry's life is better substantiated than that on November 12, 1895, he was living in Houston and had resigned his position in the Austin bank early in December, 1894." But the dates probably escaped the notice of O. Henry himself.

He started to Austin, but transferred to the New Orleans train and later sailed for Honduras. In New Orleans he remained some time, either on his outward journey or the return. *Whistling Dick's Christmas Stocking (McClure's,* December, 1899), *The Renaissance of Charleroi, Phoebe, Blind Man's Holiday,* and *Cherchez La Femme* reflect the suburban setting and the heart of the old French town. On the way to Honduras he fell in with Al Jennings, whose connection with O. Henry has since received exploitation in the daily papers and made familiar many details of their common experiences.

"Latin America fascinated O. Henry," says Stephen Leacock. "The languor of the tropics; the sunlit seas with their open bays and broad, sanded beaches, with green palms nodding on the slopes above white painted steamers lazily at anchor—quaint Spanish towns, with adobe houses and wide squares, sunk in their noon-day sleep—beautiful señoritas drowsing away the afternoon in hammocks; the tinkling of the mule bells on the mountain track above the town—the cries of unknown birds issuing from the dense green of the unbroken jungle—and at night, in the soft darkness, the low murmur of the guitar, soft thrumming with the voice of love—these are the sights and sounds of O. Henry's Central America." And he concludes, "Whether this is the 'real Central America' or not is of no consequence. It probably is not."

Meantime, Mrs. Porter, back at home, was ill. When her husband heard of her failing health, he returned. He arrived in Austin February, 1897, and went free under doubled bond until Federal Court convened. Mrs. Porter died July 25, 1897. By singular irony, his first published sketch, *The Final Triumph*, appeared in *Truth* the next month.

When Will Porter was tried, he was convicted largely because he had fled from justice and was a fugitive from July, 1896, to February, 1897. His friends have always believed him innocent of the charge against him. He himself behaved apathetically, but he wrote his mother-in-law—she and Mr. Roach remained his staunch friends—"I am absolutely innocent of wrong-doing in the bank matter, except so far as foolishly keeping a position that I could not successfully fill."

He entered the penitentiary at Columbus, Ohio, April 25, 1898. Humiliated, he was none the less obedient to rules and soon found himself in a trusted position. Except that he was detained, he was as free as though he had voluntarily chosen "the place" (his term for the prison, in letters to friends) for his abode. As night pharmacist, he did not sleep in a cell but on a cot in the hospital. Later, secretary to the steward, he was free to walk along the streets and the river. On his rounds among the prisoners, he learned their life stories. He heard the true story of Jimmie Connors, who was in erroneously on the specific charge but correctly enough in general, the story from which evolved *A Retrieved Reformation.* He heard the actual exploits which later became tales of the *Gentle Grafter.* Of the dozen or so stories written in prison and published, the best is *A Blackjack Bargainer,* which appeared in *Munsey's,* August, 1901. The story of *Georgia's Ruling* will also continue to have admirers. But at least one dramatist prefers *The Marionettes,* of this period, to all O. Henry's stories.

In these years he served his novitiate. Some of his tales were published while he was yet in prison. He sent them under cover to New Orleans, whence they were remailed to New York magazines. His editors, assumed, of course, that he was living in the Crescent City and that the pseudonym of O. Henry he had chosen in Columbus was his real name. When he was freed, July 24, 1901, two years before his time was up, he joined Mr. and Mrs. Roach and his daughter in Pittsburg. They fitted up a room for him in the hotel, of which they were proprietors, and there he settled down to continuous writing.

In 1902, Gilman Hall and Richard Duffy of *Ainslee's,* who had accepted a number of O. Henry's stories, asked him to come to New York. There was no business proposition involved; the editors simply foresaw success for the writer if he came to the city and through their publishers advanced the check that brought him.

O. Henry came, saw and was conquered. If Texas awoke in him a response to romance, and if his years in Columbus grilled him to expression, then New York gave him the material whereon he needed most to try his skill. He is "the narrator and supreme celebrant of the life of the great city," writes Dr. Archibald Henderson*, "in the parks and open squares, the cheap restaurants and bowery haunts, the crowded department stores, and the tiny homes of the aerial flat dwellers." Or, as Francis Hackett puts it: "In one sense Broadway is the spinal column of his art, and the nerve branches cover all Manhattan. He knows the side streets where Maggie boards. He knows Harlem. He knows the narrow chested flat. He knows the Bowery, Irish and Yiddish. He knows the Tenderloin, cop, panhandler, man about town, sport, bartender, and waiter. He knows Shanleys and Childs, the lemon-odored

* *Southern Review,* May, 1920.

buffet and the French *table d'hôte*. He knows the sham Bohemia, the real Bohemia. And his stories are starred with little vignettes of the town, paragraphs of unostentatious art that let us see Madison Square, or the White Way, or the Park, or the side street in springtime—all clear as the vision in the crystal!"

At first, as was natural, his stories dealt with the scenes he had left in the other Americas and Texas. He had made up his mind to keep the shadowed years secret. And the first impression he made upon his friends at Ainslee's was a "reticence of deliberateness." Gilman Hall thought, at times, that O. Henry might once have killed a man, as he had a way of looking quickly around a restaurant on entering, but Mr. Hall abandoned this theory when he discovered that O. Henry did not carry a pistol. If Mr. O. W. Firkins* is right, then O. Henry was still serving his apprenticeship before coming into his own in the New York stories. "With the exception of his New Orleans, I care little for his South and West, which are a boyish South and West, and as little, or even less, for his Spanish-American communities." At the same time, there are critics who prefer his stories of the South. *A Blackjack Bargainer, A Municipal Report, The Ransom of Red Chief*—these surely are among his ripest work. And Dr. Henderson remarks, "His own rich and variegated experiences in the Southwest and in

* *The Review,* September 13, 1919.

South America; the strange and bizarre narratives he
gleaned from his fellow prisoners—cracksmen, des-
peradoes, hoboes, men of the underworld—these by
some marvelous alchemy of the creative imagination,
he transmitted into the gold of literary art."

O. Henry's homes in New York may be traced
roughly in his stories. Mr. Arthur Bartlett Maurice*
has shown that he lived first in West 24th Street, then
across the Square in East 24th Street, near Fourth
Avenue. *A Madison Square Arabian Night* was published in *The World,* January 24, 1904; it and other
stories suggest the close connection between this locality
and his use of it. His third residence was 55 Irving
Place, "a few doors from old Wash Irving's house,"
he wrote. This number is near Gramercy Park, the
scene of part of the action of *Two Thanksgiving Gentlemen,* published in *The World,* November 26, 1905,
and not far from Allaire's Restaurant, or Scheffel Hall,
which is the setting for *The Halberdier of the Little
Rheinschloss (Everybody's,* May, 1907).

His fourth home was back across the Square in a
house next to the rectory of Trinity Chapel in West
25th Street, whence he moved to The Caledonia, 28
West 26th Street. The three squares, Madison, Union
and Gramercy Park figure repeatedly in the stories
written within the fourth period of his life. "Nor did
ever Haroun-al-Raschid and his viziers, wandering at

* *The New York of the Novelists.*

will in the narrow streets of their Arabian city, meet
such varied adventure as lies before us, strolling hand
and hand with O. Henry in the new Bagdad that he
reveals."

In 1904, O. Henry published sixty-six stories; in
1905, fifty-five. From December 6, 1903, to July 15,
1906, *The World* alone published one hundred thirteen
stories from his pen.*

Meantime, Mrs. Coleman, mother of O. Henry's
boyhood friend, Sara Coleman, "Miss Sallie," visited
New York. She returned to Greensboro to impart to
her daughter the information that the author of *Madame Bo-Peep of the Ranches,* which that daughter
had been treasuring since its appearance in *Smart Set,*
1902, was no other than Willie Porter. The two at
once entered into correspondence, renewing relations
that terminated in their marriage November 27, 1907.

From mid-year, 1906, on to the end, O. Henry sold
to the magazines, for the most part to *Everybody's,*
of which his friend, Gilman Hall, had become Associate Editor, and John O'Hara Cosgrave was Editor-
in-Chief. *Munsey's* and *Ainslee's,* however, continued
to share in his output, and occasionally *Hampton's,
The American* or *The Cosmopolitan.*

In April, 1910, he set out in search of health, revisiting the scenes of his boyhood; but he returned,

* I am indebted for these statistics to Miss Nella Braddy, of
Doubleday, Page & Co.

drawn by the appeal of New York. He was taken to the Polyclinic Hospital, and died there June 5, 1910.

It may as well be admitted that not all of O. Henry's work is so good as his best. It would be surprising if there were not unusual depressions and extraordinary high-water marks. But measured by the strictest standards of story values, his stories of first merit would need three or four volumes to contain them. Even then there would be as many popular favorites omitted as would find place in the chosen lot. The present writer would place in Volume I the following sixteen as his best:

A Double-Dyed Deceiver.
A Blackjack Bargainer.
A Municipal Report.
The Furnished Room.
The Hypotheses of Failure.
Roads of Destiny.
The Ransom of Red Chief.
Jeff Peters as a Personal Magnet.
The Marquis and Miss Sally.
The Gift of the Magi.
The Last Leaf.
The Halberdier of the Little Rheinschloss.
After Twenty Years.
Christmas by Injunction.
The Hiding of Black Bill.
The Last of the Troubadours.

It will be observed that the popular *Unfinished Story* is not included. It is just what the author called it —unfinished. Its *tour de force* closing words probably account for its vogue. Mr. Firkins concludes his article above mentioned: "When in his dream of heaven he is asked: 'Are you one of the bunch?' (meaning one of the bunch of grasping and grinding employers), the response through all its slang is soul-stirring. 'Not on your immortality,' said I. 'I'm only the fellow that set fire to an orphan asylum and murdered a blind man for his pennies.' The author of that retort may have some difficulty with the sentries that watch the entrance of Parnassus; he will have none with the gatekeeper of the New Jerusalem."

A slight rustling, not yet wholly silent, was created a few years ago when Katharine Fullerton Gerould was reported in an interview to have said that O. Henry wrote not short-stories but expanded anecdotes. Although it cannot greatly matter to the non-technician whether the name of anecdote or short-story be given to his narratives, it is true that O. Henry frequently developed pseudo-short stories in anecdotal fashion. "O. Henry's *A Lickpenny Lover, The Romance of a Busy Broker* and *A Comedy in Rubber* are anecdotes, farcial anecdotes, expanded. They are readable and enjoyable, but this fact has nothing to do with the genre to which they belong. *A Lickpenny Lover,* for example, might be put into a form no longer than this:

"The young man was imploring the young lady to be his own.

" 'Only say that you will be mine!' he cried. 'I long to fly with you from the sordidness of the life you must lead; it would be bliss to introduce to you the pleasures of a world far from Billington's Department Store. We would row to the tune of the gondolier's song, would visit India and Japan, would ride in 'rikishas and toboggan over the Himalayas——'

"She turned cold eyes upon him. 'Can't you do better than Coney for a wedding trip?'

"And she rose and left him." *

It is also true that O. Henry repeated his plots. But he could afford to do so. "There is one literary trait," says Mr. Firkins, "in which I am unable to name any author of tales in any literature who surpasses O. Henry. It is not primary or even secondary among literary merits; it is less a value *per se* than the condition or foundation of values. But its utility is manifest, and it is rare among men: Chaucer and Shakespeare prove the possibility of its absence in masters of that very branch of art in which its presence would seem to be imperative. I refer to the designing of stories—not to the primary intuition or to skill in development, in both of which finer phases

* From *A Handbook on Story Writing*, p. 49, by Blanche Colton Williams, Dodd, Mead and Company, 1917.

of invention O. Henry has been largely and frequently surpassed, but to the disposition of masses, to the blocking out of plots. That a half educated American provincial should have been original in a field in which original men have been copyists is enough of itself to make his personality observable."

The following stories all have a common plot formula, and yet the originality of each is distinct from all the others: *A Service of Love, Lost on Dress Parade, While the Auto Waits, The Shocks of Doom, Transients in Arcadia, Two Thanksgiving Day Gentlemen, Proof of the Pudding, The World and the Door, The Whirligig of Life, The Gift of the Magi.*

In connection with these plots, O. Henry must have observed that Henry James had employed the method he himself used. It is a far call from one of these stylists to the other; yet the older writer's *Broken Wings, The Real Thing,* and *The Madonna of the Future* have at their bases the very plot principle on which O. Henry rested the group just given.

, It is a truism to observe that he learned from Aldrich and Maupassant how to construct surprise; but not to remark that he progressed beyond the French author in this particular phase of technique. The following stories represent his ability to create surprise by deliberately withholding a detail which he reveals in the dénouement: *A Double-Dyed Deceiver, Christmas by Injunction, After Twenty Years.* These illustrate his ability to secure surprise by deliberate attempt to mislead and the certain wager that the reader will follow a conventional track: *"Girl,"* and *October and June.* And these effect surprise through a clever use of the angle of narration: *The Hiding of Black Bill, The Gift of the Magi, Lost on Dress Parade.* In all these, and in many others, he takes advantage of the well-known principle that the reader helps to invent the story. The reader speeds along a beaten path of foregone conclusion and finds that he does not "come out with" the author. Upon the difference between the points of the two arrivals depends the shock, the surprise. And it further depends upon the difference between the hackneyed and the original.

It may be true that O. Henry's characters are types. "Club men, fighters, thieves, policemen, touts, shop-girls, lady cashiers, hoboes, actors, stenographers, and what not," the list is long. There are those who agree with William Marion Reedy that as a depicter of New York's Four Million "O. Henry has no equal for keen insight into the beauties and meannesses of character or motive." And if he did emphasize type, he placed upon it a hall-mark that stamps it his forever.

O. Henry sums up the development of story art from Poe to the present. Stockton humor, Aldrich surprise, and Harte's exaltation of local color contributed to his flood tide. But they remain tributary.

O. Henry's volumes of short-stories:

Cabbages and Kings, 1904.
The Four Million, 1906.
The Trimmed Lamp, 1907.
Heart of the West, 1907.
The Voice of the City, 1908.
The Gentle Grafter, 1908.
Roads of Destiny, 1909.
Options, 1909.
Strictly Business, 1910.
Whirligigs, 1910.
Sixes and Sevens, 1911.
Rolling Stones, 1913.
Waifs and Strays, 1919.

CHAPTER XIII

JOSEPH HERGESHEIMER

IT occasionally happens that a writer bursts into publicity with a bomb effect, stunning his audience into admiration which is the prelude to chatter over his unexpectedness. The period of formation, the preparation of the bomb, is too slow and tedious for popular interest. It is left out of account. Booth Tarkington was "fussin' with literatchoor" for five years, an apprenticeship his happy readers knew little and cared less about as they helped to make *The Gentleman from Indiana* one of the best sellers in the last year of the nineteenth century. James Branch Cabell came into the fringe of popularity with *The Eagle's Shadow,* in 1904, and then in his winged soaring after the gleam rose far out of the lime-light glow. A dozen years later he is, in a manner, re-discovered. At least part of his public forgets that he was proving himself an artist, meantime, in *The Line of Love,* and *Chivalry* and *Gallantry,* which, fortunately, were too good for a riot of sales.

Joseph Hergesheimer wrote steadily for fourteen years before finding acceptance with the editors. Only the other day an English novelist visiting our shores is reported to have spoken of him as one of three great American artists, the others being Willa Cather and James Branch Cabell.

No reading of Mr. Cabell and Mr. Hergesheimer, however superficial, can fail to observe the striking similarity of aim and purpose joined to a dissimilarity of objective methods. The unlikeness exists by virtue of the epochs and countries, which are followed by an attendant train of divergences in the setting, the dialect and the customs, each author has chosen; it exists, also, by difference in manner, style. Their resemblance lies in the search for beauty, and in their common concept of the great and only human struggle—that between the ideal and the practical, the visionary and the real.

Mr. Hergesheimer wrote "Looking back over the whole field of my work a very few things are evident, and principally that I always write about people, men usually near forty, who are not happy. The story at bottom is nearly always the same—a struggle between what is called the spirit and what is called the flesh—the spirit is victorious—that is why, it seems to me, my books are happy books." * He and Mr. Cabell—who, in his estimation, "writes beautifully"— have also in common the gift of satire. The close of Mr. Hergesheimer's *The Lay Anthony* and Mr. Cabell's *Jurgen,* throughout, are illustrations. But as

* *The Men Who Make Our Novels,* by George Gordon.

yet Mr. Cabell uses this gift more swiftly, dextrously, and more constantly.

Joseph Hergesheimer was born at Philadelphia, February 15, 1880. Because of persistent illness in his childhood he began the period of idling which continued until the day in the early 1900's when he bought a decrepit type machine and set for himself the task of writing. His early memories, according to *Some Veracious Paragraphs* * and Mr. Gordon's articles are of his Grandfather Thomas McKellar's large mid-Victorian house and the family therein domiciled. There were the grandfather, of the short beard and steel-bowed spectacles, "rigorously Presbyterian"; two ancient great-aunts, "like shriveled and blasted apples," another "excessively genteel"; Joseph and his mother, and infrequently Joseph's father. This gentleman was an officer in the United States Coast and Geodetic Survey and the boy's earliest memories of him are of his playing the violin or bending over a large table drawing maps.

Mr. Hergesheimer vividly remembers the setting, under the Fourth of July lanterns or January snow and ice. He recalls the white marble mantels, the tall glimmering mirrors, the onyx-topped tables, and a formal parlor with a lovely Chinese cabinet and domestic paintings of the Dutch school; the walls of hall, music-room and library, lined with books, "every book a successful Scotch Presbyterian type-founder would pos-

---

* *The Bookman*, September, 1918.

sess"; the bell that clashed for prayers, morning and evening. His mother subscribed for a series of paper-bound love stories, and these young Hergesheimer read to his edification. "After a number of pleasant years in the company of The Duchess and a stainless Indian named Deerfoot," and he adds Ouida elsewhere, he started to school. *Who's Who* records succinctly: "ed. short period at a Quaker sch., Phila. and Pa. Acad. Fine Arts." Mr. Hergesheimer says that at the Quaker school he failed with the boys and with the girls, and at the end of two or three terms he definitely withdrew himself from the field of education. At seventeen, he entered the Fine Arts Academy, where he worked two days in the month. He underwent a love affair which he frankly confesses occupied him until he was twenty-one. Before he was nineteen, however, every one of his family died. On his grandfather's death he received a sum of money, which he immediately dissipated in Venice, where he had a private gondola and gondolier. He spent days floating on the placid tide beyond Murano, rolling cigarettes, and he so lived until, his money exhausted, he came home. About this point in the pursuit of Mr. Hergesheimer's reminiscences the reader suspects the veracious paragraphs of romancing. It all seems too good to be true: it is precisely the account of himself the author might have prepared as outline for a fictive autobiography. He continues by asseverating that he next manifested a desire for "low company." A nighthawk cabman who had been a prize-fighter was his special friend, with whom he went to remarkable balls. One morning, he found his mode of living less than satisfactory and determined upon change. He took the train for Harper's Ferry. There, again, the incidents that befell him are characterized by coincidence as stunning as ever befell man outside his own fiction. But the significance of his moments in the hotel lay in reading proof of a novel, which he found a challenge. He believed he could do better. Of course, he was right. But it was some years before his belief was justified, perhaps even to himself.

With a second-hand type machine he retired to a farmhouse, where he addressed himself to "the difficulties of creative writing." His first story he re-wrote a score of times. "It would be difficult," he says, "to express the depth of my ignorance at that time. I could follow the superficial logic of events, and I had a vague idea from its appearance when a sentence was completely wrong. That was the extent of my literary knowledge and background." (Query: Is the proof-reader or the author at fault for the form "ladened" which occurs with such annoying frequency in his tales?)

The script was returned. Only after fourteen years of continued writing did he succeed in selling a story. He says of his first novel that a thousand copies were exempt from royalties and nearly nine hundred were sold. *The Lay Anthony* (1914) institutes the author's dramatization of the conflict between flesh and spirit. Anthony Ball, with his memories of Eliza Dreen, strives toward chastity, finding strength only in his dream of perfect love. But his ideal becomes an obsession: his virtue becomes one of the flesh rather than the spirit. As Mr. Cabell * affirms, not one of Mr. Hergesheimer's five novels varies from the formula of men laboring toward the unattainable, and a high questing foiled. And he adduces, further, the instance of Gordon Makimmon (of *Mountain Blood*, 1915), whose vain struggle was to atone; the heroes of *The Three Black Pennys* (1917), who floundered toward the beauty of a defiant carnal passion; the five persons of *Java Head*, who struggle and "fretfully know their failure to be foredoomed, toward the capturing of one or another evincement of beauty, with the resultant bodily demolishment of three of them and the spiritual maiming of the others." And he concludes this brief: "Now the fifth and incomparably the finest and loveliest of the Hergesheimer novels is *Linda Condon*, which renders self-confesedly a story of 'the old service of beauty, of the old gesture toward the stars'—'here never to be won, never to be realized.'"

Although discussion of Mr. Hergesheimer's novels has small place here and they have been summed up through the appreciation of his fellow-artist, there is one point regarding *Linda Condon* which calls for

In Respect to Joseph Hergesheimer. Bookman, November-December, 1919.

comment not yet bestowed. The foreshortening of the story makes Linda seem much like a modern child—a child of to-day—when she appears at the beginning; yet at the end she is an old lady. Many years pass as though only a few. If the author was consciously experimenting in futurism or some other 'ism' for bringing the modern novel within the reading time of the modern reader, this is an admirable new device. Not so successful is he at the climax of her marriage. We turn from a scene between her and her suitor and gasp as we see her (on the next page) walking out, followed by her children. Oddly enough, Mr. Hergesheimer says: "I'd like to write a novel about a girl of fourteen, slender, with a black bang and blue-black eyes, in a modern hotel with porphyry columns and turkey-red carpet, against a background of cold gorged women in dinner gowns." The pertinence of this quotation with respect to the note on the foreshortening method lies in the words, "a modern hotel." He begins with to-day; more than half a century later he ends with to-day.

Mr. Hergesheimer has published two volumes of short stories: *Gold and Iron* (1917) and *The Happy End* (1919). The former consists of *Wild Oranges, Tubal Cain* and *The Dark Fleece*—three "long shorts." Iron is the theme of the second, gold of the third, while the wild oranges of the first are a sort of figurative gold for the woman beside whom other women were mere garden fruit.

Part of Mr. Hergesheimer's task which he has set himself to perform before the night cometh is the celebration of various ages of industry in America. His novels are epics, whether of long voyages to China that are the eighteenth century American version of the search for the Golden Fleece, or of the Gage Steel and Iron Works compared with which the forge of Vulcan was but a giant's plaything. His short stories are but novels in miniature. The forge, Tubal Cain, is set in Pennsylvania in the days of the iron age, and as it is abandoned by the owner, Claypole, because of his religious fanaticism, so it is reclaimed by Alexander Hulings because of his inflexible resolution to become a man of power. The iron-willed man becomes the greatest Ironmaster of the state. The author has created him not only through suggested comparison with his own iron, but through the number of tragedies put ruthlessly behind him on the way to his goal. Again, the character is that of the epic. Only fifteen words are allotted Hallie Flower, but they are sufficient to make her live as a deserted woman; little space is given to Wishon's son, but it is enough for the reader to gather that faithful service and death were the attendants of the Ironmaster's course.

This author's women are rather shadowy, mysterious, and reticent, and therefore incomprehensible; because of their incomprehensibility they are the more powerful. They frequently capitulate, most convincingly, to romance. And in this capitulation Mr. Hergesheimer has laid firm hold on a basic element of feminine character—not the only element, however. Hulings by his affair with the duelist worked on the imagination of Gisela, daughter to his rival. So Jason Burrage *(The Dark Fleece)* became, in lesser degree, a figure of romance to Honora Canderay, inspiring her proposal to him after his return to California. *The Dark Fleece* is Mr. Hergesheimer's contribution to the literature of the days of '49 when the Argonauts headed for the California coast, and as the title implies is another epic fragment.

The struggle in *Tubal Cain* is single, of the starkly simple variety wherein man wrestles with his destiny and conquers.   In *The Dark Fleece,* the interest is divided between Jason's and Olive's affairs, afterward shifting wholly to Honora and Jason's.   *The Dark Fleece* is a novel; as a story it leaves untold the fictive histories with which it first intrigued the reader's imagination.   But there is compensation for loss of the "story" in the figure of Honora; and we should not take a great deal for the dénouement wherein she horsewhips so efficaciously the unspeakable Thomas Gast. This, even though we know as Jason knew, that "Honora would always be a Canderay for him, he must perpetually think of her in the terms of his early habit; she would eternally be a little beyond him, a being to approach, to attend with ceremony."

The Happy End (1919) contains seven short stories, of average length and scope. *Lonely Valleys,* a tale

of some eight thousand words, is technically interesting in that the plot dénouement becomes the first page
of the finished narrative. It succeeds in baring, by
half concealment and altogether beautiful restraint,
the pathos in the lives of men and women who inhabit
lonely valleys. The girls go away to the city, to escape,
and fall on evil days; the boys stay at home, to conquer,
and miss life, shut in by the high green mountain
walls. In its pessimism, suggested however and not
urged, the story is of the *Main-Travelled Road* variety.
Moreover, the method is romantic, rather than after
the realism of Mr. Garland. Depression settles upon
a reader who finishes the tale of Calvin Stammark
and Lucy, daughter of Hannah, as it descends upon
him at the close of Mr. Garland's *A Branch Road*. The
late William Dean Howells wrote of the latter: "It is
all morally wrong, but the author leaves you to say
that yourself. He knows that his business was with
those people, their passions and their probabilities."
Without the change of a word the same comment might
be made of *Lonely Valleys*. The price of Calvin's
protecting Lucy seems too great for the lukewarm and
immature affection he will receive, just as her surrender seems too pitifully absolute for her compensation.

Mr. Hergesheimer's Scotch Presbyterian inheritance
emerges in the piety that characterizes Olive of *The
Dark Fleece* and Lemuel Doret, of *The Egyptian
Chariot*. Lemuel's spirit struggles; then having lost

daughter and wife he turns to the city to find June Bowman. But the song, "God's chariot out of Egypt" brings him to his knees and he turns again from the city, leaving vengeance to God.

These are two of six stories in *The Happy End,* of what Mr. Cabell has called beautifully written moral tales. He finds the seventh, *The Flower of Spain,* "well-nigh perfect and a profoundly immoral work of art." But there are two flaws in the story, from an artistic point of view. One is the literal lugging in of a bull that Mochales may show his prowess; another is the happy end for Lavinia and Orsi through the sudden death of the bull-fighter in an elevator accident. A realist might have used the elevator accident; but for the romanticist it smacks too crisply of the intention implied in the title of the volume. The women in this tale are among the most individual Mr. Hergesheimer has created. Lavinia is a sister of Linda Condon, though one is of Italy, the other of America.

The Thrush in the Hedge, which relates the story of Harry Baggs, tramp, and Old Janin who played the violin at the Opéra Comique, emphasizes music as a theme. This musical *motif* is touched here and there throughout the author's works with a sureness that is pledge for his interest in the art of sound rhythm as his word pictures are gauges for his study of color rhythm. Perhaps the violinist, Mr. Hergesheimer's father, is to be thanked that his son "has an ear."

Tol'able David is the most popular of this author's short stories, though to the nicely critical mind it may appear to be a striving to "convey his (Hergesheimer's) apprehensions of life via some such always acceptable vehicle as the prehistoric fairy-tale cliché of the scorned and ultimately victorious third champion." One manifestation of Mr. Hergesheimer's talent lies in his seizing upon prehistoric or historic types and making them at home in the twentieth century, as the conflicts wherein they take part are modern representatives of old myths and epics. Jason of the Golden Fleece and Anthony of the temptation are the companions, in their age-old names and rôles, of Tol'able David.

Since the publication of *The Happy End,* Mr. Hergesheimer has published in *The Saturday Evening Post,* a carefully wrought narrative of some ten thousand words, *Blue Ice,* done after the manner of Maupassant; and in *The Century,* one of the strongest human interest stories of 1920, *Read Them and Weep.*

The most remarkable accomplishment of Mr. Hergesheimer is the process by which as author he apparently undergoes a backward or reverse reincarnation. It is as though he were one man after another, or before another, in various historical eras. His assurance about the setting, to the detail of a bell rope, about the speech, to the last inflection of a syllable; about the dress, to the sound of crinoline swish **or** the angle of a parasol,—this assurance affirms that he was present in all the scenes he evokes. Of course, we say, the unparading review simply means that he has read and has synchronized his movements to those of the past. None the less, we aver that he might have been Hulings, he might have been any one of the three Black Pennys—who lived, it will be remembered, some generations apart—he might have been the hero of *Java Head* or the returned bearer of the dark fleece. It is enough to make one turn metempsychosist.

Again, no present day writer is more delicately adjusted physically and æsthetically than Mr. Hergesheimer. Surely, if keen appreciation of atmospheric moods, sensitiveness to light and shadow, and swift reaction to color—lilac and orange in particular—are signs, he would have made a great artist of the brush. But we should have lost, thereby, his odors. Through them he calls life into his word pictures, whether he does so through whiskey, oranges, or goya lilies. These æsthetic sensibilities joined to skill acquired by long practice mean sharp and sure representation of realities. As Mr. Cabell puts it, "to turn from actual life to Joseph Hergesheimer's pages arouses a sensation somewhat akin to that sustained by a myopic person when he puts on spectacles."

Mr. Hergesheimer's creations further illustrate the pertinence of an old saying that art is nature passed through the lens of temperament. For it is his way

of visualizing and his peculiar individuality that stamp upon his work *"Joseph Hergesheimer fecit."*
Mr. Hergesheimer's Short Stories:

Gold and Iron, 1918
The Happy End, 1919.

CHAPTER XIV

I WAS born October 19, 1889, in Hamilton, Ohio," writes Fannie Hurst, "although I usually pass the honor on to St. Louis, Missouri, since I was taken to Hamilton for the exclusive purpose of being born there in a gem of an old grandparental homestead, and returned to St. Louis while still in the beety, underdone infantile stage, where I grew up a naughty, rather spoiled only child."

Life for her was easy from the beginning. Paradoxically, her only battles have been against a well-ordered, smooth-graded existence. Perhaps in early years and through high school the level smoothness grew monotonous to the eager girl athrill with life. She "did" her lessons dutifully; she practised her scales; she accomplished a precocious amount of reading, and she escaped atrophy through self-expression. One fancies her, heavy dark braid thrown over her shoulder after the fashion of her *Star-Dust* heroine, before her small desk writing verses and romances.

By the year 1903 she had accumulated a quantity

237

of rejected poems, among them a blank verse masque sent back from *The Saturday Evening Post.* Two years later her completion of Coleridge's *Christabel* fared not more successfully with *Poet Lore.* Poetry comes first in the history of the individual as of the race. Miss Hurst's development proved no exception to the rule.

The fiction writer may be born; but he is indubitably made—by his habits. While yet of dancing school age, Miss Fannie conceived the astounding business project of mailing her contribution on Saturday that it might reach the editor for whom it was designed on the following Monday. There is a legend, for which she is responsible, that she gave up a party, new frock and escort and all, on a particular St. Valentine's Day to remain at home for completing her hebdomadal offering.

This story, *Upon the Irony of Fate,* she received back from the shy and recalcitrant editor. But no critic could read the script without recognizing in its author the potentialities of the present artist. She pictures in it, with the same verisimilitude and the same regard for detail which to-day convince her readers, an Indian girl and her dress down to the uttermost bead. The "story" reveals her combination of the romantic—melodramatic, of course, in that early effort—with the realistic. In short, it represents her power in embryo. Already she is passing realism through a romantic temperament, and so producing characters of Dickens kind, who act with Ouida intensity against a back-drop of prosaic William Dean Howells fact. It is easy to see this *flair* now; but not less surely should it have been easy then to affirm, "Granted health and persistence, this writer will go far."

After four years of high school and continued writing, Fannie Hurst braved opposition at home and entered Washington University. There she wrote so many short-stories she herself has forgotten how many: the number is variously stated as twenty-one or thirty-five returned by one national weekly alone. These, however, were published in her college paper after she became editor. She also sold for three dollars a vignette to *Reedy's Mirror*. Three or four years later, when she was asked by another editor to try her hand at a personality sketch of the most interesting man she knew, she wrote an appreciation of William Marion Reedy. Her lamentable requital after three weeks of effort was that she had treated interesting material in an uninteresting manner.

In 1909, mid-year, Miss Hurst took her baccalaureate degree. She immediately endured a brief and unsatisfactory career as teacher in a St. Louis school. Her resignation followed close upon her entrance into the teaching world for the *bona fide* reason that her nerves would not stand the strain. Verily, writers are born—and teachers. In spite of perfect health and perfectly controlled nervous system, the girl's temperament flatly refused to adapt itself to the grind of lessons.

Still short of her twentieth birthday, she turned her face to New York, fighting against the passive appeal of her comfortable home and the active will of her parents that she there remain. If one was ever drawn by a sense of destiny, Fannie Hurst was drawn. The skyey towers of Manhattan were her beacons; she had no choice but to follow their gleam.

She arrived in New York in the summer of 1909, where very briefly, with the aid of a telephone directory, she compiled a list of editors, magazines, and newspapers. Within the month she had become a familiar figure, she says, "to the office boys of journalistic New York." Sustained by checks from home, she saved up against her parents' decision to abet no further her wild but obstinate determination. Hurst *vs.* Hurst! After six months they discontinued her allowance. But a woman acquaintance sent her an unsolicited loan of three hundred dollars, and her mother, weakening, slipped her in secret two hundred more. On her hoardings and these windfalls, she lived, to write and rewrite, to suffer rejection and re-rejection. In 1910-1911 she took a course at Columbia University, probably as a sop to her loving guardians, surely to acquaint herself with Anglo-Saxon. In the autumn, still having found no takers of her scripts she became an actress at a salary of $20 a week. "The Concert," with Mr. Leo Ditrichstein as hero, had been running ten months when Miss Hurst secured, quite by accident, as she states, a part that called for twenty words.

"In Act One I appeared as follows: 'O Master, Master!' Then, 'I bring you lilies of the valley.' After a wait of two acts, I again appeared: 'Dear, dear Master.' 'The Master is resting,' and, finally, 'Oh, Master, Master!'"

In the somewhat elongated interval between Acts One and Four, she wrote *The Seventh Day*. It was accepted by *Smith's Magazine* for thirty dollars, just as the concert started on tour. The lady who had apostrophized the Master remained in New York.

She sold nothing else for six months, but in this time she acquired much factual knowledge and experience, which became the bedrock of her imaginative structures in her subsequent fiction.

"There were whole weeks of rambling among the vivid poor of the vivid East Side." This sentence of hers explains the possibility of *In Memoriam* (in *Every Soul Hath Its Song*) from the hand of a girl carefully nurtured, as protracted living 'among the vivid poor' explains its counterpart of later years, Anzia Yezierska's *The Fat of the Land (Century, 1919)*. Or consider the following paragraph chosen after the turn of a single page, from *The Squall* (in *Just Around the Corner"*):

"Upon a fire-escape level with her own window, a child, with bare feet extended over the iron rail, slept on an improvised bed; from the interior of that same apartment came the wail of a sick infant. A woman nude to the waist passed to and fro before the open window, crooning to the bundle she carried in the crook of her arm." If the passage is not precisely as it is because Fannie Hurst lived a month in an Armenian family over a tobacconist's, or roamed the by-ways of the East Side, the reason is that her imagination needs only a slight stimulus to create definitely and completely, and that her play-ground gave to her a general stage and class types, out of which she evolved her individual scenes and characters. She herself says that she has never "lifted" a character from life; but she would be the last to assert that conditions and the genus had nothing to do with her settings and particular specimens.

"I apprenticed myself as a salesgirl in New York's most gigantic cut-priced department store." Who could doubt that she had worked most of her life in one, except for the years spent in Childs' Restaurant and the years in a Polish sweat-shop and the years in a half-dozen other places! Yet she remained in the department store only a week. "Four and one-quarter yards of ribbon at seven and a half cents a yard proved my Waterloo there, and my resignation at the end of one week was not entirely voluntary." Again, if *White Goods* (in *Humoresque)* does not rest upon this single week of hard work, it is because her imagination needed no ground whatever on which to rest its supports.

A period of an actual six months covers these "years" by the magic known to the fourth dimension and the fiction writer. Ernest Poole once replied, when directly questioned, that he had taken notes on one or two mornings of the scenes described in *The Harbor* as viewed from the Heights of his volume. One would declare that he had lived there always. Local color may not be altogether fancied, nor altogether acquired from a single visit. But given a sympathetic heart and an understanding mind, the writer who is inspired by fresh scenes will embody local color without the ado some sticklers for long residence demand.

The Character Woman grows logically from Miss Hurst's few weeks in the theater; so, perhaps, do *The Wrong Pew* and others of her tales. Her success is particularly.effective when she combines a New York setting with one in St. Louis; the habitual scenes of childhood match equably and smoothly those discovered in New York. *The Wrong Pew,* for example, contrasts the little chorus girl's life in the two cities under conditions that draw sympathy for her in each, and a fine sense of her struggle—ending as it should end: "At nine thirty and with dirty daylight cluttering up the cluttered room, the alarm clock, full of heinous vigor, bored like an awl into the morning."

In 1911 Fannie Hurst met Robert H. Davis of *Munsey's* Magazine. "Fannie Hurst," he told her, "you can write." As if by white magic or miracle, all obstacles fell. Shortly she was selling her first "big pay" story for $300; shortly afterward that magnificent $300 had dwindled beside her high four-figure price. To-day she is one of the best-paid American writers. And, like Jack London, she draws large sums for "work performed." For her published stories—a hundred, or very near that number—are being filmed. *Humoresque,* written in 1919, was published the same year and was produced on the screen in the spring of 1920. At the Criterion, on Broadway, the attendance broke all previous records; thousands looked upon the dissolving views and wept, as though they sat before flesh and blood actors. Its success lies in Miss Hurst's story-writing success; she has mastered the mechanics of emotion; she makes a strong human appeal.

August 6, 1916, *The New York Times Magazine* published an interview which Joyce Kilmer—now among the great dead of poet-warriors—had enjoyed with Fannie Hurst. At that time, Miss Hurst said, "Up to the present moving pictures have been little else than a destructive force where American fiction is concerned. Picturized fiction is on a cheap and sensational level. . . . Motion pictures are in the hands of the laymen and they show it. The scenario writers, so-called 'staff-writers,' have sprung up over-night, so to speak, and from what I understand, when authors venture into the field they are at the mercy of the moving picture director."

Either the motion picture has advanced or Miss Hurst's ideals have capitulated. The growth of the one is well-known, but not better known than Miss Hurst's devotion to art as she sees it. She has refused tempting offers again and again to work for six-figured salaries where the glitter of her name would undoubtedly compensate in a short time the seemingly reckless proposition makers; for she has questioned the effect on her writing. She refused a magazine assignment to hob-nob with the Queen of a realm in a not altogether far-country and to write stories centering about her and the Great War—because, again, she doubted the effect of the shift in style and method on her own sway in the realm of art. "There are those for whom I seem to have a message," she says, "and that, even in its lowest realization, is tinctured with the sublime." She would keep her message and let the money go. And because this is true, she retains also the shekels. The integrity of her art will not fail her.

That she delayed her entry into film-land exemplifies her good judgment. For whereas her sympathetic interpretations of Jewish life might easily have degenerated through poor scenario handling, they now suffer small loss through the comparative present adequacy of the motion picture.

But back to 1911. Between that epoch-making date and the present, Miss Hurst's way has been ideal for one of her chosen work. She continues to make New York her play-ground. She has lived in many sections of the city, once occupying the house at 108 Waverly Place, without having lived in which, it might seem, no American writer may be sure of clasping the golden horn of success. She has had quarters in Carnegie Hall; she has lived in West End Avenue; and again maintained her studio in West 59th Street, hard by the Plaza. She has taken, when the spirit moved her, her maid, her dogs and her typewriter and gone a-traveling to the Adirondacks, to the Rockies or to Sorrento, for a week or a month at a time. By this escape from routine she has never found staleness in the city, where still her genius is whetted to sharpest writing point.

After her first run in *The Saturday Evening Post,* which introduced her to millions of readers, she signed up for a number of stories delivered duly to *The Metropolitan.* Later, she went over to *The Cosmopolitan.* And her work has grown as she has written. It runs true to form, but always toward a larger and completer self-expression, which is yet obtrusively none because it is lost in the objectivity of her drama. And that is as should be, always, for the writer of fiction, as for other artists.

Four volumes of her tales have been collected and published by *Harper's.* The first of these (1914) uses the significant part of O. Henry's dictum that there may be a good story "just around the corner " Of this collection, the best is *The Good Provider,* though all are of a quality so high as to draw the ever-easy criticism that her first work is her best. It is odd that this bromide should be uttered anew against every writer. It is damning in itself of those who speak it. It means a blunted perception to distinction. A writer of short-stories should stand for a definite style, mood, and recognizable types of character; and this is by no means to say a thin-worn repetition of the same theme or the immediate individual.

Shortly after the publication of her first book, Fannie Hurst was married, in the presence of necessary witnesses and a friend or two, at Lakewood, New Jersey, to Jacques S. Danielson, pianist and composer. For five years they kept their marriage quiet; and if other friends guessed it than those to whom they revealed it, all alike respected her desire that nothing was to be said about it. When, therefore, on May 4, 1920, it was at length announced in the newspapers of the metropolis, there was a stir which lasted more than the usual nine days.

"Pray why," one may inquire, "did she wish to keep it secret?" Since her step may become historic, and since on the other hand the reasons for it may become lost in the mist of memory, it may be worth while to set down here a recapitulation, or summary, of her own stated reasons:

"When I met Jacques Danielson, I found my youthful determination that marriage was not for me suddenly undermined. But my determination that marriage should never lessen my capacity for creative work or pull me down into a sedentary state of fat-mindedness was not undermined . . . I made certain resolutions concerning what my marriage should not be.

"First of all, I am anxious to emphasize that our marriage was neither the result of a fad or 'ism,' but simply the working out of a problem according to the highly specialized needs of two professional people.

" . . . We decided that our marriage should in no wise interfere with my work or my studies . . . We decided to live separately, maintaining our individual studio apartments, and meeting as per inclination, not duty.

". . . We have maintained our separate group of friends.

"We decided that the antediluvian custom of a woman casting aside the name that had become as much a part of her personality as the color of her eyes had neither rime nor reason. I was born Fannie Hurst and I expect to die Fannie Hurst.

"We decided that, in the event of offspring, the child should take the paternal name, until reaching the age of discretion, when the decision would lie with him.

"We decided that accounting for our time to one another would prove irksome and for five years have enjoyed our personal liberty precisely as we did before marriage, using, rather than abusing, the unusual privileges we grant one another."

If the plan did not "work," they would at the end

of a year go quietly apart. "The one year has stretched into five and—well, we are announcing instead of annulling."

"We live separately and shall continue to do so."

Every Soul Hath Its Song appeared in October, 1916, containing nine stories, the most remarkable of which is *Sob Sister*. The *Times* reviewer expressed the opinion of best critics when he wrote of it, "It is brutal but it is also strong, a bit of realism that grips in every line of its tense dialogue, in its impassive objectivity." "The collection reveals, even more strongly than her first book, her ability to make all her characters do the work. She places them upon the stage, with an East Side or a Riverside background; they stand up and march and play their parts.*

Gaslight Sonatas was published April, 1918. Its chief new contribution is that of propaganda in behalf of the War Cause. *Bitter-Sweet* opens the volume, a propaganda story circulated in separate form after its first publication in the *Cosmopolitan*. *Sieve of Fulfilment* and—the best of the seven—*Get Ready the Wreaths* also strike the war note. This "sonata" ring is extended into her next volume, *Humoresque,* published March, 1919.

It will have been noticed that three of her four vol-

---

* By an odd contradiction, her people transferred to the boards have not succeeded so well. *The Good Provider* failed to hold its audience, as did also a later venture, *The Land of the Free.* She will probably yet conquer the technique of the drama as she has that of the story.

umes draw upon music for their titles. In *Humoresque* she has popularized the song as Dr. Van Dyke's *Humoresque* failed to do; in *Star-Dust*, her first novel (published 1920), she accidentally repeated a title used by Jack London in an essay (recorded in Chapter XXIII of *Martin Eden*). With these exceptions, and a possible one or two others, her stories are christened with a novel freshness.

Fannie Hurst has been called, by some critics, the immediate descendant of O. Henry. It is quite likely that not one writer who learned the tools of his trade after 1900 has been able to avoid the influence of the most American of short-story writers of the first twentieth century decade. His tricks of epigram, caustic humor, surprise, and his real democracy are too inimitable to escape imitation. But to Miss Hurst has fallen only a due portion of his spirit. Her "beat" is not his beat; her length of story is not his length. She works on a larger canvas. Her sentence rhythm is staccato; his deliberate and even lazy. If Fannie Hurst could not have written his terse *After Twenty Years,* neither could O. Henry have achieved the epic, *Get Ready the Wreaths.* The ending of *Heads* has back of it the stunning dénouements of O. Henry, admittedly; but also back of it—and him—Aldrich and de Maupassant.

Her first noteworthy characteristic lies in a minuteness and picturesqueness of description, which any one of her stories will illustrate. Take, for example, the first paragraph of *Power and Horse-Power,* the first story in her first volume: "In the Knickerbocker Hotel there are various parlors; Pompeian rooms lined in marble and pillared in chaste-fluted columns; Louis Quinze corners, gold-leafed and pink-brocaded, principally furnished with a Vernis-Martin cabinet and a large French clock in the form of a celestial sphere surmounted by a gold cupid." And so on, for a hundred words or so, she takes you through the parlors, trailing off with the one where the manicurist, Miss Gertrude Sprunt, presides. By the time you have consumed a half minute in walking through the domain you are acquainted with the lay-out and ready for the heroine.

Or turn to her latest volume and to the tale of freaks, *Even as You and I.* Read the word picture of the fat lady and refrain, if you can, from following her fortune to the close: "What matters it that her skin was not without the rich quality of cream too thick to pour, when her arms fairly dimpled and billowed of this creaminess, and above her rather small ankles her made-to-order red satin shoes bulged over it, the low-cut bosom of her red and sequin dress was a terrific expanse of it, her small hands cushions of it, her throat quivery and her walk a waddle with it. . . . Between her eyes and upper lip, Miss Hoag looked her just turned twenty; beyond them, she was antediluvian, deluged, smothered, beneath the creamy billows and billows of self."

Her second characteristic is the accomplishment of a purpose. To suggest a need or a remedy or to open a reader's eyes and to do it so skillfully he does not know he has been "treated" is effectively to combine art with propaganda. *The Other Cheek* illustrates as well as any of her tales this distinguishing mark:

"Besides, hers were the problems of the six-million dollar incorporateds, who hire girls for six dollars a week; for the small-eyed, large-diamoned birds of prey who haunt the glove counters and lace departments of the six million dollar incorporateds with invitations to dinner; and for the night courts, which are struggling to stanch the open gap of the social wound with medicated gauze instead of a tight tourniquet."

A third striking feature lies in her ornamentations: mythological allusions, ancient history references, figures drawn from science: "At Sixth Avenue, where the great skeleton of the Elevated stalks mid-street, like a prehistoric *pithecanthropus erectus,* he paused for an instant in the shadow of a gigantic black pillar," etc. *(Hers Not to Reason Why).* Some critic leaped fervently upon this long-named beast, crying out that he was smallish. But the answering critic was right: the shape of the prehistoric creature and the sound of his name carry over the idea needed.

From *Heads:* "By the great order of things which

decreed that about the time Herod, brother to no man, died, Jesus, brother to all men, should be born; and that Rabelais, moral jester, should see light the very year that Louis XI passed on," etc.

From *Marked Down:* "Daphne fleeing from Apollo could not have been more deliciously agitated," etc.

This sort of one thing, one argues, is too simple. A learned reference may be dragged in with a peculiarly showy effect. But it is part of her work and pleasure —the study of the past—and one of the paradoxes that mark her throbbing reflection of the present. Rather it is the background against which she sets off the present, and by virtue of which it exists. Her study, furnished in Italian pre-renaissance style, has the asceticism of Savonarola's; most frequently to be found on her desk under the wide sky-light are those volumes which are the heritage of the past.

The short-stories of Fannie Hurst illustrate happily the best artistry to be found in present-day *conte* writing. Each develops in a series of perfectly selected scenes, vivid, picturesque, staged with accessories of time and place, which, to the minutest detail, reflect the operations of life. Her men and women exemplify in their personalities the creative faculty of their author, a faculty working as life works, not to copy the already existing, but with infinite variety to produce new specimens of their kind.

So Leon Kantor of *Humoresque* lives, a distinct creation, like his brothers in the flesh, keenly aware of a compulsion to keep a rendezvous with death; but always himself—Leon Kantor. So Hester of *Back Pay* lives; one of a sad, eternal sisterhood, but alone, distinct, Hester.

Her characters move in a kingdom of their own, not burlesque, not caricature; for the author sympathizes. Whatever the reader's cause for laughter, it works in the most objective way. One might ask, "Does Miss Hurst know this is funny?" And she might answer, "I've nothing to do with his being either laughable or pathetic. Don't accuse me of pulling 'sobstuff' or slanting toward humor. I'm interested in things as they are."

Technical excellence, excellence that comes after years of study and practice, reveals itself in well-wrought structure not less than in distinguished style. Nobody will gainsay that Miss Hurst is a stylist. If any one is marked by a difference, that one is Fannie Hurst. The architectural values, moreover, are well-nigh flawless. Her stories are well constructed from starting point to climax of action.

It is an old story now, that of the French engineer whose three successive exclamations marked his gradual approach to Brooklyn Bridge. But the triple truth is still true and equally true when applied to a story by Fannie Hurst: "How beautiful! How well-made! How well thought out!"

"No one with the love of the grotesque which is the American portion of the human tastes or passions,"

wrote William Dean Howells, "can fail of his joy in
the play of the obvious traits and motives of her He-
brew comedy, but he will fail of something precious
if he does not sound the depths of true and beautiful
feeling which underlies the comedy."

Volumes of stories by Miss Hurst:

Just Around the Corner, 1914.
Every Soul Hath Its Song, 1916.
Gaslight Sonatas, 1918.
Humoresque, 1919.
The Vertical City, 1921.

CHAPTER XV

J ACK LONDON died November 22, 1916. In the years that have elapsed he has suffered both praise and damnation; in the future, if only the topmost peaks are too high for him, only the lowest depths will be too low. There will be a necessary divergence over the quality of his work dependent fundamentally upon the difference between age and youth, conservatism and radicalism, literary attainment and narrative value. A short-story critic and a short-story lover will pronounce Jack London engaging, thrilling and satisfactory. The critic of literature, concerned not primarily about the success of a particular genre or type, but about expression and large content will declare him at best a third rate writer.

He cannot be ignored. George Wharton James stated the simple truth (*The Overland*, May, 1917), when he remarked: "For good or evil he has made a profound impression upon his generation." Aside from his vogue in America, he is the most popular foreign author in Sweden and has been hailed as a prophet in Russia.

Opposing forces will agree upon certain essential

256

characteristics of his forty-odd volumes, all of which were published within the space of twenty years. He was a pioneer in marking out unexploited geographical areas for the setting and action of his narratives. He was the first to entertain us with tales of Alaska; and the increasing number of his followers, from Rex Beach to Oliver Curwood, testify by their popularity that he evaluated correctly the definite appeal of the frozen North. The struggle it offered to civilized man, through its ice and snow and primeval beasts and primitive races, he seized and wrought into brief epics. Nor is he, with an exception or two, less the pioneer in the South Seas. It is true that Herman Melville, and, later, Robert Louis Stevenson had introduced the region to nineteenth century readers. But never had they popularized, in short-story form, tropical islands and equatorial seas and the men who dwell upon them. Conrad was to surpass him, in his own day, in depth and magnificence but not in clearness and vividness of narrative action. And it would be difficult to estimate his influence upon current writers, such as Frederick O'Brien of *White Shadows* fame. Jack London, then, struck a circle through the extremes of heat and cold; he made the area his own, but gained contrast and picturesqueness by emphasizing the territory near the extremes.

He celebrated the physical prowess of man as perhaps no other short-story author has ever succeeded in doing. Whether mushing on over an endless trail against the forces of hunger, disease, wild animals and arctic cold; or whether wrestling with the typhoon in a summer sea, while small pox and mutiny rage aboard ship, his heroes valiantly battle and endure.

In the realm of pure spirit, however, Mr. London rarely finds himself. His problems of morality and ethics arise from the physical struggle or lead to it. The subtlety of a Henry James temptation or an Edith Wharton punishment would mean nothing to his sturdy and vigorous characters. Fancy Wolf Larsen substituted for Ethan Frome—but the hypothesis is inconceivable.

Perhaps the deficiency just indicated explains why he has added not one living character to our literature. He photographed and created men; but they are men among others. And if, as has been said, his Indians rank with Fenimore Cooper's, it is as a class, not because of Chingachgook or Uncas exceptions. And if, as again has been said, he liked psychology but wrote adventure because the editors wanted it, the truth is that he followed his bent and his ability. He emphasized action, not without ideas and themes as we shall presently illustrate; but he overlooked the workings of the human soul.

Over his style opinions also differ. He is radical or refreshing, according to the point of view. He frequently uses English in a way that shocks, even though into admiration. Verbs for nouns and nouns for verbs he interchanges when he sees fit. "He muscled his body down into the hole" is peculiarly vivid to a reader interested in the act; it is a distorted mannerism to one observant of expression. But the chances are that he will prove to have been one of the first by whom the new are tried; one whom others will approach, not from whom they will depart.

Jack London was born in San Francisco, January 12, 1876, the youngest of ten children. A significant characteristic of his immediate ancestry was the nomadism of his father. Trapper and scout, John London transmitted to his son a spirit of adventure which carried him to the far places of the earth. Important, too, in explaining the boy's character was the racial variety of his progenitors: English, Welsh, Dutch, Swiss, French and German—all combined to produce a unique and yet a representative American. And he worshiped the Anglo-Saxon, in comparison with whom he recognized certain lesser breeds without the law.

For the first nine years of his existence he lived in Oakland, in Alameda, near the Coast in San Mateo County, and in Livermore. His childhood might have been embittered by poverty; but he escaped through a dual life, outwardly poor and rough, inwardly reflective and contemplative. His passion for romance early created for him a world of his own. "Read Ouida's *Signa,*" he advises. "I read it at the age of eight. The story begins: 'It was only a little lad.' The little lad was an Italian mountain peasant. He became an artist with all Italy at his feet. When I read it, I was a little peasant on a poor California ranch. Reading the story, my narrow hill-horizon was pushed back, and all the world was made possible if I would dare it. I dared."

At an early age he read, also, Trowbridge, Paul du Chaillu's *Travels,* Captain Cook's *Voyages,* and Washington Irving. Even before he was ten he wished he might be a writer. His mother once urged him to try for a prize offered by *The Call* for a descriptive article of 1000 words or less . He wrote 2000 the first evening, but later cut to the required length and won the prize.

Between the ages of eight or nine and fourteen he sold papers, worked in the canneries, the jute mills, and the power-house. At the same time he managed to secure the beginnings of an education.

On his graduation from grammar school he entered upon an adventurous career on San Francisco Bay. Down on the water-front, he underwent experiences which later furnished material for *Tales of the Fish Patrol* and gained for him the sobriquet, The Prince of the Oyster Pirates. In these years he learned to handle a schooner and to acquire the seamanship which enabled him, a self-taught navigator, many years later to sail the *Snark* across the Pacific.

At fourteen or fifteen he became interested in sociology and from his street corner harangues was known as The Boy Socialist.

In 1892 he turneα tramp, compelled not through his study of sociology; but, as he himself wrote, "because of the life that was in me, of the wanderlust in my blood that would not let me rest." The immediate motivation he recounts in *The Road*, in the chapter entitled *Road Kids and Gay-Cats*. From his first monica, "Sailor Kid," he passed to "Frisco Kid" and at length to "Sailor Jack."

Concluding this first tramp experience, which led him over many of the States and Canada, he said: "The Road had gripped me and would not let me go; and when later I had voyaged to sea and done one thing and another, I returned to the Road to make longer flights, to be a 'comet' and a profesh, and to plump into the bath of sociology that wet me to the skin."

The sea-voyage to which he refers is the one made in 1893, when he shipped before the mast, on the *Sophie Sutherland*, to Japan. There he caught the spell of the Orient which gripped him forcibly in after years and held him in the South Sea Islands. "I looked on the world and called it good," he wrote, in *The War of the Classes*, of his life at this time.

After he came back from his voyage to the East he wandered over America by the under-beam route. He set out in the spring of 1894 with General Kelly's Army of Protest two thousand strong, and ended, alone, in Niagara, in June, where he was arrested as a hobo and sent to prison. The extremities he suffered in the Erie County Penitentiary confirmed and strengthened his socialistic proclivities. A study of his life at this period, so frankly set forth in *The Road*, will convince the reader that he had found food for thought, even while he roamed, the Playboy of the Western World. It dawned upon him that he was eighteen years of age, that he was beneath the point at which he had started, and that he was down in the cellar of society. He had learned that muscle and brain have selling values and that the latter brings more. He determined to be a vender of brains.

In the brief space from the fall of 1894 to the spring of 1897, not quite three years, were compressed the training and preparation most men of fair education require ten years to cover. His first step was to enter the Oakland High School, where he maintained himself by a janitor's work. He remained only three months. With the fervor of one who comprehends suddenly the value of time, he recognized the need for haste and set out to reach the University by the shortest route. He was distant from it two years. But there was a training school, Anderson's Academy, which offered preparation. Jack London became the scandal of the Academy by accomplishing in four months an incredible amount of work. His tuition was returned and he was requested to leave, since he would discredit the place by his performance. He then studied alone, nineteen and twenty hours a day, without equipment save books and his imagination.

His new life gave him friends of a different "set." He met Bessie Maddern, her friend Fred Jacobs the librarian, and Mabel Applegarth. Mabel introduced him to poetry; he "grew drunk with Swinburne and mad with Verlaine." He devoured the libraries. *The Age of Fable,* Emerson's Essays, Paine's *Rights of Man,* Montaigne, Kant and Schopenhauer represent the diversity of his reading. And he was writing stories, impossible romances most of them, but all helping him to a mastery of his tools. He crammed the two years' course in three months and passed the University examinations.

He was not to remain at Berkeley, however, for more than part of his Freshman year. He worked in a laundry and with his pen; but the task was too great. The support of his mother's family fell upon him. He left the University, not to return. When the elder London once more found work, the boy continued his Blickensdorfer efforts. Perhaps he had reached, already, the conclusion that "reading Chaucer doesn't teach any one to write," and that only by practice comes success. It should be remembered that all along he was under the necessity of making a livelihood for himself and sometimes for others.

The first chapters of *Martin Eden* reflect faithfully the spirit of his life in 1894 and 1895, if not always the actual events. He has been described by one who knew him then as having a radiant personality and abounding in life energy.

In 1897 he joined the rush to the Klondike. In the late summer he landed at Dyea Beach and entered upon his heritage. He found in the Alaskan wastes the material upon which to exercise his craft, his skill acquired through training rigorous and difficult, and he found himself. "There nobody talks. Everybody thinks. You get your true perspective. I got mine." After a year, with characteristic decision he set sail in an open boat and stoked his way over the nineteen hundred miles to San Francisco.

In 1898 he was where he had started, but with a definite acquisition. While he labored to support the family at cutting wood and shoveling coal, he wrote, widened his reading and fell in with his former friends. Herman Whitaker and George Sterling were the men who meant most to him in those days; and he saw much of Bessie Maddern, whose fiancé, young Jacobs, had died. His interest in biology and philosophy deepened through study of Darwin, Hegel, Kant, Huxley, Berkeley, Hume and Nietzsche. But the important fact is that he was writing, and in less than six months after his return from the Klondike he met with initial success.

The Overland bought *The Man on Trail*, first of the Malemute Kid series, then *The White Silence, The Son of the Wolf* and eight other stories. But these, the perfected result of six years' work, he sold for the sum of fifty-three dollars. Even this amount he had difficulty in collecting if Martin's adventures with the editors of *The Transcontinental* (in Chapter XXXIII of *Martin Eden*) are at all representative of the facts. *The Black Cat* paid him forty dollars for *A Thousand Deaths* (published, May, 1899). But they took nothing else from him. He began to fear that he was beaten. And then came a check from *The Atlantic Monthly,* a check for one hundred and seventy-five dollars. It meant the sharp dramatic climax of his career.

At the age of twenty-four Jack London had crossed the threshold of the literary life and was shortly to find his seat among the elect. Life should have appeared brighter. On April 7, 1900, he married Bessie Maddern. His first book was about to appear with the imprint of a long-established house. His publishers had advanced funds to maintain him while he wrote, and he was writing regularly one thousand words a day. (It is worth noting that he never afterwards departed from this craftsman's habit.) He had arrived at his own interpretation of life and at a credo he was to exemplify throughout his works: Reason rules the universe; all life is related to biology; courage, love and loyalty form a trinity than which nothing is more divine. He maintained his friendship with Sterling, Anna Strunsky and others of his socialistic group. By comparison with the past, surely he had every cause for happiness. But at the dawn of his new life, he grew morbid. "Inarticulate discontent awoke in his soul." *The Daughter of the Snows* written at this time reveals the struggle between his own instincts and those about him. The publishers refused it; he owed those publishers more than a thousand dollars, and in this temporary setback his first daughter was born, January, 1901. He wrote unceasingly, buoyed by Whitaker and Sterling, until the outbreak of the Boer War. Then he started to Africa, stopped in New York, and ended by investigating the London slums.

He came back to Piedmont, still out of harmony with the world, but persisted doggedly at his writing. His family relations were strained; he continued his friendship with Charmian Kittredge, a friendship that had begun with the publication of his first novel. Meantime, his volumes were appearing: *The God of His Fathers*, 1901; *A Daughter of the Snows*, 1902; *Children of the Frost*, 1902; *The Cruise of the Dazzler*, 1902. Of these, *Children of the Frost* is most significant with respect to the sum total of the author's accomplishment. It contains many of his best North Country stories, and notably the one Jack London liked most of all his narratives: *The League of the Old Men*. In 1903 appeared *People of the Abyss*, which embodied the results of his vagabond life in London. It has been compared favorably with General Booth's *Submerged Tenth;* the two authors speak with authority, from different angles, of conditions too frequently skimmed by the dilettante in letters and life. The *People of the Abyss* vividly describes scenes which filled the author with a fierce passion for the downtrodden.

In 1903 appeared, also, *The Kempton-Wace Letters*, which grew out of the correspondence between Jack London and Anna Strunsky. And, then, in the same year, *The Call of the Wild*.

Upon the publication of the last-named the author found himself famous. *The Saturday Evening Post* paid seven hundred dollars for the manuscript, a considerable sum in those days; Macmillan's gave two thousand dollars for the book rights. The creator of Buck meant to illustrate in the big dog the Darwinian theory of reversion to type; but this intention escaped, perhaps fortunately, the lay reader who enjoyed the fortunes of the animal hero as those of a human being and who was concerned only about the external adventures. The fight between the brutes was for nine out of ten a capitally described dog-fight, not, as the author intended it symbolically, a case of the survival of the fittest. Jack London may have been swept to success on the Kipling wave, as his detractors assert and his admirers do not believe. But it is undeniable that many animal stories published since 1903 were swept into publication by the success of *The Call of the Wild*.

At the outbreak of the Russo-Japanese war Jack London set sail for Japan, hoping to serve as reporter, but when he discovered that opportunity was lacking to get near the battle-front, he came home. He was met at the dock by a lawyer who served him with papers of his wife's divorce suit. A year later he married Charmian Kittredge.

In 1905 he planned the voyage of the *Snark* and began to build the schooner. In 1906 he was writing in Sonoma, in the Valley of the Moon. By September of this year he had published thirteen books, all done in five years. Yet, again, if the testimony of *Martin Eden* is acceptable, much of this successful material must have been on hand longer, "work performed," as Martin said bitterly.

In April, 1907, the *Snark* was ready; on the 25th he and his wife, with a small crew, set sail from the Golden Gate. May 17, 1907, they sighted Maui. In June, Mr. London showed signs of serious illness; but they remained for eighteen months in the land they both loved, and left only that he might recuperate.

Charmian London has told in *Our Hawaii* many interesting details of life there and of her husband's work: "—he shrugs his wide shoulders under the blue kimono, girds the fringed white obi a little more snugly, picks up a note pad and long sharp pencil and makes swift, sprawling notes for a Klondike yarn on which he has been working, *To Build a Fire*. This, staged in the Frozen North, is bound to captivate editors and public alike, who think every other subject but the Klondike out of his 'sphere.' " So she makes entry under date of May 22, 1907, rightly commenting upon a tale which in the judgment of many critics is his best story of the arctic regions.

Again, May 31: "He is commencing an article on amateur navigation, for *Harper's,* which he calls 'Finding One's Way About';" and, July 11, "Jack has lost no time finishing the promised article, 'The Lepers of Molokai'." Repeatedly she quotes his "Mate, are you glad you're alive?" indicative of his happiness. August 21: "Jack has located a shady corner for his work, out of range of the distracting landscape, and is swinging along on that autobiographical novel he has so long contemplated. The hero is 'Martin Eden' and the author cannot make up his mind whether to use the euphonious name for title, or call the book 'Success.'"

In 1908 he visited the Solomon Islands. In 1912 the Londons were at Seattle after five months of wind-jamming from Baltimore around Cape Horn. In 1914 the author spent two months at Vera Cruz in the American occupation of that city. Back in Honolulu in 1915 he finished *Jerry* and had about completed *Michael* when they sailed in July for San Francisco.

In 1916 Jack London resigned from the Socialist Party "because of its lack of fire and its loss of emphasis on the class struggle." "My final word is that liberty, freedom and independence are royal things that cannot be presented to, nor thrust upon, races or classes. If races and classes cannot rise up and by their strength of brain and brawn wrest from the world liberty, freedom, and independence, they never in time can come to these royal possessions."

Meantime, at his home in the Valley of the Moon, his long sickness was upon him. He died November 22, 1916, not sorry nor yet glad to go. He had insisted that nobody be present at his funeral but his wife and sister and the poet Sterling. Buried on a site he had selected for himself, he recalls in his resting place as in his life, Robert Louis Stevenson and their common love for the open spaces.

Instant regret assails one who considers that the boy who fought long and hard before achieving the barest foothold for an equal fight, died before he had scarcely halved his allotted three score and ten. But if one agrees that he had made in *Martin Eden* his last attempt to write for the love of good writing, and that, a disillusioned man, he was a child grown tired of his playthings, then it may be best for his after-fame that he passed young. If he burnt out his life by enjoyment of it, then he greatly enjoyed.

Jack London loved adventure, as we have seen; he loved clean sports—swimming, canoeing, boxing, swinging the sledge, throwing the hammer, and riding horseback. He said he would rather dig ditches than write, a statement to be taken with allowance when we remember his long study and rigorous practice. He loved reading, as we have also seen. Next to his own stories he loved the verse of George Sterling (Brissenden, in *Martin Eden*). He was not an academician, and more than once jars the sensitive ear; for example, when he refers to the study of Chaucer as "Saxon." He loved music. There is a touch of pathos and prophecy in Mrs. London's statement that Jack loved nothing better than the funereal rhythms of Handel's Largo and the processionals of Chopin and Beethoven. He loved his home, his estate of over a thousand acres which he bought in the first flush of his success, and on which he planted an incredible number of eucalyptus trees. The thing he professed to like most of all was personal achievement. And always he loved romance, the call of the faraway.

Jack London's supreme gift was that of story telling. It has been asserted not without just claim that there is nothing among all his work which cannot be called a story. And on the negative side, he failed when he tried Carlylean philippics or drama. According to Oliver Madox Hueffer, who knew him at Vera Cruz, the stories he spoke were better than those he wrote. His success lies in his knowledge gained first hand; in his sense of the dramatic and picturesque, and in his love for the struggle. It is not odd that he built upon some phase or instance of the Eternal Conflict.

The most significant aspects of his narrative work appear, at first glance, to be his amazing fertility and his wide range of subject matter. Underlying the range, however, clearly unifying principles proclaim themselves: interest in sociology and evolution runs like a cable throughout the length of his life-work. Yet it is not, usually, obtrusive. Witness *The Call of the Wild*. One may read *Li-Wan, the Fair* without an oppressive awareness of its illustrating Spencer's consciousness of kind, or *The Son of the Wolf* without worrying over its exemplification of the survival of the fittest, or *The Sea Wolf* without reflecting that it pushes to the *n*th degree Nietzsche's theories about the Blond Beast. The reader of the story will enjoy the adventure, the concrete; the analyst will find in it a new illustration of a social principle.

Now and then, it is true, the theme receives emphasis at the cost of narrative interest. Consider *The Scarlet Plague*, a long short-story which demonstrates first, that an insignificant germ can delete in an inconceivably brief time an entire nation; second, that the survivors who are left to found a new civilization will only repeat evolutionary processes. The narrative conforms agreeably to short-story technique, but leaves the reader pondering on its theme long after characters and setting and the related action have departed into oblivion. Similarly, *Before Adam,* a comprehensive work on anthropology, reveals the author's interest in prehistoric man and holds attention by its speculations of what life was like in the Mid-Pleistocene Age.

His stated interest in sociology occurs, mainly, outside his volumes of short-stories. Occasionally, however, he incorporates some socially significant principle; for example, in *The Heathen,* he insists upon the brotherhood of man. In *The House of Pride,* he illustrates the truth that manhood lies beneath the veneer of civilization and depends not at all upon it or worldly position.

His technique grows, logically, out of his conception of life. As he says of Martin, "It was always the great universal *motif* that suggested plots." After the idea came location in time and place and the particular persons for its embodiment or demonstration. In accordance with his genius, he evolved the physical struggle, as we have repeated, and as stories chosen at random will exemplify. In *Love of Life* a man traverses a snow-covered plain against the forces of hunger, disease, and a starving wolf; in *The House of Mapuhi,* the hero weathers a typhoon on Hikueru; in *Demetrios Contos* a patrolman on San Francisco bay captures, after an exciting chase, a Greek pirate. *To Build a Fire* records the vain attempt of a man half frozen to secure warmth and life. *All Gold Canyon* presents a fight to the death between two men for a pocket of gold. *The Game,* a favorite of the author, describes with the skill of the artist and the knowledge of the initiated, a prize-fight as no prize-fight had been described previously. And if, occasionally, he tries a slightly different type of conflict, as in *The Shadow and the Flash,* he none the less conveys the feeling of personal strife. In all these stories of physical contest or endurance the character is a man of fortune. He may be adventuring for gold because he is an outcast, or a rover, or because he has left an easier life in the hope of "making his pile." But his personality, though fitting to the time and place, is ordinarily subdued to the action. This point argues well for the story: the story's the thing, however deeply in character it may be rooted and should be rooted. That he has contributed no portraits to the fictive hall of fame means that he was a raconteur, rather than a novelist. There is one glory of the moon and another of the stars. Few writers have wrought with greater vision, whether story-tellers or novelists; few have analyzed with keener mental processes the structure of the social fabric.

Asked only a short time before his death what he considered the factors of his literary success, Mr. London tabulated them—eight. First, good luck. He might have suffered, as he said, before the age of seventeen the fate of his comrades of the oyster beds. They were drowned, shot, killed by disease or declining in prisons. Second, good health, in spite of the liberties he took with it. His open air life, rough and hard, fostered the good body nature gave him. Third, good brain, derived from a noble American lineage, mainly English and Welsh. Fourth, good mental and muscular correlation. Fifth, poverty. Sixth, reading *Signa* at the age of eight. Seventh, the influence of Herbert Spencer's *Philosophy of Style*. Eighth, his early start.

But no reader of *Martin Eden* can doubt that untiring, unswerving application to his art and his business of story writing contributed most to his success. As he has recounted (Chapter XXIII) he read the works of men who had arrived, "he noted every result achieved by them, and worked out the tricks by which they had been achieved—the tricks of narrative, of exposition, of style, the points of view, the contrasts, the epigrams . . . He did not ape. He sought principles." He induced the general principle of mannerism; he collected lists of strong phrases, "phrases that bit like acid and scorched like flame, or that glowed and were mellow and luscious in the midst of the arid desert of common speech. He sought always for the principle that lay behind and beneath. He was not content with the fair face of beauty . . . having dissected and learned the anatomy of beauty, he was nearer being able to create beauty itself. . . . And no matter how much he dissected beauty in search of the principles that underlie beauty and make beauty possible, he was aware, always, of the innermost mystery of beauty to which he did not penetrate and to which no man had ever penetrated."

The works of Jack London:

The Son of the Wolf, 1900.
The God of His Fathers, 1901.
A Daughter of the Snows, 1902.
The Children of the Frost, 1902.
The Cruise of the Dazzler, 1902.
The People of the Abyss, 1903.
The Kempton-Wace Letters, 1903.
The Call of the Wild, 1903.
The Faith of Men, 1904.
The Sea Wolf, 1904.
The Game, 1905.
War of the Classes, 1905.
Tales of the Fish Patrol, 1905.
Moon Face and Other Stories, 1906.
Scorn of Woman (a play), 1906.
White Fang, 1907.
Before Adam, 1907.
Love of Life, 1907.
The Iron Heel, 1907.
The Road, 1907.
Martin Eden, 1909.
Lost Face, 1909.
Revolution, 1910.
Burning Daylight, 1910.
Theft, 1910.
When God Laughs, 1910.
Adventure, 1911.

The Cruise of the Snark, 1911.
South Sea Tales, 1911.
Smoke Bellew Tales, 1912.
The House of Pride, 1912.
A Son of the Son, 1912.
The Night Born, 1913.
The Abysmal Brute, 1913.
John Barleycorn, 1913.
The Valley of the Moon, 1913.
The Strength of the Strong, 1914.
The Mutiny of the Elsinore, 1914.
The Scarlet Plague, 1915.
The Star Rover, 1915.
The Little Lady of the Big House, 1916.
The Turtles of Tasman, 1916.
The Human Drift, 1917.
Jerry of the Islands, 1917.
Michael, Brother of Jerry, **1917.**
On the Makaloa Mat, 1919.

CHAPTER XVI

I N *The Cambridge History of American Literature*
(Chapter VI, Volume II) occurs a significant
paragraph. It begins, "1884 was the climactic year
in the history of the short-story inasmuch as it produced *The Lady or the Tiger?* and *In the Tennessee
Mountains,* each one of them a literary sensation that
advertised the form tremendously." It ends, "The
year was notable, too, because it produced Brander
Matthews' *The Philosophy of the Short-Story,*—the
first scientific handling of the art of the form since
Poe's review of Hawthorne." If, in the first sentence,
some of us might prefer "*a* climactic year," with the
second nobody can disagree.

Brander Matthews' contribution to short story history, criticism, and literature is considerable. No book
about our story writers can afford to omit his work,
yet his fame will rest upon other labors. From *French
Dramatists of the Nineteenth Century* (1881), which
grew out of his enthusiasm for the recent French play,
through *The Development of the Drama* (1903),
wherein he sums up comprehensively his knowledge of

successive dramatic ages, to *Molière* (1910) and *Shakespeare as a Playwright* (1913), studies in detail of the two great dramatists, Mr. Matthews has progressed to the place of first authority in matters histrionic. As the last named title indicates, he is technician no less than historian. *A Study of the Drama* (1910), *A Book About the Theater* (1916), and *The Principles of Playmaking* (1919) testify with further explicitness to this interest. He has written a number of plays. Not to mention his earlier French adaptations or his less successful original ventures, his *A Gold Mine* and *On Probation* were acted several seasons. He is an indefatigable play-goer, and as he states in *These Many Years* (1917) he has seen, probably, almost everything that was worth seeing in the theaters of New York in the half-century which elapsed between 1865 and 1915. He knows the theaters and actors of Paris and London only not quite so well, perhaps, as those of New York.

He has written about verse forms. *The Rhymester,* or *The Rules of Rhyme,* by Tom Hood, he edited with additions, in 1882, and *A Study of Versification* he published in 1910. In his story *The New Member of the Club* (1893), some one remarks of Arthur Penn (a pseudonym of Mr. Matthews) that he knows a sonnet when he sees it, "and he can turn off as good a topical song as any man in New York." In earlier years he frequently exercised this talent for lighter verse and at the age of sixty presented to his friends a few of his scattered poems humorously entitled *Fugitives from Justice.*

He is, *par excellence,* the great college professor, the one at Columbia University who for the longest time has been before the public eye. Twenty years after he took his A.B. degree, he returned to his alma mater as assistant professor of English literature, later (1899) occupying the first chair of its kind to be established in this country, that of dramatic literature. He will live longest through his books; he will live best loved by the boys who have sat in his class-room year after year, to whom he is not only a rare instructor but "a good fellow," and most admired by all the men and women to whom in large numbers he has lectured, out of the plenitude of his richness, on the development of the drama. These lectures are indescribable rushes of information that soothe by their emollient urbanity, delight by their scintillant humor, incite to keener appreciation through poignant darts of criticism, vivify the subject with anecdotes of foremost writers and actors, and illuminate through the electric glow of a unique personality. He thinks he is not a "born orator"; but he must have been a talker shortly after that auspicious event.

Such a personality cannot but have lived greatly. In the course of his three score years and more Mr. Matthews may boast of the acquaintance or friendship of most representative professional folk throughout the globe. To read *These Many Years* is to see unfold from his angle the last quarter of the old century and the first years of the new.

Not only on the broad highway of literature did Mr. Matthews early set forth. From the beginning he strayed into byways, taking time for curiosities of literature as of life. Parodies, fans, notes on swearing, hypnotism, crystal gazing, tumbleronicons, "carols of cookery," and sixteen years without a birthday—these merely illustrate the countless diversified topics that have received attention from his pen. The variety of his interests, serious and diverting, has meant a number of outlets for expression. So it is that he has published in all the prominent periodicals at home and many in London and Paris. He writes no reviews of the current drama because he is a member of the Players Club, to which no critic of the current stage may be admitted. His large popularity first arrived, it may be added, through one of the volumes resulting from his professional career: his *Introduction to the Study of American Literature*.

These Many Years sets forth entertainingly the facts of his life and work. To sum up the full chronology would be a labor of supererogation. But it is interesting to read that he was born in New Orleans in 1852, that he moved with his father and mother to New York when he was a child, that he was brought up to the profession of millionaire but turned with amazing ease to the earning of his own livelihood, that he read Beadle's Dime Novels, that he became a trapeze performer and expert parlor juggler, that he rapidly widened his reading, that Arnold's *Essays in Criticism* and Lowell's *Among My Books* initiated him into the principles and practice of criticism, that he taught himself writing by a weekly letter to *Figaro* (London), that he took a degree in law two years after his A.B. degree in 1871, that the same year (1873) he was married to Miss Ada Smith of London, and that he remained four or five years in his father's office before turning definitely to his lifework. It is interesting to find many illustrations of his love for club life. After eighteen years on the waiting list for the Athenaeum he was admitted—the first American; he is a familiar figure at the Savile. At home he frequents the Century, the Authors, and the Players. He is an enthusiastic advocate of reformed spelling; he has aided in the organization of certain leagues and societies; he is the fifty-second member of the American Academy of Arts and Letters; he is a member of the (French) Legion of Honor. It is pleasant to read, further, of his happy experiences in collaboration with Laurence Hutton, Bronson Howard, George H. Jessop, and Henry Cuyler Bunner. Above all, it is heartening to see that he has fulfilled one after another of his early ideals; his ambition to write a history of dramatic literature was formed in 1873 and gratified in 1903, to write the biography of Molière was conceived in 1872 and in fruition nearly forty years later.

It may seem matter for wonder that he has found

time to study mere fiction or to practice its composition. Yet for a period of years he wrote novels and short stories, to the exclusion more or less of other forms, and was probably deterred from further, so-called, "creative" writing only by his duties at Columbia University. His best known novels are *A Confident To-morrow* (1899), *The Action and the Word* (1900), and *His Father's Son* (1895), each of which has for sub-title, *A Novel of New York*.

In fiction, as in the drama, he has followed a wholly logical method of procedure. His analytical habit of mind precedes or accompanies the synthesis of composition. From the beginning, in fiction as elsewhere, the manner of accomplishment has concerned him more than the matter. Hence, he has written on aspects of its philosophy and technique.

He is not without suspicion that his first serial, now forgotten, was modeled on the dime novels he had read with such assiduity. But when he began seriously to practice the art of narrative, he took for his master Thomas Bailey Aldrich, "From whom," he says in the dedication of *The Story of a Story* (1893), "I learnt the trade of story-telling." He studied to write the tale "with an amusing twist of surprise at the end of it." He may be appraised in this particular in *A Family Tree* (title story of the volume, 1889), in which the "inexorable end of a Greek tragedy" is shifted to a happy conclusion, justified by the statement that "Love is too strong for Fate"; or in *The New Member of the Club* (*The Story of a Story*), where the pleasing shock turns on a raconteur's having not one brother-in-law but eleven; or in *The Rival Ghosts* (in *In Partnership*, and later in *Tales of Fantasy and Fact*), which makes the somehow totally unexpected revelation that the antagonistic spirits were of opposite sex; or in *An Interview with Miss Marlenspuyk* (*Outlines in Local Color*), in which the piquant flavor is added at the very last.

As Mr. Matthews has recorded, Aldrich was his predecessor in another respect. *The Documents in the Case* reveals a series of events through letters, telegrams, news paragraphs, pawn tickets, and similar evidence. This novel framework advanced beyond the letters of *Marjorie Daw,* which none the less furnished the idea to Mr. Matthews and his collaborator, Bunner. Both authors liked experimenting with the letter-form. Witness Bunner's *A Letter and a Paragraph,** and Mr. Matthews' *Two Letters* (*The Story of a Story*), *Idle Notes of an Idle Voyage, Chesterfield's Letters to His Son,* and the titular piece of *A Family Tree.*

Two Letters, One Story Is Good Till Another Is Told, and *The Story of a Story* illustrate a third device in technique. Complementary points of view in *Two Letters* convey the correct account to the reader. *One Story Is Good* was written in collaboration with George

---

* *Love in Old Cloathes,* where it is reprinted from *In Partnership.*

H. Jessop, as a similar experiment: "We simply narrated twice the same sets of incidents as seen through two different pairs of eyes." In *The Story of a Story,* he uses the angles of author, editor, artist, printer, publisher, critic, and four readers, in order to carry a complete estimate of the "story." These efforts, as well as others, such as Henry James's *The Point of View,* succeeded the famous example of Browning's *The Ring and the Book.*

The Story of a Story illustrates, further, the author's insistence upon the struggle element in fiction. The artist says, "There's a fight in it"; the girl remarks, "There was too much fighting in it"; the blacksmith declares, "I'd like to have met the man that fought that way"; and the small boy "picked it out because there was the picture of a fight in it."

Suggestion, too, Mr. Matthews believes to be indispensable to short-story success. This principle emerges in the selection just discussed; notably, again, in *Chesterfield's Letters,* wherein the postcards reveal by strong implication, the adventurous life of J. Quincy A. Chesterfield; and in *By Telephone,* which conveys one end of a conversation through the expressed other end. This device is shopworn now, even on the discard shelf; but in the late eighties it could have been not otherwise than new.

Fantasy, according to this author in his *The Philosophy of the Short-Story,* is a desirable constituent. Nowhere has he reached this ideal better than in *The*

Rival Ghosts. Tales of Fantasy and Fact (1896) when most fantastic are less story-like. *A Primer of Imaginary Geography, The Kinetoscope of Time,* and *The Dream Gown of the Japanese Ambassador* are the works of Mr. Matthews which deserve the title of incursions in beauty. The author modestly says of these tales that they may reveal invention only; but surely through reminiscence of high imaginative peaks they carry the illusion of imagination. They are, however, not among his best narratives. They are, rather, of the later Vision literature, exemplified, for instance, in Addison's *Mirza.* In *The Dream Gown,* moreover, after effecting a fair story, he explains too explicitly the motivations for the dreams. Always interested in watching the wheels revolve, he must tell the other man how they move. In an earlier story, *On the Battlefield,* he could not resist describing in detail the construction of the cyclorama. This interest in discovering how a thing is done he illustrates in *A Confidential Postscript* to *The Tales of Fantasy and Fact.*

Close circumscription in time and place conduce to unity of action, effect and single intention. *In a Vestibule Limited* (1892) and *Check and Countercheck: A Tale of Twenty-five Hours* (1892)* illustrate in their very titles a conscious conformity to the laws of the Greek "unities."

* Reprinted from *Lippincott's Magazine,* 1888, where it bears the sub-title, *A Tale of Twenty-four Hours.*

It is not surprising that from his over-sea travel, Mr. Matthews occasionally used, in his earlier stories, the ocean for setting or background. The story of *The Rival Ghosts* is told at sea, presumably; jottings during a supposed voyage became *Idle Notes*. *The Secret of the Sea* (title story of the volume published 1886) is perhaps the best of the lot, in its recountal of how an ocean liner is forced by a yacht to surrender the specie it carries.

But as the author has stated, he uses New York most often for his setting.   And the greatest service he has performed in the field of the short story exists in three volumes about the Empire City: *Vignettes of Manhattan* (1894), *Outlines in Local Color* (1897), and *Vistas of New York* (1912).   The first of these has become a classic for its *Spring in a Side Street, In the Little Church Down the Street, Vista in Central Park* and other numbers: delicate miniatures, all of them, regarded by certain critics as the author's best work in fiction. *Vistas* includes *In a Hansom*—to which Richard Harding Davis's *A Walk Up the Avenue* is the only companion-piece—*On the Steps of the City Hall, Under an April Sky*, and repeats, from another collection, *In a Bob-Tail Car*, for the loss of any of which, literature about New York would be the poorer. For *Outlines* we have a strong personal preference, from *An Interview with Miss Marlenspuyk* to *Men and Women and Horses*.

These thirty-six tales—there are twelve to the

volume, one for each month—present the city in the late nineteenth century, with a dash of twentieth century spirit. There are the landmarks dear to every New Yorker: Central Park and Fifth Avenue, the East Side and the East River; the region below Fourteenth Street—so different a few years ago from its present aspect; Wall Street and Broadway; Riverside Drive and the Hudson. There are the Gotham customs and pleasures, which have passed or may pass, but not from the hearts of those who have known them: the horse show in Madison Square Garden; Thanksgiving Day parade; the giving of potted plants at Easter. The cable car, the jeweler's at Fifteenth Street (already he is farther uptown), the Statue of Liberty, Normal College (now Hunter College in honor of its founder), Trinity Church, the Squares, and the Jersey Shores—nothing is too large or too small to receive attention. In fact, reading with his purpose in mind, one cannot but feel that the landmarks press a trifle closely and obviously. He is more successful with the aspects of the city; April rain Fourth of July heat, and January snow are more than mere "weather." They are garments that express the moods of Manhattan.

Since the first of these books appeared, it has become the fashion to stage the action of stories in New York. But Mr. Matthews observes that when he and Bunner first discussed the topic of the individuality, the picturesqueness and the charm of the city as a novel setting, about the year 1880, there were only a scant half dozen books so using it. "I attempted to catch certain aspects and attributes of New York merely because I found keen enjoyment in making these snap-shots of the metropolis, and because I kept on observing conditions and situations which seemed to me to be essentially characteristic of the city I loved." Etchings, thumb-nails, the author appropriately terms these adventures in local color. He knows they have the merit of sincerity and directness; for they grow from intimate knowledge. He never went out of his depth. "Sometimes I was able to utilize a real happening, brought to me by word of mouth and therefore more malleable than if it had been snatched from a newspaper; and sometimes the germ of my story had to evolve by spontaneous generation in my own head, conjuring up the ghost of a plot to permit me to reproduce the atmosphere of the special spot and the special moment I had chosen."

The author would agree with a former student of his, George Hellman, that the tales interest through the social milieu and the enjoyable conversation, that there are no strong characters—it was not part of his purpose to present them—they are real people one might have met in any of the circumstances set forth. They occur and recur in his episodes, as they might in real life. But Mr. Hellman is wrong in thinking the plots not strong. Mr. Matthews' schooling with the "deft playmakers of Paris", his own dramatic con-

struction, and his sense of architectural finish predetermined proportionate success in this regard. If we
keep in mind, always, his place in the development of
the short-story, he is one of the prime "plotters."

Besides his debt to Aldrich, he owes something to
Francois Coppée and Ludovic Halévy. When Walter
Learned translated ten of Coppée's tales, Mr. Matthews
wrote the introduction for the book (published 1891),
as he did also for *Parisian Points of View* (1892),
translated from Halévy by E. V. B. Matthews. His
bright dialogue conceivably lost none of its sparkle
from study of the most Parisian of story writers, none
of its neatness of construction from study of the man
who achieved *The Substitute*. Henley's comment upon
The Last Meeting (1895) is just: the crackle of cleverness makes one long for a flash of stupidity. In general, his stories read colloquially, a recommendation or
otherwise, according to taste.

In his *The Philosophy of the Short-Story*, first contributed to *The Saturday Review* in 1884, Mr.
Matthews set the fashion of writing "Short-story,"
the compound being the only expression the language
affords for a form equivalent to, or comparable to,
the *conte* of the French. Unfortunately, this suggestion has not resulted in fixed custom: "short story"
and "short-story" flourish side by side, either serving
for the more severely defined form or the story merely
short. Among the essentials of the Short-story Mr.
Matthews places "an idea logically developed by one

possessing the sense of form and the gift of style";
the supremacy of plot—"The Short-story is nothing if
there is no story to tell"—neat structure and polished
execution. Elsewhere he says, "The Short-story must
do one thing and it must do this completely and perfectly: It must not loiter or digress, it must have
unity of action, unity of temper, unity of tone, unity
of color, unity of effect; and it must vigilantly exclude
everything that might interfere with its singleness of
intention."

Since he has the power of dissociating himself from
his work and of judging it objectively, and since he is
unsparingly stern with himself, Mr. Matthews has
made the most stringent criticism that may be offered
against it. "In all these essays in fiction the frame
now appears to me to be more prominent than the
picture itself." But undoubtedly, the social historian
of the twenty-first century will find them, as their author hopes, useful.

Mr. Matthews' Short-Stories:

> *The Last Meeting* (novelette), 1885.
> *A Secret of the Sea and Other Stories,* 1886.
> *A Family Tree,* 1889.
> *In the Vestibule Limited,* 1892.
> *Check and Countercheck* (with G. H. Jessop),
>   1892.
> *The Story of a Story,* 1893.
> *The Royal Marine: An Idyl of Narragansett
>   Pier,* 1894.

Vignettes of Manhattan, 1894.
Tales of Fantasy and Fact, 1896.
Outlines in Local Color, 1897.
Vistas of New York, 1912.

CHAPTER XVII

OF all American writers who have converted to fictive purposes the science of logic, two are preëminent. They grew up, some fifty years apart, in the same section of the United States, and by a pun the surname of one is the superlative of the other. They are Edgar Allan Poe and Melville Davisson Post.

The first of these formulated the laws of the short story. He originated the detective story, his model for which served writers half a century. That model is well known: a crime has been committed, or is about to be committed, and the agent of the law bends his efforts to apprehending the criminal or to preventing the crime. It was left for the second to invent a new type of detective tale.

As Mr. Post has himself remarked, the flood of detective stories succeeding Poe's poured forth "until the stomach of the reader failed." He, a lawyer of parts, who has pleaded before the bar of the Supreme Court of West Virginia, the United Circuit of Appeals, and the Supreme Court of the United States, recognized that, notwithstanding stories of crime, "the high ground of the field of crime has not been explored; it has not even been entered. The book stalls have been filled to weariness with tales based upon plans whereby the *detective* or *ferreting* power of the State might be baffled. But, prodigious marvel! no writer has attempted to construct tales based upon plans whereby the *punishing* power of the State might be baffled.

Deducible from the preceding paragraph is the originality of Mr. Post's inventions. And by inference emerges the truth that only a lawyer or student of criminology has the precise knowledge adequate to the task. To write a series of detective stories wherein the criminal must go unpunished presupposes ability to differentiate between crime in the sense of social wrong and crime punishable by law. For law is not reason: not all wrongs, great though they may be, are crimes.

Here, at once, enters a new need. Poe had required an acute and subtile intellect, a highly trained ratiocinative mind, for his detective. These he incorporated in Monsieur Dupin. Mr. Post required, first of all, an unmoral intelligence, preferably that of a skilled unscrupulous lawyer who would instruct men how to evade the law. Hence, arose the figure of Randolph Mason.

Of the stories in *The Strange Schemes of Randolph Mason* (1896) *The Corpus Delicti,* reprinted by *The Review of Reviews* as a masterpiece of mystery fiction,

is the most gruesome and the most powerful.   But if
it brings a shock to the layman, it conveys only a striking instance of legal lore to the lawyer.   Samuel Walcott, in danger from Nina St. Croix, goes in his dis-
tress to Mason.   Mason gives directions that must be
faithfully followed.   The reader is then treated openly
to the performance of a diabolically contrived crime.
In the guise of a sailor, Walcott enters Nina's home,
stabs her to death, dismembers her body, destroys it
by means of decomposing agents and through the bath
tub drain removes all traces of his ghastly work.   He
is arrested, however, as he leaves the house and is
brought to trial.   To the astonishment of the Court,
the defendant Mason moves that the Judge direct the
jury to find the prisoner not guilty.   In the bout that
follows between himself and the prosecuting attorney,
Mason observes: "This is a matter of law, plain, clear,
and so well settled in the State of New York that even
the counsel for the people should know it. . . . If the
corpus delicti, the body of the crime, has been proven,
as required by the laws of the commonwealth, then this
case should go to the jury. If not, then it is the duty
of the Court to direct the jury to find the prisoner
not guilty." The Judge so directs, and the undeniably
criminal Walcott walks out, a free man.

Now, had Poe or Conan Doyle told this story, he
would have bent the energies of the detective to discovering what had become of the body (the reader
would have learned only when Dupin or Sherlock

Holmes saw fit to spring his discovery), and would have hailed the criminal before a bar at which he would be convicted. Mr. Post frankly gives away the murder, and shifts his emphasis to showing how the State was baffled.

Of other stories in the same volume, *The Sheriff of Gullmore* and *Woodford's Partner* are, perhaps, the most satisfactory. In the latter Mason finds a criminal way, not, however, a crime before the law, to protect an honest young man from whom has been stolen twenty thousand dollars entrusted to him. An extreme application of the sophism that the means justifies the end, it draws to some extent upon the reader's sympathy. In the former, a sheriff who has defaulted, and whose bondsmen may be called to cover his defalcation, shifts the responsibility to his successor as he goes out of office. If here, as in succeeding stories, Mr. Post has seemed to show the villain how to circumvent the consequences of his villainy, he has also, as he maintains, warned the friends of law and order.

Mr. George Randolph Chester, whose *Get-Rich-Quick Wallingford* stories resemble in certain respects those of Mr. Post, was once asked whether sharpers had not received pointers from Blackie and Wallingford. "They have," he replied with something like enthusiasm, "but they are now behind prison bars!" One does not like to read with the feeling that some criminal may profit by the plan unfolded; it is more pleasant to harbor the thought that the law will take note, as well as the lawless . . . In any event, Randolph Mason has the fascination, and the repulsion, of the serpent.

The succeeding volume, *The Man of Last Resort* (1897), informing by its sub-title that the stories deal with the clients of Mason, has been praised as a strong plea for moral responsibility made in vivid and earnest style. The author observes in the Preface that a few critics contended the first volume was dangerous because it explained with detail how one could murder or steal and escape punishment. He answers them by the fact that law-making ultimately lies with the citizens, and changes in the law must come about through public sentiment. "If men about their affairs were passing to and fro across a great bridge and one should discover that certain planks in its flooring were defective, would he do ill if he pointed them out to his fellows?" Perhaps the close of the volume further enforces the cause of righteousness: Mason is in a bad case of acute mania, raving like a drunken sailor: "The man of last resort was probably gone. There was now no resort but to the steel thing on the table."

One more volume, however, appeared with this trickster for central character: *The Corrector of Destinies* (1908). An element of novelty enters in the fact that Randolph Mason's secretary, Courtlandt Parks, heretofore spoken of in the third person, becomes the narrator.

A strong appeal Mason has for the reader is the

eagerness with which he welcomes a struggle against Fate or Destiny. It appears as a determinant of his acts throughout. With Chance, or Fate, or Destiny, Robert W. Chambers evolves a light or pleasing love story; with the same forces Melville Post effects a revision of the Greek concept. "Fate is supreme," says Sophocles through the Œdipus trilogy. "Perhaps," says Post through the triptych of Mason volumes, "but probably not. Fate may be averted." He admits, through his dramas, that sometimes there is the inevitable "come-back," as in *Mrs. Van Bartan* (in *The Man of Last Resort*).

Mr. Post recognizes that in a story, the story's the thing, that no degree of literary excellence can atone for lack of plot. He addresses himself at once to the popular and the critical reader. If there lives a writer of stories who is the "critic's writer," he is the man. He expressed himself unmistakably in *The Blight**: "The primary object of all fiction is to entertain the reader. If, while it entertains, it also ennobles him this fiction becomes a work of art; but its primary business must be to entertain and not to educate or to instruct him." In answering the question, "What sort of fiction has the most nearly universal appeal?" he holds that the human mind is engaged almost exclusively with problems, and that "the writer who presents a problem to be solved or a mystery to be untangled will be offering those qualities in his fiction which are of the most

* *Saturday Evening Post*, December 26, 1914.

nearly universal appeal." Men of education and culture—but never critics of stories!—have taken the
position that literature of this character is not of the
highest order. He cites Aristotle's *Poetics:* Tragedy
is an imitation, not of men, but of an action of life
. . . the incidents and the plot are the end of a tragedy."
The plot is first; character is second. The Greeks
would have been astounded at the idea common to
our age that "the highest form of literary structure
may omit the framework of the plot." The short
story is to our age what the drama was to the Greeks.
Poe knew this. And he is the one literary genius
America has produced.

Yet Mr. Post's ideal of plot is no mere mechanical
contrivance. He once expressed his pleasure to the
present writer that "there are people who see that a
story should be clean cut and with a single dominating
germinal incident upon which it turns as a door upon
a hinge, and not built up on a scaffolding of criss-cross
stuff." In all these underlying principles of his work,
principles stated with the frankness of Poe, Melville
Post strikes an answering chord in the critic who finds
in his stories the perfect application of the theories he
champions.

Mr. Post also holds a brief for his large employ-
ment of tragic incident: "Under the scheme of the
universe it is the tragic things that seem the most real."
He pleases the popular audience because he writes of
crime. He knows, as Anna Katharine Green knows,

its universal appeal. Mrs. Green once wrote: "Crime must touch our imagination by showing people, *like ourselves,* but incredibly transformed by some overwhelming motive." Further, we are interested because what most interests us in human beings is their hidden emotions; crime in normal people must be the result of tremendous emotion. We like to read detective stories of crime because we like to figure on the solution of the mystery. Motive and mystery, in short, are the sources of entertainment, rather than the crime itself. But murder is interesting because of its finality: it is the supreme crime, because it is irreparable.*

Mrs. Green thinks that nine times out of ten the crime is selfishness, which has many forms. If one form of selfishness is the desire to be freed from some obligation or duty, Mr. Post uses it as a motive in *The Corpus Delicti.* Walcott murdered Nina because he desired liberty and because she was about to disclose the secret that would have disgraced him and cost him his life. But he also employs unselfishness as a motive. In *Woodford's Partner,* William Harris commits crime to save his younger brother from disgrace. Camden Gerard, of *The Error of William Van Broom,* becomes a thief unpunishable by law, that he may pay the school bills of his sister.

Uncle Abner (1919) is proof that Mr. Post had by no means exhausted his fecundity in creating the unmoral Mason. His sense of justice and his sense

* *American Magazine.*

of balance have produced a hero the antithesis of his hero-villain. Whereas Mason delighted in struggling against pagan Fate, Uncle Abner finds joy in furthering the beneficent operations of Providence. These two men express, respectively, the heathen and the Christian ideal; and they are as complementary as Jekyll and Hyde. This is the significant accomplishment of Mr. Post. He has demonstrated that wrong may triumph over man-made laws, which are imperfect after all the centuries; but that right must win under the timeless Providence of God. Uncle Abner as described by his nephew, Martin, who recounts most of the exploits, is an austere, deeply religious man, with a big iron frame, a grizzled beard and features forged by a smith. His gift for ferreting out crime, which is as great as that of Sherlock Holmes and, in accordance with the author's purpose, requires not nearly so long to arrive at conclusions, works to throw down the last barrier behind which the criminal is entrenched. Small space is required to mete out justice. Take *The Concealed Path*, for example: after four thousand words or so ending in the revelation of the murderer, Abner's pronouncement of doom is swift. . . .

"He raised his great arm, the clenched bronze fingers big like the coupling pins of a cart.

" 'I would have stopped it with my own hand,' he said; 'but I wanted the men of the hills to hang you. . . . And they are here.'

"There was a great sound of tramping feet in the hall outside.

"And while the men entered, big, grim, determined men, Abner called out their names:

" 'Arnold, Randolph, Stuart, Elnathan Stone, and my brother, Rufus!' "

The death of a criminal may be the subject of investigation, as in *The Doomdorf Mystery*. The flawlessness of this story was appreciated by every critic who read it on its appearance in *The Saturday Evening Post*, July 18, 1914. For unity, strength, and integration of detail no better story has been written. Abner and Randolph arrive at the house of Doomdorf, meaning to remonstrate with him over his illicit brewing. They find the circuit rider Bronson on his big roan horse in the paved courtyard. They knock and are admitted by a little, faded woman. They continue to Doomdorf's door, which, finding bolted, they burst open. Doomdorf is lying on his couch, shot through the heart. The mystery lies in the manner of the murder: the locked door and the barred windows seem to preclude human agency; suicide is eliminated inasmuch as the gun rests on its rack. The mystery is not lessened when the circuit rider declares he is responsible and when, later, the woman declares, "I killed him!" In the dramatic revelation, the reader is held breathless. The bottle of distillate on the table catches the sunbeam and focusing it upon the lock of the gun on the wall ignites the percussion cap. The symmetry of the story is perfected through the preacher's prayer that the Lord would destroy Doomdorf with fire from heaven, and through the woman's practice of magic which urged her to create a wax image and to thrust a needle through its heart. Doomdorf had died by immutable and natural laws working through his own hell-brew to poetic justice; or in answer to prayer, as the circuit rider believed; or through her sorcery, as the woman believed; or by the mysterious justice of God, as Abner saw it.*

As in *The Concealed Path,* murder is used for chief interest in *The Wrong Hand, The Angel of the Lord, An Act of God, The Age of Miracles, The Straw Man, The Adopted Daughter,* and *Naboth's Vineyard.*

A difficult task lay, one might think, in convincing the reader of the murder in *The Adopted Daughter.* Suppose you are told that a crack shot has put a bullet through a man's eyeball so as to leave no mark of death. Impossible, you say; the bullet must come out somewhere. But the author allows his murderer to use a light charge of powder that lodges the bullet in the brain. Well, you counter, why wouldn't the shrunken eyelid betray the death-wound? That is the center about which the author has woven the web of his story. You may also reflect that expert marksman-

*An interesting comparison lies in the end of his long story, *The Nameless Thing,* 1912.

ship is required. Mr. Post treats you to a dramatic instance or so of impromptu efficiency that requires *more* skill than is needed to shoot a man through the eyeball. He knows the value of the *a fortiori* argument.

To the critical eye the weakness of most of these tales is apparent; but they are not obstrusive to a reader who seeks entertainment. For example, in *The Adopted Daughter,* Shepjard Flornoy's eye has been shot out by his brother Vespasian. The latter saws off the head of an ivory pawn and forces it into the bullet hole to round out the damaged eyeball. No criminal would be likely to keep the pawn after sawing off the head. Yet it is this tell-tale object which, joined to suspected motivation for the fratricide, excites Abner's suspicion.

The scenes of these adventures are in Virginia in the days before the carving out of West Virginia. Although the stories more nearly approach the Poe type than do the Mason group, yet novelty is secured through shift of emphasis and through the setting. Dupin recalls to us the crime of the city; Sherlock Holmes lives in London. Abner is a man of the hills, whose detective work leads him among the hill people.

In *The Mystery of the Blue Villa* (1920) the author reveals knowledge of settings into which, in real life, his travels have led him. Port Said figures in the titular story—a story which lacks the freshness of Mr. Post's plots in that it is a variant of an old one.

It has found subsequent treatment by Albert Payson Terhune in *A Catch in It Somewhere*.* But it is only fair to note that the fine hand of coincidence may have directed both Mr. Post and Mr. Terhune.   Paris, Nice, Cairo, Ostend, and London, with Washington and New York thrown in for home flavor, make up the settings of these tales.   In this volume, as in the first, the reader thrills to a series of climaxes in plots so logically built as to seem a natural growth of events leading to or away from the dominant incident.   They add nothing, perhaps, to the writer's fame, save in their indication of his broadening interests and in their suggestion of the Great War as an occasional background.   *The Miller of Ostend*, indeed, is a superb example of war horror.   *The Witch of Lecca* points to study of witchcraft and the Black Art, and develops with amazing resourcefulness a single incident.   The author's manner is everywhere derived from the American plus the French: he combines the ratiocinative processes of Poe with the dramatic presentation of Daudet and Maupassant.

Among Mr. Post's most absorbing interests and pastimes, if one may judge by his articles in current magazines, are codes and ciphers.   Readers of *Everybody's* will recall a cover picturing a code letter such as was discovered in the days of the War, and illustrating a factual story by Mr. Post.   He has used a similar code letter in *The Pacifist* (in *The Mystery of the*

* *The Blue Book,* July, 1920.

Blue Villa). His constant curiosity about the ways
men seek to outwit their fellow creatures promises
further entertainment to his large class of readers.
But it is to be remembered that before the age of fifty
he had established himself in narrative one of the im-
mortals.

Mr. Post has written not only the type of story
with which he has scored so successfully again and
again. Besides *The Gilded Chair* (1910), a novel of
love and adventure, he published in 1901—between the
second and third Randolph Mason books—*Dwellers in
the Hills*. It is impossible to read this work, which as
to plot is a short story, and in deliberate use of irrele-
vant but enriching detail a novel, without the certainty
that it is from Mr. Post's own experiences, and that
he is limned in the narrator, Quiller. For the alien to
read it is to acquaint himself with life in the hills of
West Virginia some two score years ago. For the
rural Southerner of Mr. Post's generation to read it
is to ride in memory a gallant steed—like Quiller's El
Mahdi—along a country road bordered by sedge and
ragweed; to note the hickories trembling in their yellow leaves; to hear the partridge's "bob white" call,
the woodpecker's tap, and the "golden belted bee boom-
ing past"; to cross the stream fringed with bullrushes;
to hear men's voices "reaching half a mile to the graz-
ing steers on the sodded knobs"; to meet a neighbor's
boy astride a bag of corn, on his way to the grist-mill;
to stop at the blacksmith's, there to watch the forging

of a horse-shoe; or at the wagoner's, to assist in the making of a wheel; to taste the sweet corn pone and the striped bacon, and to roast potatoes in the ashes —to re-live a sort of natural "mission furniture" period of existence.

To read the book is also to construct the boy that was Melville Davisson Post, a process the more compelling because of the half-hidden, half-expressed relationships. If you know, for instance, from *Who's Who* or other source, that his father was Ira Carper Post, you will notice that "Carper" creeps out in this book (as it does in the *Randolph Mason* books for other characters), and you find yourself wondering just the kinship between fictive heroine and actual human being. His use of family and State names is constant throughout his volumes: Randolph, Davisson, Blennerhassett and Evelyn Byrd are a few that set ringing the bells of history, conveying a mood that holds long after the peals have died away. . . .

Mr. Post was born April 19, 1871, and grew up, you are sure, to appreciate the art of riding (which consists in becoming part of your horse.) no less than his lessons in the classics. From his fiction you are so sure of these truths that you hardly need for confirmation his factual articles testifying to the value of Aristotle, nor a published photograph that portrays him in riding togs with a noble dog at his side. Through the dramas he presents, you somehow have borne in upon you that he is a community man and a statesmen, one ready to take his part in all that affects the good of neighborhood or nation. You turn to the record and find your deductions or vaporous guessings established facts. He has not all these years devoted himself wholly to writing nor yet to the law. He has been interested in railroads and coal, in education and in politics. His art of story-telling has been strengthened by his legal training and—what does not always follow from mere recognition of critical canons—by application of scientific standards to his own fiction. He learned before he was thirty that the mastery of an art depends only upon the comprehension of its basic law; that the short story, "like any work of art, is produced only by painstaking labor and according to certain structural rules." He is convinced that "the laws that apply to mechanics and architecture are no more certain or established than those that apply to the construction of the short-story." In his enthusiasm for economy, he would brand into the hand of everybody the rule of Walter Pater: "All art does but consist in the removal of surplusage."

Mr. Post's books of stories:

The Strange Schemes of Randolph Mason, 1896.
The Man of Last Resort, 1897.
Dwellers in the Hills, 1901.
The Corrector of Destinies, 1908.
Uncle Abner, 1919.
The Mystery at the Blue Villa, 1920.

CHAPTER XVIII

THAT story telling is the most popular of all kinds of discourse, spoken or written, has been exemplified from the time of Homer to the present. Whatever other elements may be conducive to longevity, it is narrative which draws numbers to the fireside, the printed page, or the screen. It is for her foremost ability to tell a tale that Mary Roberts Rinehart is successful. The fact that frequently there is small residuum after the "story" is subtracted is one proof of this ability. She knows this fact, knows that she is a narrator and modestly states that some day she may be a novelist. For she is aware that the novelist is biographer, analyst, philosopher—in many respects so much more than the story teller. But, as she must also know, the story teller's compensations are many in the direction of the dramatic, the picturesque and the vivid.

She is popular because she not only knows how to tell a story but how to tell the sort that most people seek to-day for entertainment. No other writer reflects more accurately the age of the motion picture. This is neither to assert nor to deny that she has been influenced by motion picture technique. It is to say that, being a child of the twentieth century, she recognizes the demand for rapid action and the eagerness for one unique visual impression after another. She supplies the demand by unreeling film after film from a mind fertile in invention and prodigal of picture-story stuff which, translated in terms of black and white, reel off before the reader. There is the same lack of depth, or "thickness," in her narrative which the motion-picture play illustrates. It is art of two dimensions. Bearing in mind that comparisons are odorous, but without invidious comparison, we find distinguishing characteristics in the narratives of three women writers who have been associated with the Steel City. Margaret Deland's stories have the depth of life, Willa Cather's have the finish of the sculptor, Mary Roberts Rinehart's have the finish of the screen play. Each method is well in its way; and if the first two contribute, in the main, to more enduring literature, the third contributes, on the whole, to the entertainment of the greater number. Moreover, each method shares with the others.

Take, for example, Mrs. Rinehart's "Tish" stories. After reading them, one knows that Tish is a daring eccentric spinster in the neighborhood of fifty; that to tell her a thing is dangerous means no power can restrain her; that she has mastered, in middle age, motoring, riding and skating; that she has run the hazards of camping out in Maine and the dangers of climbing the Rockies; that she has solved a mystery or two—that she is, in short, the representative of a contemporary type worthy to rank with the best creations of Mrs. Rinehart's contemporaries. For Tish, though typical, is an individual creation. She is promise of what the author of her being may do when she writes the novel as she will wish to write it. And yet, to revert to the point under discussion, when one reads about Tish it is the chronicle of her adventures that gives pleasure. One recalls from *Mind Over Motor* Tish triumphantly whizzing around the race course in Jasper's new car; from *The Simple Lifers,* Tish with a clamshell, "Indian nippers," advancing upon Percy's beard; from *Tish's Spy,* Tish, buoyed by a life-belt, headed for Island Number Eleven; from *My Country Tish of Thee,* Tish capturing a band of real bandits. All the pictures are screen studies, or pictures that cry out for screen presentation.

"Any one who has a sense of proportion can write a short story," Mrs. Rinehart has said to interviewers. "The main thing is to realize its essentials. The instinctive sense of what to tell and what to leave to the reader's imagination is what makes the born story teller." In addition to knowing that action is demanded by men readers, who go to baseball and polo, even if women, who are more introspective, are content to read analytical paragraphs, she believes that suspense is the vise that holds the reader. Therefore, she clamps it on early in the action, quite often hinting at just enough of the dénouement to cause curiosity as to what it was all about and how it all happened. She is a master of the art of suggestion. She believes that in a story the story's the thing: "You must have a good plot" (a particular in which the story is different from the novel). She recommends acquaintance with the market, since the writing of short stories is a game, and certain subjects are more or less in demand. Some subjects she regards as taboo—for instance, religion.

Mary Roberts was born in Pittsburgh, August 12, 1876. After being graduated from high school, she took the training school course for nurses offered by the Pittsburgh Homeopathic Hospital. That she draws largely from her hospital career is evident from her most successful fiction, from *The Amazing Adventures of Letitia Carberry* (1911) (albeit the title doth protest too much), through *K* (1915), the first long story of its kind, and *Love Stories* (1919). Though not a few authors have written hospital sketches, yet not one of them before Mrs. Rinehart wrote a body of narrative contributing definitely to local color and setting through hospital scenes and business. Even when she writes a story that has its action outside the hospital, she introduces bits of lore obviously gathered in her training career, odds and ends that rise spontaneously and become part of the whole. They form, incidentally, part of the realistic detail by which *à la Defoe,* the author, conveys the illusion of reality. For instance, you are rather sure Tish was in the Maine Woods; for you remember that a leech attached itself to her leg and was allowed to remain (by Aggie's advice): "One must leave it on until it was full and round and couldn't hold any more, and then it dropped off."

On April 21, 1896, according to *Who's Who,* Mary Roberts, not yet twenty, was married to Dr. Stanley Marshall Rinehart. In 1905, after the birth of her three sons, Mrs. Rinehart began to write. For the magazines she wrote poems and short stories—her first story went for $35—and in 1907 she produced her first play, *Double Life.* About this time Robert H. Davis, of *Munsey's,* suggested that she try a serial. The result was *The Circular Staircase* (1908), a mystery story, which she sold for $400. In 1914 she said she would not sell it for less than $20,000. This long story brought her popularity, popularity increased by another mystery, *The Man in Lower Ten* (1909). *When a Man Marries* was also published in 1909, after which followed *The Window at the White Cat* (1910). Her deftness in plot construction, her skill in arousing suspense, her ability to hold off the climax relentlessly while apparently advancing relentlessly toward it, and her final seeming clever solution of the mystery—all are manifest in *The Window at the White Cat.* There is the lawyer narrator, Knox, whose employment as mouthpiece makes for reality; there is

the disappearance of Allen Fleming, a piece of paper
bearing the sign of Eleven Twenty Two, the only clue,
there is his daughter Margery, who comes to the
lawyer (the love story is drawn in, at once, with a
tempestuous tug at the ears) ; there is the rival, young
Wardrop, former secretary of Allen Fleming, about
whom suspicion is thrown (with a rather strong odor
of red herrings) ; there is the concomitant disappearance of Miss Jane, sister of Letitia (not the Letitia
who is Tish, however) ; there are the stolen pearls, the
lost traveling bag, the murder of Fleming and the
final solution of the mystery at *The White Cat.* Clever
"detective story" stuff it is, much like that of Anna
Katherine Green and numerous followers of Poe,
without particular distinguishing marks.

The Amazing Adventures followed, 1911. The
volume includes three stories, in which the first, a
mystery, introduces the heroine of all. *Three Printers
of Penzance* and *That Awful Night,* which fulfill the
requisites of the short story, fill out the book; but the
two hundred pages in which Letitia turns detective at
the hospital are the most important. Mrs. Rinehart
may have found the germinal idea in Poe's *The Murders in the Rue Morgue.* So similar is the likeness
at one point that, just as the reader begins to wonder
whether she will solve the story similarly, she takes
occasion to mention *The Murders* in such manner as to
convey that her dénouement will be different. The

solving, however, lacks the convincingness of Poe's
story, as the manner lacks his clarity.

The author recognized the value of the material in
her enterprising old maid and utilized it in stories
published from 1912 on. In 1916 five of them were
collected under the title, *Tish*. For the title of one,
instanced above, we have not been able to forgive her:
My Country Tish of Thee. She likes punning as well,
almost, as the Elizabethans and, admittedly, she
ordinarily succeeds better than in this perpetration.
When Aggie of *The Amazing Adventures* broke the
thermometer in her mouth, Tommy Andrews remarked
of her that having been quicksilvered she'd now probably be reflecting; when Lizzie, the other crony, who
narrates *My Country* fell from her horse, which stepped
on and over her, Tish said something about his
having walked across a "bridge of size." On the
whole, this volume is the best collection Mrs. Rinehart
has published. To "Pendennis," of *The Forum,* she
said in 1918: "Every man is a hundred types; he's a
Puritan and a rake, a coward and a soldier, a shirker
and a worker, a priest and a sinner. All the writer does
is to take the dominant characteristic of that man
and lay stress on it." Surely, she put much of herself into Tish, wide as seems the gap between the
incorrigibly eccentric spinster and the lady of "erect
force, of swift judgment, of irreproachable dignity; in
manner gentle, feminine." They share a love of nature:
Tish's mountains and woods are to her a forest

of Arden no less than to Mrs. Rinehart; doubtless the latter shares the sense of discomfort the three spinsters felt, but never would she have turned back with Aggie and Lizzie; she grimly enjoys the conquering of difficulties, one fancies, as Tish enjoyed struggling; and, in diverse ways, they share a sense of humor.

It is, again, the background of reality, of such settings as Mrs. Rinehart has seen summer after summer, which fixes the all but unbelievable adventures of the three maiden ladies. So much, then, for the three tales of *Tish* which show her going back to nature. That the author has insight into character of another sort is displayed in *Like a Wolf on the Fold* wherein the astute Syrian, Tufik, is as individual and as typical as toothless Aggie, fat Lizzie and enterprising Tish, all of whom finally flee from his outrageously calculated dependence upon his "mothers." The presentation of his character gains from the method best adapted to narrative—the objective. Tufik acts, and his acts are colored by the comments of the ladies; but the author keeps out of his mind and proves, again, her ability to succeed by steering clear of the psychological.

Meantime, beginning about 1909, Mrs. Rinehart was writing stories of another sort, which appeared that year, in 1913, 1914, and 1915 in various magazines and which were gathered up under the title of *Affinities,* and published in 1920. Apropos of her nomenclature, the author was asked in 1914 whether it was difficult to get names for her people. She smiled. "Once I was invited," she said, to an affinity party. I did not go, but it suggested a story to me. Of course, I was very careful not to use the names of any one whom I knew. After the story came out I had a letter from a man in the West saying that his name was Ferdinand, and that his wife, his affinity, in fact the whole set, had names identical with the ones I had used in my story."

The title story may be cited, further, by way of indicating the all but unavoidable O. Henry influence. Fanny (the assumed narrator) and Ferd Jackson are affinities. The complication, at the basis of the surprise, lies in the fact that Day (Fanny's husband) and Ida Jackson (Ferd's wife) are also affinities, and unknown to the narrator and her picnic party are with another group on a neighboring island. After an exciting incident of a borrowed boat and a thrilling automobile race across country, Fanny and Ferd reach home. The shock emerges in the knowledge each acquires of the parts played by Day and Ida. Similar in construction are *The Family Friend,* and *Clara's Little Escapade,* testifying to Mrs. Rinehart's mastery of surprise. In all, the passing fad of a few years ago for affinities is treated in humorously satirical vein. *The Borrowed House* and *Sauce for the Gander* entrench upon the débutante ground which Mrs. Rinehart worked to best advantage in *Bab—A Sub-Deb.*

The book was published in 1917, after appearing as a series of stories in periodicals.

Mrs. Rinehart has stated that her creed is service, and she has illustrated how her books bear it out by reference to these whimsical fabrications of Bab's sub-débutante days. Bab, she says, is typical of the service we give to that brilliantly adorned figure of our first dream ambitions—romance. So again, as in the person of Letitia Carberry, Mrs. Rinehart draws upon her own personality for the psychology of Bab or draws upon what she might have been. In Bab Mrs. Rinehart has succeeded in approaching and describing, through narrative, the mental condition of a young girl who, surrounded by wealth and culture, is eager to escape from the reality of life, who as indicated, is romantic. She is another of the gauges the author has flung down to her future novel. The fact that little Mary Roberts Rinehart, 2nd, who made a grandmother of Mary Roberts Rinehart, 1st, at 43, is familiarly known as Babs, may be an indication that the fictive heroine is popular in the family.

Tish and Bab are frequently spoken of as though characters in novels. But it is to be remembered that they figured, first, in a series of short stories. The quite unexplainable tradition among publishers that books of short stories do not sell so easily as novels is probably accountable for such works as Mr. Tarkington's *Penrod* and Mrs. Rinehart's *Bab* appearing in novel disguise.

From 1912 to 1917 Mrs. Rinehart published, from
time to time, a number of hospital stories in which
love is supreme. They are included in *Love Stories*
(1919). There are critics who think the strongest
element of her success lies in her appreciation of the
joys and sorrows of the tender passion. *Twenty-
Two, Jane, I.: the Pavilion, God's Fool,* and *The
Miracle* run the gamut of this emotion as it may be
found, in varying aspects, in the private ward or Ward
G, in the heart of the guiltless or the guilty. There
is the young probationer, N. Jane Brown, who by a
daring act loses her newly achieved position but saves
a boy's life, and whose case is happily solved through
the interest of the patient in Twenty-Two. There is
another Jane, whom temper alone has brought to the
hospital and who is conquered by the application of
the principle that fire drives out fire. There is the
nurse who marries, just to oblige him, a supposedly dying gentleman, and for whom he recovers. There is
the Magdalen of *The Miracle,* which touches the misery
of the degraded woman with an unusual sympathy and
which shows the regenerating influence of the child. Of
them all, *God's Fool* offers the one character worthy
of being placed alongside Tish and Bab. The volume
includes a war story, *"Are We Downhearted? No!"*
which we should have liked to see published, rather,
with *Twenty-Three and a Half Hours' Leave* (1919).
The latter is one of the most humorous stories resulting from the Great Conflict and grows out of the au-

thor's intimate acquaintance, through her soldier son
and her own war work, with actual conditions.

It is not to be forgotten that in these years Mrs.
Rinehart's most impressive accomplishment has lain
in her longer stories, her drama, and recently, in the
motion picture dramatization of *Dangerous Days* and
It's a Great Life. It has been urged that some genius
may do for the movies what Shakespeare did for the
drama. This person might well be Mrs. Rinehart. She
has the gift in that direction; she has evinced increasing interest in the medium. Only the other day she
had a moving picture projector installed in her own
home, finding it helpful to study picture production
at close range. The New York *Tribune* of July 18,
1920, is responsible for the statement that the moving
picture addition to her work necessitates her going to
the California Coast about three times a year.

Her earlier long stories were continued in *Where
There's a Will* (1912), *The Case of Jennie Brice*
(1913), *The After House* (1914) and *The Street of
Seven Stars* (1914). The psychic tale *K* was followed
by a romance of lovable Otto IX. *"Long Live the
King!"* (1917) and *The Amazing Interlude* (1917),
a war theme of feminine courage. *A Poor Wise Man,*
her latest long work, was first published serially in *The
Ladies Home Journal* (1920). Among her dramas
are *Seven Days* (1909), and *Cheer Up* (1913).

Through Glacier Park revealed this author a powerful writer of expository and descriptive prose. Her

articles on the war, conceded to be among the most vivid and accurate written, were sent from the various army fronts she visited. On one occasion, according to her story, she reached France as a stowaway across the Channel. She interviewed the Queen of England, the Queen of Belgium, General Foch, and was decorated by the Belgian Queen.

Mrs. Rinehart lives at Sewickley, but has her office in Pittsburgh, where she works daily. After the manner of the modern professional, she waits not for inspiration, but picks up her pen and writes.

On her office wall hangs this motto: "Ideas and hard work are the keys to all success."

Mrs. Rinehart's Short Stories:

The Amazing Adventures of Letitia Carberry,
    1911.
Tish, 1916.
Bab, A Sub-Deb, 1917.
Love Stories, 1919.
Twenty-three and a Half Hours' Leave, 1919.
Affinities, 1920.

CHAPTER XIX

NOT many moons ago we heard an anecdote about an editor. Asked to name the best short story he had published in the year he immediately responded: "Why, that one by Jones-Smith—the one, you know——"

"And why is it the best?" the gadfly insisted.

The editor reviewed his story standards and somewhat dazedly replied that, after all, he hadn't measured the yarn; he just liked it. According to his tapeline—well, Green-Brown's about so and so was superior.

When asked in the days when William Sylvanus Baxter was seventeen, "Who is your favorite short story writer among the men?" we replied without hesitation, "Booth Tarkington." Of late, we have to admit that, rated by certain standards, he must give place to A and B and C.

First of all, Mr. Tarkington is a writer of long stories: he is neither short-story writer nor novelist. For though dissenting from Gouverneur Morris's remark to the late Joyce Kilmer (*New York Times,*

June 20, 1915), that in America we have had only one novel—*Huckleberry Finn*—and though ranking *The Turmoil* highest among Mr. Tarkington's works as a novel, we agree with Mr. Morris that it lacks the weight of such a work as *Henry Esmond*. In the second place, Mr. Tarkington or his publisher has the vexatious custom of running his best recent short stories into books so split into chapters that the story boundaries are obliterated. Witness *Penrod* and *Seventeen*. In the third place, his stories lack plot value. He is, himself, not concerned about plot. (Query: What does James Branch Cabell mean, in *Beyond Life,* when he says: "For the rest his [Mr. Tarkington's] plots are the sort of thing that makes criticism seem cruel"?) As a corollary, he rarely comes up to his promises. He fumbles the dénouements of his stories, the long ones in particular, which work up greatly and expectantly to a height, only to fall Luciferwise, not into a pit of horror, but to a level of disappointing mediocrity. He seems, in completing some of his stories, to say: "There, now I've done enough. The tale will go through on its own momentum." In two or three instances, the latter part sheers off so abruptly from the first half or three-quarters of the action as to drop the reader with a thud into real life out of pages the author's workmanship has been at pains to make climactic in the fourth dimension. Witness *The Magnificent Ambersons.* The book *Seventeen* is an exception. In the words of

Mr. Cabell, its "winding-up" is "just the species of necromancy attainable by no other living author." In the fifth place—but why continue objecting? The reasons we adduce against his stories weigh little in comparison with our confessed admiration.

This admiration rests on something deeper than merely technical grounds. His way of looking at life, through successive periods of interest in realism, romanticism, and satire; his experiences and observations translated into fiction with unsurpassed artistic skill; his modernity, by which he has represented a quarter century of American life just elapsed—these are more human and therefore more powerful contacts. His understanding, his sympathy, and his infectious humor make for the universality of his appeal. Frequently we hear extolled the crackling thorns of a mordant wit, or, at the other extreme, horse-play and silliness; then we hesitate to admit the tender impeachment that we have a sense of humor. But when we read Booth Tarkington our confidence is restored. And if we have only appreciation of humor as he points it out, we prefer keeping that appreciation. It is difficult to say with the requisite degree of difference what should be said about Mr. Tarkington's work. In the end, it is necessary to take refuge in some platitude which of a sudden glows with new meaning; for example, the old shopworn epigram, "Style is the man." It is the man Tarkington, the personality revealed in his works, who compels admiration.

Newton Booth Tarkington was born at Indianapolis, Indiana, July 21, 1869. When he was four or five years of age he revealed a gift of extraordinary imagination, or at least qualified as a youngster of make-believe and let's-pretend proclivities. He surrounded himself by a family bearing the descriptive cognomen of Hunchberg (Did it evolve, jobberwocky fashion, from *The Schönberg-Cotta Family* and *Hunchback*?). If he kept the original characters and nomenclature in the story he wrote thirty-five years later, he created at the age of four or five Mr. and Mrs. Hunchberg; the young gentlemen, Tom, Noble and Grandee; the gay and pretty young ladies, Miss Queen, Miss Marble, and Miss Molanna; the Uncle, Col. Hunchberg, and the amiable but decrepit Aunt Hunchberg. It is not on record, however, that he owned an imaginary dog, by name Simpledoria, or that he was an invalid child, like Little Hamilton Swift, Jr.

When he was eleven years old he established a friendship with James Whitcomb Riley, by whom he was influenced so long as the Hoosier Poet lived, and to whom he dedicated the Hunchberg story, *Beasley's Christmas Party* (1909).

After a year at Phillips Exeter Academy, Mr. Tarkington studied at Purdue University; then he went to Princeton, where in 1893 he took his first degree. In 1899 his alma mater conferred upon him the degree of Master of Arts, in 1918 the Doctorate of Literature.

Of the Tarkington tradition at Princeton there is no need to write. Everybody has heard of the gay youth from the Mid-West, who seemingly sang his way through the halls of learning and whose "Danny Deever" has become the subject of ballad and limerick. Robert Cortes Holliday, author of the entertaining volume, *Booth Tarkington* (1918), comments on this accomplishment of "Tark" and upon the fact that many of his characters sing. Pietro Tobigli of *Aliens (In the Arena)* sings; David Beasley's darkey sings; Penrod sings; the serenaders in *Seventeen* sing. And, however delectable or horrible the sounds may be to the audience of the vocalist, the result for the reader is, in Mr. Holliday's word's, "an infectious air of youth and good old summer time."

Just after leaving college, Mr. Tarkington was associated (in 1896 and 1897) with a group which published a small magazine, *John-a-Dreams.* As staff artist, he signed his name to the drawings; but as literary contributor he used the *nom de plume* of Cecil Woodford. There is a legend that having written a playlet, *The Kisses of Marjorie,* he set about illustrating it and that as he looked upon his handiwork he received inspiration for *Monsieur Beaucaire.*

One has only to glance at the drawings in Asa Don Dickinson's booklet, *Booth Tarkington* (Doubleday, Page and Co.), to agree with Mr. Holliday: "Of course, it is very 'nice' that Mr. Tarkington liked to 'draw,' and (though it is difficult to say why) everybody likes him the better for it; but the upshot of the matter is, it is perfectly splendid that he concluded that he couldn't."

Beyond his connection with *John-a-Dreams,* Booth Tarkington seemed to do very little for half a dozen years after leaving Princeton. He idled, enjoyed the life of his home town, a gallant among the ladies, a guest at such grand-scale gatherings as he has recorded in *The Magnificent Ambersons.* And as certainly as Penrod and William Sylvanus reflect not only the boyhood and adolescence of his nephew but also his own youth, so must Lucius Brutus Allen draw upon his adult experience.

In reality, the author was extracting from those years just the sustenance he needed. He was living, and he was teaching himself to write. No writer can survive without the indissolubly joined matter and manner: only life affords the first, only individual effort the second. "Writing is a trade," Mr. Tarkington said, "and, like any other trade, it must be learned We must serve our apprenticeship; but we must work it out alone. We must learn by failure and by repeated effort how the thing should be done." He kept on writing and re-writing poems, plays and stories. And for eight years he received rejection-slips. For five years his gross returns were $22.50. *Cherry* and *Beaucaire* long remained unsold. It was after he published his first novel, *The Gentleman from Indiana,* that *McClure's* accepted *Beaucaire* (published in book form in 1900); and after seventeen rejections that *Cherry* appeared in 1903.

These early works, with the addition of *The Two Van Revels* (1902), embody the leading characteristics of the author's genius: realism merging into romanticism, exemplified in the story of The Great Harkless; realism and satire illuminated by imagination, revealed in the story of Sudgeberry of Nassau Hall in the days before the American Revolution; romance triumphant in the story of the dashing Frenchman and Lady Mary Carlyle of the days when powder and patches and courtliness prevailed; romance exaggerated in the love story of the Mexican War period. Humor and wit vitalize all the works. *The Gentleman from Indiana* has been praised as the wittiest of American novels.

Mr. Tarkington is primarily a realist, a humorist, and a satirist of the scalpel order. But his orientation was somewhat obscured in the zenith of the romantic revival, and he followed the fashion set by Stevenson, a fashion exploited by Stanley Weyman, Winston Churchill, Mary Johnston, and Paul Leicester Ford. His place in the chronology of literature accounts for the indubitably hybrid nature of his efflorescence.

In 1902-1903 Mr. Tarkington was a member of the Indiana House of Representatives. It is interesting to surmise, from reading *In the Arena* (1905), a collection of "real" short stories—the only collection, we believe, left intact as stories—that if he had "gone in big" for politics, he might have produced The Great

American Political Novel. But when we consider, further, that he might have foresworn writing altogether, we are thankful that his political career is regarded as a sort of mild joke. It is said that he was never able to speak. The probable reason is, though we have not heard it alleged, that he scorned the palpable sham and fustian back of most oratory, without which it was probably difficult to gain attention. One has only to read *The Need of Money, Hector,* and *Mrs. Protheroe,* to be convicted of the truth that those three R's, poor old Uncle Billy Rollinson, the Hon. Hector J. Ransom, and fatuous Alonzo Rawson, represent the three types of orators beyond which there are few others. Can one imagine Booth Tarkington, with his perfectly good brain and an abnormally developed sense of humor, making a spectacle similar to one of these—even the Hamlet-like Hector J.?

In the Arena reflects remarkably the author's comprehension of political tactics and situations and their availability for story material. For diversity of subject-matter subordinated to the ruling topic, for realism made palatable by the flavor of humor, and for restraint the collection ranks first among political stories. Restraint is practiced almost too obviously; it is a virtue displayed even in the dialogue, as in Alonzo's conversation with Mrs. Protheroe:

"Do you remember that it was said that Napoleon

once attributed the secret of his power over other men
to one quality?" the lady asked.

"I am an admirer of Napoleon," returned the Sena-
tor from Stackpole. "I admire all great men."

"He said that he held men by his reserve."

"It can be done," observed Alonzo, and stopped,
feeling that it was more reserved to add nothing to
the sentence.

Boss Gorgett illuminates the devious way of the
political boss. Farwell Knowles threatens the penitentiary for the henchmen of Lafe Gorgett who have
planned to stuff a ballot-box. Gorgett retaliates with
a threat to expose the private life of Knowles.
Knowles is innocent of wrong intention, but he has
been indiscreet. In the end, the reader is ready to
sanction the dictum of the Boss: "The only way to
play politics, whatever you're *for,* is to learn the game
first."

Mrs. Protheroe, companion-piece to *Boss Gorgett,*
throws light of equal brilliance on the why and where-
fore of the lady lobbyist. But our preference among
the six stories is *Hector.* The characterization is better
than life; for the subordinate qualities of each individual are omitted or subordinated to his dominant
trait. And the plot, growing logically out of character,
is sufficient to support the warp and woof of the
story fabric.

The Conquest of Canaan, a novel, was published in

1905, the same year of *The Beautiful Lady,* a novel-ette. The latter reflects the French influence, as it is reflected in *Beaucaire,* but with less of action and more of feeling, through the Italian gentleman, Ansolini, who became a bill-board that he might educate his nieces, through the Prince Caravacioli and through its setting. The young American, Lambert R. Poor, Jr., and the Beautiful Lady supply contrast. As a delight-ful trifle, Mr. Tarkington's biographer thinks the work should be preserved in the World's Literature of Great Trifles.

Mr. Tarkington numbers among his favorite French authors (according to Mr. Dickinson) Dumas, Balzac, Daudet and Cherbuliez. He likes Rome, Naples, the Island of Capri, and Paris. *His Own People* (1907) recounts the adventures of a young American abroad and his experience with a false Countess, but his ability to handle locale is superior to the story which is other-wise negligible. *The Guest of Quesnay* (1908) is a sort of metaphysical side-step or excursion. After *Beasley's Christmas Party,* however, the author carved another tremendous trifle in *Beauty and the Jacobin* (1911). This work was a turning-point in the sequence of the Tarkington stories and dramas. In *The Flirt* (1913) he revealed the triumph of the satirist; he was yet to develop the power and art of the vivisectionist. This art which he approached in the boy Hedrick Madison, brother of the coquette, he conquered and carried off in the heroes of *Penrod* (1914), *Penrod and*

Sam (1915) and *Seventeen* (1916). Meantime, in *The Turmoil* (1915) he became the sociologist.

In refusing to be pigeon-holed and in maintaining that the only thing which matters is *how* a book is written, Mr. Tarkington is very properly indifferent to type and to whether he has produced a short story, a long one, or a novel. Perhaps Benedetto Croce is right in his views on literary types. Surely, it can matter little whether one reads *Penrod* as a volume or as a series of magazine stories. But to evaluate them as separate narratives, it is necessary to read them in *The Cosmopolitan* and *The Metropolitan* before they are lost in the continuity and chapter divisions of the books.

To read the volume, *Penrod,* is to behold an unfolding panorama of boyhood, to know in particular the history of one boy, ten or eleven years of age, a boy with a friend Sam and a dog Duke. It is to recall others of his kind, Aldrich's *Tom Bailey*, Matthews' *Tom Paulding;* his near kinsmen, *Tom Sawyer* and *Huck Finn,* and his not too remote ancestor, Peck's *Bad Boy*. It is to live life with Penrod and Sam. But to read each story as it appeared was to receive a definite impression of a single conflict worked out to a satisfactory if sometimes rueful issue. There is the famous attempt of Penrod to escape the ignominy of appearing in trunks cut down from his father's red flannels by covering them with the janitorial overalls, and so regaling the audience assembled for the pageant.

The Children of the Table Round. There is his violent opposition to the epithet, "Little Gentleman," with the consequences of his fight against its application to himself by the Rev. Mr. Kinosling, *et al.* Incidentally, the Kinosling gentleman receives his come-uppance in one of the most delicious bits of satire the author has achieved. There is the famous fight between the tough guy, Rupe Collins, and the colored troops commanded by Penrod, a battle wherein Herman urges enthusiastically the cutting out of Mr. Collin's "gizzud," a battle from which Rupe makes an exit that forbids further relations with Penrod and Sam and Herman and Verman.

To read *Seventeen* is to read an epic of adolescence. William Sylvanus Baxter is one of the most humorous figures of fiction; he is funny because having passed through similar trials and tribulations, we who are older look down upon him from a superior height; he is funny because of the incongruity between the deadly seriousness of life as he finds it and the triviality of his affairs as the reader sees them; he is funny because of the author's exuberant devices for emphasizing this incongruity. To think of him after reading the book, is to think of him as brother to the irrepressible Jane, son to a considerate mother and matter-of-fact father; a boy who liked his own age and kind and found insupportable the intrusions from elders or children or darkies of the Genesis order or dogs of the Clematis breed; a young man who suffered the tortures of young love and the fervors of verse writing. But to read the stories was to follow a series of individual conflicts: between William and his Mother regarding the disposition of his father's dress suit; between himself and the Big Fat Lummox for the favor of a lady; between him and Fate, a fate which prevented his presence when he should have been at home to his friends, a fate which barred his dancing "on and on" with the Baby Talk Lady of his affections at the farewell party. We are glad to have the books; but we shall be happier to recall the tales which unfolded, month by month, in the magazines so fortunate as to publish them.

In the Arena, Penrod, Penrod and Sam, and *Seventeen* and the tales that appeared in *Everybody's* about Lucius Brutus Allen are the cream of Mr. Tarkington's short stories. And of these, *Seventeen* and *Penrod* are the heavy cream. His novelettes, particularly *Cherry, The Beautiful Lady* and *Monsieur Beaucaire,* have gained for him—probably because they preceded these later works—greater popularity. *Monsieur Beaucaire* is one of a very few American productions to have been sung in Grand Opera. But from the type point of view and from the literary point of view, the short stories included under the titles named, disguised as they are, are his high-water accomplishments. Those of us who do care about form cannot but regret that the gems have lost their individuality, cut up and strung, bead-like, throughout the volume. They will be forgotten, in short, as stories, because of the amorphous state to which chapter division has reduced them. Not that it matters; but the destruction of form has significance with respect to views held by their builder, and rescue of the old structure is probably hopeless.

As story-maker, Mr. Tarkington succeeds through his struggle element. His plots are insignificant. This truth again does not mean criticism of his works from a literary point of view; character is the ultimate remainder, and that is as he would have it. If Mr. Holliday's definition of a short story be accepted, then Booth Tarkington is a king of story-makers: "A good story, after all, is a fabrication in which real people seem to do very real things." "Fabrication" challenges a twinkle; for a fabrication is a structure; but, of course, it may mean literary invention.

Mr. Tarkington is interested in people, and as he said in a symposium in *The New York Sun* (April 17, 1915), which arraigned a number of replies against Melville Davisson Post's *The Blight*, "It seems strange that he does not perceive the profounder interest of the mystery and surprise of character."

Mr. Tarkington is a hard worker. By dint of eating little and carrying on for eighteen hours or so at a stretch, he frequently accomplishes ten thousand words a day. He loves the open and enjoys his summer home at Kennebunkport, Maine. He writes best, he has said—whether seriously or humorously—"in a dirty, dark, dull place."

Mr. Tarkington's Novelettes and Short Stories:

Monsieur Beaucaire, 1900.
Cherry, 1903.
In the Arena, 1905.
The Beautiful Lady, 1905.
His Own People, 1907.
Beasley's Christmas Party, 1909.
Penrod, 1914.
Penrod and Sam, 1916.
Seventeen, 1916.

CHAPTER XX

IN 1899 appeared a slender volume of two hundred and twenty-nine pages, containing eight short stories under the inclusive title, *The Greater Inclination.* In the following five years the author established her high place in contemporary fiction, in ten years her definite leadership, and in another decade her priority among women writers in America. In her novels her talent has found exercise, through freer expression, to her greater popularity; in her short stories, through a more restricted medium, to her perfection of art.

Among the causes that elevated Mrs. Wharton to her enviable altitude are her birth into a world smooth-gliding socially; her dower of intelligence and genius; her education in belles lettres; her interest in a diversity of subjects common to a limited range; her love for a cosmopolitan life, in the broadest sense; and her artistic conscience, satisfied with nothing less than perfection.

Edith Newbold Jones was born in New York City

in 1862. Presumably, she grew up after the fashion of young girls, gently bred, who both suffered from and profited by mid-Victorian ideals. That she studied under tutors at home, that she traveled, that she read widely, and that she was married at the age of twenty-three to Edward Wharton, of Boston—so much the public is privileged to know. But when her authorized biography is written, it is to be hoped that in it the incidents of her early life may find a generous place; for if the literary output of a writer is conditioned by the first four years of existence, it would be illuminating and instructive to grow four years old with Miss Edith Jones.

Her removal from the commercial metropolis to the metropolis of culture—as Boston allowably was even through the last quarter of the nineteenth century—meant further entrenchment in books and art. Not that she did not relish humanity; but while through one-half of her brain she lived, with the other she criticized life. And in her accompanying studies or reading she learned a way to use her own appraisements. Her obvious acquaintance with the masters early invoked the charge that hers was a literary point of view, dissociated from actual life. The truth is that her own angle either completed that of her classic authors or merged with it. Her art is dead, says one critic; it is bookish, says another. Her body of expression undoubtedly develops from the writer's treatment of subjects observed through the writer's eyes. There are those of us, however, who place her art the higher because of this verity. And if the life she relentlessly analyzes is fortified by convention and removed from lowlier planes of existence, it is— whether to the credit or discredit of civilization—one of the topmost strata; and it is brought through her art into closer relation with the rest of the world.

This relation had already been effected, in part, through a fellow-New Yorker, the late Henry James. At the time Mrs. Wharton began to publish, in *Scribner's Magazine,* in the late nineties, Mr. James had reached the height of his career. Her admiration of his work, plus a heritage, social status, and interests the counterpart of his, resulted in her following his blazed path, foremost of the trailers, and later in outstripping his pioneer leadership.*

From almost the beginning he was her encouraging critic and friend. In 1902 he thanks Mrs. Wharton's sister-in-law for two of Mrs. Wharton's books. "I take to her very kindly," he wrote from England, where he had established his abode, "as regards her diabolical little cleverness, the quantity of intention and intelligence in her style, and her sharp eye for an interesting kind of subject." On his American tour in 1905 he established acquaintance with her and her husband, who were living at the time in Lenox, and enjoyed the whole country-side by the aid of their

* "Comme Henry James, Mrs. Wharton ne fréquente que l'élite"—Régis Michaud.

high speed automobile; in 1907 he visited them at Paris, later taking a motor tour with them over Western and Southern France. Mrs. Wharton's *A Motor Flight through France* (1908) is a testimony to her love for adventure, in a rapid car, with lingering moments at a favorite cathedral or the home of an admired writer—George Sand, for instance—and illustrates what Mr. James called her "great heroic rushes and revolutions," "her dazzling, her incessant braveries of far excursionism."

Since no discussion of Mrs. Wharton, however brief, ever has omitted the influence of Henry James, it should be pointed out that she was by no means susceptible to over-influence. The resemblance, as has been indicated above, is rooted in life itself; she is more than the first of his "school"; she is the originator of her own. In 1906 Mr. James wrote her, apropos of her taking up life in Paris, "Don't go in too much for the French or the 'Franco-American' subject—the real field of your extension is *here* [England]—it has far more fusability with *our* [American] native and primary material; between which and French elements there is, I hold, a disparity as complete as between a life led in trees, say, and a life led in . . . sea-depths, or in other words, between that of climbers and swimmers." * In the face of this

* *The Letters of Henry James*, Selected and Edited by Percy Lubbock, Charles Scribner's Sons, 1920.

caution, she produced one of her greatest accomplish-ments, *Madame de Treymes.*

After the spring of 1907, Mr. James's letters to Mrs. Wharton dropped the formal introduction. She became "Dear Edith," "Dearest Edith," to whom he was, in the complimentary close, her "faithfully fond old Henry James." For the nine years until his death there existed between them an intimate sympathy and a mutual appreciation which, revealed in *The Letters of Henry James,* render the two volumes invaluable human documents. In 1908 he visited her in Paris; later, in the same year, he wrote Mrs. Henry White, "We have been having here lately the great and glori-ous pendulum in person, Mrs. Wharton, on her return oscillation, spending several weeks in England for almost the first time ever . . ." And between the two visits he had written her, in a dark period of her life, "I don't pretend to understand or to imagine . . . Only sit tight yourself *and go through the movements of life.*"

To return to *The Greater Inclination.* The stories of the volume which best represent the scope of the work, the author's power, her keen understanding of mental processes, and her perfection of finish are *The Muse's Tragedy, A Journey, The Pelican,* and *Souls Belated.*

In *The Muse's Tragedy* the following plot unfolds: Danyers meets and falls in love with Mary Anerton. This lady has been the friend, the inspirer, of the poet

Rendle, now dead, and Mrs. Anerton enjoys a pseudo-celebrity as the Sylvia of his poems. Danyers proposes and is rejected. Mary Anerton writes him that Rendle had never really loved her. She had felt, after his death, that perhaps she had been too old, too ugly to stir him, and she had—not entirely with calculation —let Danyers fall in love; for she wished to prove her theory or disprove it. Her punishment lies in the disproof, and in the attendant fact that she sees for the first time "all that she has missed."

This story will serve for a point of departure for a brief discussion of a question, frequently stated as an affirmation that Mrs. Wharton's technic has changed but slightly from 1899 to the present. Formerly of the opinion that the abrupt shift from the point of view of Danyers to the letter of Mrs. Anerton would have been rejected for a more consistent angle of narration had the author written the story later, and finding our own conclusions buttressed by a similar opinion on the part of Frederic Taber Cooper,* we were the more impressed by a comment Mr. James made concerning *The Reef* (1912). "I suffer or worry a little," he wrote Mrs. Wharton, "from the fact that in the Prologue, as it were, we are admitted so much into the consciousness of the man, and that after the introduction of Anna (Anna, so perfectly named) we see him almost only as she sees him—which gives our attention a different sort of work to do." . . . One

* See *Some American Story Tellers.*

may argue, however, that the novel in general allows the shift whereas the short story does not, and that in her later short stories the point of view is usually maintained. The large point at the moment is that the master technician noted the same kind of jar in *The Reef* which readers of *The Muse's Tragedy* had experienced.

The Muse's Tragedy illustrates, too, Mrs. Wharton's development of a situation; she converts a misunderstanding to an understanding; she pursues with punishment in kind the yielding of a sensitive soul to a subtle temptation. It further orientates her best-worked field, that of literature and art, and one of her best-loved settings, Italy.

A Journey has shared honors with *Ethan Frome* (1911) in being accounted "the best short story" America has yet produced. In close circumscription of place —a train from Buffalo to New York, in brevity of time—part of a day only, and in its successful struggle of the heroine to bring the body of her husband into the city before his death is discovered, it fulfills economically the requirements of the short story. But poignancy the author sacrifices to intellectual probing and dissection.

Souls Belated is a study in the infringement of social laws. Mr. Cooper has called attention to Mrs. Wharton's "rather rigid prejudices of social caste," and Mr. John Curtis Underwood to her "patrician exclusiveness." Here, as in other stories, the social background is an eternal verity against which the individual struggle is posed in high relief. Lydia Tillotson and Ralph Gannett are traveling in Italy when they receive news that Tillotson has obtained a decree of divorce. Lydia tries to hold out against marrying Gannett, struggling not only against custom but her feeling for the marriage tie. Her ethical sense that the ceremony of marriage will not undo the evil goes down against the combination. The story introduces a second line of interest and uses it for effecting a slight complication: the two main characters are paralleled by another couple in a situation similar to their own.

So far, the examples chosen have dealt with crucial moments. But in *The Pelican* the author tries her hand at character degeneration. Mrs. Amyot, a young and charming widow, who must support her baby, takes the lecture platform. From Greek art she passes to evolution and succeeding subjects, discussing each from a storehouse of information no greater than the encyclopedia affords, supplemented by chance aid from more or less academic friends. Successful, so far as her superficial purpose is concerned, she keeps up the pretense that she is maintaining her boy long after he has finished college, is married and himself a parent. This story which has excited both favorable and unfavorable critical reaction should have been written as a novel or a novelette. The Folletts * suggest that Mrs. Wharton's treatment of the short story meant the development of a new kind of novel; that her practice broke down barriers between the types. There is much in this point of view; but, after all is said, there are norms from which departure occurs in greater or lesser degree. In *The Pelican* Mrs. Wharton used material for a successful novel in a comparatively unsuccessful short story. This statement is not to hedge the opinion that it is one of four numbers in the volume which represent the power of the author and her feeling for perfection. Even the dénouement, which dramatically presents the son of Mrs. Amyot turning upon her in ungentlemanly manner, and which has been criticized as a flaw, is not markedly below her level.

The Touchstone (1900) may be discussed as an instance of the "cross-type" Mrs. Wharton early achieved, partaking as it does of both the short story and the novelette characteristics. Glennard, an impecunious New York lawyer, reads an advertisement in the London *Spectator* to the effect that Professor Joslyn, who is writing the life of Margaret Aubyn, wants letters from the famous woman, now three years dead. Glennard has hundreds of letters from Margaret Aubyn, for she had loved him. Her intellect had drawn him, whereas her physical self had

---

* *Some Modern Novelists,* by Helen Thomas Follet and Wilson Follett, Henry Holt and Co., 1918.

repelled him: "He saw her again as she had looked at their first meeting, the poor woman of genius with her long pale face and short-sighted eyes . . . so incapable, even then, of any hold upon the pulses." Now, Glennard is poor and he is in love with Alexa Trent. The basis for the moral struggle—and the critic who sees no struggle in this author's stories is myopic—lies in the incident of Glennard's hushing his inner voice while he sells the letters for something like ten thousand dollars. The double sequence is, of course, his marriage to Alexa and the publication of Margaret's letters in a volume which becomes the literary event of the season. The rest of the story has to do with remorse and punishment. At first, Glennard keeps the transaction from his wife, then he allows her to see a slip from the publishers stating that they are sending him a royalty. Alexa makes no sign. By and by, from his unendurable torture he confesses to the last degree the depth of his degradation. The dénouement shows how purification comes through Alexa. Mrs. Wharton says elsewhere,—"The plain man is a touchstone who draws out all the alloy in the gold." From start to finish the angle is that of Glennard, and in this essential the technic is that of the short story. If he were, throughout, the dominant character, he would make still further for short story unification. But here enter the claims of the novelette: Alexa assumes first place, and although her promotion is so gradual as to prevent jar in the switch-

ing of relative importance, yet a more expanded canvas
would have developed her proportionately to her value
revealed in the dénouement. The title, too, emphasizes
her rôle. In England the work was published, perhaps more appropriately, as *A Gift from the Grave*,
which brings into greater relief a larger thesis. It
subdues Alexa—as the touchstone—preserves the
relative position of Glennard, and establishes the significance of Margaret Aubyn.

The Touchstone felicitously illustrates Michaud's
view, that by a curious inversion in Mrs. Wharton's
books, sensibility lies with the men and logic with
the women. Glennard suffers; Alexa understands and
reasons.

Crucial Instances (1901) continues the use of Italy
as a setting in *The Duchess at Prayer*. In *The Confessional*, *The Recovery* and *The Moving Finger* the
action shifts shuttle-wise between America and Italy
or France. As the French critic has remarked of Mrs.
Wharton, "L'Amerique ne lui suffit pas. Elle s'en
vient en Italie at en France chercher des impressions
et des sujets." Art continues to provide interest in
The Recovery, *The Rembrandt* and *The Moving Finger*. A new note is struck in the fantasy of the last-
named: the portrait of Grancy's wife is changed by
the portrait painter, from time to time, to grow old
with her husband, and at last gives a revelation to the
artist, himself: "I swear it was her face that told me
he was dying, and that she wanted him to know it!"

It may be chance that a sentence in this story reflects Mrs. Wharton's concept of art and its function as measured by her own attainments: " 'Pygmalion,' he began slowly, 'turned his statue into a real woman; I turned my woman into a picture.' " For the sum of criticism, laudatory of aim or otherwise, is that she does just this thing. . . . It is surely not by chance, however, that *"Copy": A Dialogue* throws a gently shaded saturnine light on the processes of the writer, male or female. Brief as it is, it deserves study as a companion piece to Barrie's *Sentimental Tommy.* Ventnor's charging Mrs. Dale with being a "marvelous dialectician" might have been taken from current comment on Mrs. Wharton's methods. Perhaps with Ventnor she recalls the time when "we didn't prepare our impromptu effects beforehand and copyright our remarks about the weather," and with Mrs. Dale when "she did not keep her epigrams in cold storage and her adjectives under lock and key." From the beginning she has been a creator of phrases, a fabricant of word combinations. If a writer deliberately chooses to be so clever in the particular thought or picture or mere manner as to draw attention from the larger unit—whether it be sonnet or short story—she must suffer the corresponding diminution of interest in her integral effect. Apparently the practice does not pay; and yet the writer who does not painstakingly labor with words and phrases rarely achieves the **wizardry of** style.

The Duchess at Prayer is an interesting variant of an old plot used by Poe and, earlier, by Balzac. Burying a person alive they employed to tragic, if not melodramatic, effect; Mrs. Wharton subdues tragedy to psychology. The same process is found working in *The Confessional,* wherein the old story of a substitute for a Father Confessor and the ensuing confession is poignantly varied. The scene in which Roberto Siviano defends his wife's honor is one of the most dramatic in the author's repertoire, built on careful analysis of motive and conflicting ideals.

In *The Descent of Man* (1904) Mrs. Wharton adds to her catalogue of interests that in biology. The title story and *The Debt,* the latter in her *Tales of Men and Ghosts,* reflect her attitude toward the subjects of evolution, scientific research and progress. If the burden of this task sounds heavy for fiction, her easy victory in bearing it off should meet louder applause. The irony of *The Descent* and the seriousness of *The Debt* combine to represent the academic and the social point of view of a writer just learning the use of her deadliest weapon—humor. For in her hands its mordant edge not even the reader may escape. No gentle thud on the shoulder, knighting the reader to a superior position whence he looks down upon and laughs at the objects of her comedy, immeasurably below him; but a flashing cut and thrust, from which he flinches, sooner or later sure he will meet the blade: this is her play of humor.

The other eight stories in *The Descent* handle society more satirically. *The Other Two* (presenting Waythorn and his wife, who had been twice married, at tea with her former husbands) is a social comedy, measured by the problem play of the earlier *Souls Belated*. Jane, of *The Mission,* uniquely brings about understanding between the husband and wife who have adopted her; *The Reckoning, The Quicksand,* and *The Dilettante,* though more sympathetic and evincing real interest in the situations disclosed, are not without their barbs; *Expiation,* in its union of the Church, the social world and the world of letters, achieves a triple thrust. Notwithstanding the adaptation of the volume title, no other could so well describe the nature of the several numbers composing it.

Her manifest interest in marriage and divorce joined to her first hand knowledge of French custom rises triumphant in *Madame de Treymes* (1907). For breadth of sympathy, for comprehension of opposing French and American standards, for acute play of intellect expressed through the persons of her drama, she has nowhere surpassed herself in this pendant to Henry James's *Madame de Mauves.* Pendant it is usually termed, but unfairly, for it is superior to the first work.

It should not be forgotten that before the publication of *Madame de Treymes* Mrs. Wharton had published two noteworthy novels: *The Valley of Decision* (1902), whose characters lived in an Italy of the past, and *The House of Mirth* (1905), whose Lily Bart has not been outranked by any contemporary New York lady of fiction. *Sanctuary* (1903) should be added to these, rather than to the list of the author's long short stories. Works more or less factual and descriptive are *Italian Villas and Their Gardens* (1904), and *Italian Backgrounds* (1905). After *Madame de Treymes* came *The Fruit of the Tree* (1907), the least satisfactory of her novels.

An unhappy period of Mrs. Wharton's life may be responsible in part for her descent in *The Hermit and the Wild Woman* (1908). In any event, the collection adds nothing to her fame if it does not, even, subtract therefrom. The titular story, to be sure, creates a slight surmise that the author has developed an interest in medieval Christianity; but the rank and file follow without distinction the beaten path.

Since the *Motor Flight,* mentioned above, Mrs. Wharton has spent most of her time abroad. She added Germany to her countries of invasion, visiting Munich in 1909, and some time later having translated Sudermann's *Es Lebe das Leben,* published it as *The Joy of Life.* In 1909 her volume of verse appeared: *Artemis to Actæon.* A revival of the supernatural theme, first struck in *The Moving Finger* marks the publication of her *Tales of Men and Ghosts* (1910). Unless "ghosts" be interpreted freely, the stories deal separately with the two terms of the title. *The Bolted Door,* for instance, is a remarkable story

of a criminal, who having gone unsuspected for a number of years meets only incredulity upon his con-
fessing.   The door opening to restitution, which he
agonizingly desires to make, is "bolted." It is characteristic of Mrs. Wharton's genius that she reverses
the theme Maupassant worked out in *A Piece of String*
(*La Ficelle*), and which Tchekov varied in *The Death
of an Official*. It is so much more difficult to follow
seriously the criminal who vainly wishes to be found
guilty than the innocent man who tries to prove himself guiltless. All readers of this book will recall the
story in which a pair of detached eyes haunt the character, Frenham. As he finishes his rehearsed tale, his
hearers see his reflection in the mirror and recognize
that he had been haunted by an image of that which
would come to express his character development. The
powerful moral lesson in no manner weakens the dramatic appeal of *The Eyes*. *Afterward* resembles, as
a type of the supernatural story, Henry James's *The
Turn of the Screw,* which preceded it by a dozen years
or so. Of other stories in the volume, *The Daunt
Diana* is the most beautiful; not only so: it is the most
beautiful of all the author's art stories, and this is
equivalent to saying that nowhere does she surpass it
in its reaction, upon the reader, of pure spiritual exaltation. *The Letters* represents her in the social
world, again, making the most of a situation in which
a wife comes across letters she had written her husband before they were married. The discovery that

he had not troubled to break the seals is the poignantly small thing that becomes the crucial moment.
Mrs. Wharton is aware of the value intimate holo-
graphs have as stage properties: *The Touchstone* and
"Copy" are other instances to this conclusion.

Ethan Frome (1911) has indisputable claim to rank
as the greatest short story in America. Its close unity,
its three main characters, its Greek exaltation of Fate
as supreme ruler of man and his affairs, its circumscription of place, and more, lend to it the salient marks
of the brief fictive form, though its length places it
in the novelette class. In discussing the flaws of Mrs.
Wharton's art, opinions differ widely over her use
of detail. This story offers the best example for a
brief note upon this point. It will be recalled that
Mattie Silver and Ethan Frome, in their pitiful at-
tempts to make merry while Zeena is away, break a
pickle dish. Mr. Percy Lubbock says that such an
instance is the natural and sufficient channel of great
emotion. "The most distinguishing gift of the true
novelist is his power of so completely identifying himself with the character through whose eyes he is seeing
that his field of vision, both in extent and particular-
ity, is exactly no more and no less than that of the
man or woman he has imagined." * If this power of
Mrs. Wharton is best shown in *Ethan Frome,* as he
thinks, the breaking of the dish must be acknowledged

* *Quarterly Review,* January, 1915.

as one of her greatest accomplishments in drama. But Mr. Underwood thinks that the plot focuses "rather farcically" around this breakage. Critics of the latter opinion forget the dropping of the handkerchief in Othello, which has served for several hundreds of years, and among characters to whom the act might have been attended with less significance.

From 1910 to 1913, Mrs. Wharton was most of the time in Paris, with a week now and then in London, which she again visited in 1914. *The Times Literary Supplement* published her article entitled *The Criticism of Fiction* this year, a work about which Henry James expressed his appreciation. Earlier in this *annus mirabilis* she had toured through Algeria and Tunisia, as later she was throwing herself heart and soul into the struggle of France. Meantime, *The Reef* appeared in 1912, and *The Custom of the Country* in 1914. *The Book of the Homeless* (1915) and *Fighting France* (1915) preceded the latest collection of brief tales from Mrs. Wharton's pen: *Xingu and Other Stories* (1916). •

The titular story is the complement, in a certain sense, of *The Pelican,* which it will be remembered follows the fortunes of the shallow and showy lecturer, Mrs. Amyot. Osric Dane of the later satire is by no means inadequate in her rôle of honored guest, nor is Mrs. Roby, the supposedly ignorant and frivolous member. If Mrs. Wharton likes to betray her sex, as has been urged, at least she betrays it to reveal the shams and weaknesses attendant upon ineptness in literature in art, ineptness joined to pretense. In this instance, she lets fly her barbed shaft against the ladies who "pursue Culture in bands, as though it were dangerous to meet alone." In it one may discern a rise of irony and critical alertness, which may be or may not be the result of the author's seeing her countrywomen from the superior age and culture of an older world—a world with which she had at last identified her sympathy and point of view through long residence—and which may be indicative of the author's growing disposition to satirize. Better than her atmosphere of bright irony is that of twilight seriousness in which her ghosts have their being. *The Triumph of Night,* upon its first appearance in *Scribner's,* August, 1914, was acclaimed as matchless. For us, it is one of three best ghost stories ever written: the others are *The Turn of the Screw,* by Henry James; and *They,* by Rudyard Kipling. Not unworthy of a place under the same covers is *Kerfol,* the tale of the dog ghosts that return once a year to the house where they met death successively and where they, in turn, had enacted revenge upon their slayer.

The Marne (1918), a long short story of some eighteen or twenty thousand words, closes the list of Mrs. Wharton's stories in book form, and of subsequent magazine publications nothing worthy of record has appeared. Her novel, *The Age of Innocence,* begun in the *Pictorial Review* in midsummer 1920, and published in book-form in the autumn, delineates New York society of forty years ago.

Of Mrs. Wharton's superb work during the war there is space for only this comment: it would seem to be a special dispensation of providence that one of our best should have trained for the great conflict—that, in short, it was Edith Wharton who was there to evaluate the "beauty and the terror of it all."

This summary of Mrs. Wharton's work has been futile if it has not indicated, at least, that her initial accomplishment in the realm of art, culture and intellect, drew together, through her cosmopolitan sympathy, the new world and the old; that her later work as woman, no less than writer, has strengthened the ties between America and France. She is, always, as Michaud puts it, the writer of psychological novels from Fifth Avenue to the Argonne trenches. Her books, Percy Lubbock has declared, are "from the earliest to the latest, more than a collection of penetrating and finely finished stories; they are linked episodes in one continuous adventure, the adventure of her rare and distinguished critical intelligence." And if we venture to disagree with him when he asserts that one leading quality of her talent is swiftness, we shall the more eagerly join with him in extolling the other, which is acuteness.

Mrs. Wharton's collections and volumes of stoties:

The Greater Inclination, 1899.
The Touchstone, 1900.
Crucial Instances, 1901.
The Descent of Man, 1904.
Madame de Treymes, 1907.
The Hermit and the Wild Woman, 1908.
Tales of Men and Ghosts, 1910.
Ethan Frome, 1911.
Xingu and Other Stories, 1916.
The Marne, 1918.

CHAPTER XXI

MAXWELL STRUTHERS BURT*

*S*CRIBNER'S MAGAZINE contained in the issue
for July, 1915, a short story entitled *The Water-
Hole*. It was signed by a name hitherto unknown
in fiction—Maxwell Struthers Burt. The narrative at
once implicitly promised to reward the reader for his
outlay of time and energy, promised by a beginning
that definitely conveyed the shaping up of material and
subtly suggested forces drawing together for action.

As the story progressed it pictured the shimmering
Arizona desert under a steel-blue sky, in a heat so intense "the horn of the saddle burned your hand." It
recounted a search for hidden treasure, abandoned
when, through two logical mishaps, the water supply
failed. It described realistically the tortures of thirst,
assuaged the torture, and pointed the climax at the
water-hole. No other than a man who knows adventure at first hand in the great West could have written
the tale; nor other than one whose past had been spent
among books and ideas.

The hero of *The Water-Hole* is represented as tell-

* This chapter on Mr. Burt was first published in *The Bookman.*

358

ing his story to three classmates. At the end is the twist of surprise which links the narrator with the love element, delicately inwoven. Only by the surprise does the author disclose his apprenticeship, and that may have been, admissibly, a concession to the fashion in fiction. By every hallmark the story is the sure product of the craftsman.

The Water-Hole was the forerunner of other stories, nearly all of which combine the mountains and plains of the West with the club life of the East, stories of restaurants where men get together over glasses of— leave it at that, over glasses—and the most exotic food; or where ladies and gentlemen gather in a dining room around impeccable linen, plate, and crystal. As his West identifies Mr. Burt with adventure, so the East identifies him with gentlefolk. The first quality in his fiction is truth to life as he knows it, life envisioned through the temperamental lens of the artist.

Of a Philadelphia family, Mr. Burt was born in Baltimore, October 18, 1882. "I am an *echt*-Philadelphian," he says of himself, "bred in the bone for many generations; but since the age of eighteen, when I went to college, I have been what I think is called 'an escaped Philadelphian.' My family still live there, but I don't."

He was educated in private schools in Philadelphia, "very badly," he thinks, "as most men of my generation were." Getting through school somewhat earlier than is usual, he worked for two years as reporter on

the Philadelphia *Times,* under the man who had been
private secretary to Lincoln, Colonel A. K. McClure.

At the tender age of sixteen the boy was probably
the youngest Philadelphia reporter in newspaper days
of hard drinking and fakes. "My last week I had one
murder, two suicides, and three fires, if I remember
correctly," he says. "I don't think that was very good
for a boy of seventeen."

When he was old enough he went to Princeton,
where in 1904 he took his bachelor's degree; later to
Munich for a year, then to Merton College, Oxford.
Throughout his prose and poetry the academic shadows
of Princeton and Oxford towers lie lightly over the
brave exploits of his heroes, subduing their adventures
to a mellowness never approached by unmodified high
lights of risk and hazard. To Princeton, Mr. Burt
avows himself indebted even for his love of nature or
appreciation of nature in certain phases. In *Gifts** he
lists a number of things he has learned from his alma
mater: warm winds bringing elm scent; love of the
sun, open fields and windy weather, and love of bells
across the fields at dusk.

He intended to take a degree at Oxford, but when a
vacancy occurred at Princeton they called him back to
teach and there he remained for three years. He had
already won distinction in student days, "being very
much mixed up in the Triangle Club, for which I wrote
two librettos."

* *In the High Hills.* Houghton Mifflin Co. 1914.

Meantime, while teaching, he spent his summers in the West, gradually acquiring interests in various ranches. Ultimately, he settled in Jackson Hole, Wyoming, where he owns a partnership in Ranch Bar B. C. As the nomenclature indicates, this is a cattle ranch. Another, the partners devote to "dude ranching." For the uninitiated Mr. Burt patiently explains that a "dude" is a non-resident of a country; the word carries with it none of the contemptuous connotation of "tenderfoot." A "dude ranch" is a sort of glorified summer hotel, where people are given horses, taught the ways of the West, and taken on pack trips.

Mr. Burt's summer home, his much wandering over the West, and his wide interests, account for his pictures and his knowledge: of the blazing heat of Arizona, its rattlesnakes and scorpions; of the Big Cloud river region, its groves of aspen trees delicate in ghostly silver; of the Pelly lakes and the river Frances, its black rocks upjutting through the white spray of its falls; of the Southern Wyoming desert, its "yellow and red buttes and stunted cactus; all of it under a sky of piercing blueness." Out there men drive cattle in blizzards over gray expanses of sage brush; or in time of drought see them die stark mad while "dust devils dance along the ridge." Out there, too, men know peace under slumberous fir tops; or under myriad hosts of tall pines, white under the magic of the moon.

The Jackson Hole country is the most beautiful in the United States, he thinks. And in this view he is supported by the testimony of the late Colonel Roosevelt and of Owen Wister.

Mr. Burt's love of contrast, of widely dissimilar states and kingdoms, urges him to know life from opposing outlooks and to mirror their diversity in his art. When tired of his ranch, when desirous of gayety, he turns like the narrator of *The Glory of the Wild Green Earth** to the East. "I wanted to come back to the unexpected quiet and aloofness of a club," says he, "to low-voiced, well-scrubbed servants; to a bed of cool sheets, to a morning of a valet and a porcelain tub and new and beautiful clothes." If he becomes nostalgic for the West, he turns again to

> . . . the great
> Scarred beauty of a lonely land, and seeks
> Ever to keep renewed an hundred dreams,
> Of plains that brood by wide unwearying streams,
> Of how archangels hold red sunset peaks,
> Winged with a flaming splendor desolate.

This love of the West is inherited, as his love for the conventions is bred in the bone. His great-grandfather, he suspects, must have been some sort of Sinn Feiner, for, having to leave Ireland between sun down and sun up, he turned fur trader in the West. Then there was an uncle who, when he left Princeton, became a cattle man in Arizona and California. It was from this uncle that Struthers Burt learned when he was eight years of age how to throw a rope, an art he never forgot.

*John O'May. Charles Scribner's Sons. 1918.

Between the indoor comforts of civilization and the outdoor thrills of the rancher's life, Mr. Burt experiences a *joie de vivre* that manifests itself minutely and concretely in his poems and his prose.   Though he loves the mountain peaks—"big ones, with snow"—and pine forests better than anything else in the world, he waits not upon them but finds contentment in a lake between the hills, surrounded by sedges, murmurous with bees.   He savors the immediate sweetness of damp hay, or a garden wet with showers, with as keen relish as he whiffs the air blown cold from the snow-capped Tetons.*

In his love for nature he is a descendant of Wordsworth, as in his modernity he is a kinsman of Rupert Brooke and Alfred Noyes.   He must have delighted in the rhythm of *Grantchester* before composing his sprightly *Spring in Princeton,* which celebrates the Jersey meadows—golden with daffodil, resonant with bird song—and the little town of towers "silvery gray and high":

> There as the sun folds down its wings,
> On every lawn a robin sings,
> And kindly people take their tea,
> Under an elm or maple tree.

It is this same poem which captures a picturesque moment of New York:

* See, passim, *Songs and Portraits.*   Charles Scribner's Sons. 1920.

> I think there's nothing like at dark
> To see the lamps in Central Park
> Turn yellow in the purple gloom
> To huge gold lilies dripping bloom;
> And watch the great walls through the night
> Ripple to towers of fabulous light.

Other verses ring echoes of Mr. Noyes, as these from *The Flute-Player:*

> And barrel organs everywhere
> Make songs for little children's feet,
> And, O, the chestnut trees are sweet!

With Mr. Noyes he has more than a passing acquaintance, as one may infer from the fact that he and the English poet are coeditors of *A Book of Princeton Verse* (1916).

Although it is true that the greater number of his poems proclaim Mr. Burt the celebrant of external nature, even as his stories declare him, yet a few of subjective mood reveal him the nature mystic, interested in the soul of nature, as his stories show him concerned in essential human character, half concealed under the outer man. After the death of a loved sister, Jean Brooke Burt, an author of promise who died July 4, 1918, he published a series of sonnets entitled *Resurgam.* In the final one, the fifth, he has an equivalent of Shelley's, *He is made one with Nature,* in the line, "All this, I know, is part of your new dream." Yet he is not successful in achieving the faith of the nature mystic, as Wordsworth was successful. Rain, which he loves to consider objectively, becomes a cold and dreary thing in his quatrain, *Question*.

Of fantasy he has a gift like that of the earlier American, Joseph Rodman Drake—a gift which enables him to write, in *Märchen*, of

> A little man with cap of red,
> And horn-brown lamp of glow-worm light.

This dower of fantasy, again, rises to imaginative heights in his story, *Wings of the Morning*, which suggests the return of a ghostly aviator. More artificially and less happily it appears in *Fishing*, in an Oscar Wilde strain:

> Beside the kitchen stove the cat
> Blinked twice with eyes of gold,
> And yawned with infinite contempt,
> For sleep is new, and old is fishing;
> on the Nile,
> Once with mysterious, feline guile,
> In moon-lit, temple-shadowed bays,
> Were caught bright fins, in other days.

It is not possible to find in Wilde's *The Sphinx* a stanza of which this is reminiscent, but the resemblance in subject-matter and rhythm is unmistakable. The title of the poem intimates another interest of the author, quite in keeping with his expressed love for fly fishing and camping out.

The folk of Mr. Burt's poems are treated much in the same way as those of his stories. Poem and story express his feeling for nature; they show his opinion of people to be conditioned on intellectual appraisal. Mr. Latimer, of the poems, has his counterpart in Sir John Masters, of *A Cup of Tea* (in *John O'May*); each is able to buy his mood or his heart's desire—and yet not quite successfully. Uncle Jim, of the poems, he who came to a marvelous harmony with the hills, has for his prose parallels the seekers and wanderers in *Closed Doors, Le Panache* and *A Cup of Tea.*

In poems to his family there is an affectionate linking of the human being and nature. One need hardly read Mr. Burt's own words about his wife, "Fortunately she loves the West as much as I do," to be aware of this truth after reading *K. N. B.* (in *Songs and Portraits*), and various other lines in which reference to her is evident. Then, of course, Mrs. Burt's *The Branding Iron* and *Hidden Creek* speak for her love of the open. *Primavera: To My Daughter upon Reaching Four* ends on a picture of himself and the child walking afield to trace out the piping of Pan.

Maxwell Struthers Burt met Katharine Newlin at Oxford, in 1912, while he was on a vacation from his ranch. They were married in 1913. "Our families had known each other always," Mr. Burt remarks, "but apparently it was necessary for us to go to Oxford to meet. There is a tradition that two writers do badly to get married to each other, but that certainly has not been the case with us. My wife is my most useful critic and I trust I am hers. We are very savage with each other, but that doesn't seem to hurt our feelings."

Mr. Burt's psychological interest in men and women remains his greatest asset for his narrative. In *Closed Doors* the narrator says of Murray that he should have been on his way to being a great painter; but he wasn't. Hewitt explains.

"The fault lies in the boy's character," he spluttered. "How the devil can you paint a portrait when you can't get inside, and don't want to get inside your subject's mind? When you don't know what getting inside a mind is? Sense of beauty? Oh, yes, he's got a marvelous sense of beauty; but you can't even paint a great landscape unless you have a perception of humanity. In the end, as in everything else, you've got to know the taste of blood and smell of sweat."

It is the recognition of this truth joined to his love of the outer world which gives depth and beauty to the fiction of Mr. Burt.

His stories are, as he occasionally implies, biographies. A unique character gives him material for a series of chronological incidents all bearing on the man's individuality. So far, with one illustrious exception, his chief characters are men. These incidents rise to a nominal climax, as notably in *Le Panache* and *John O'May*, to the death of the hero, but leave the reader wondering, questioning about him whose life has been partly bared and so irretrievably ended. You would have liked to know these men, you say; yet you are rather sure you never would have understood them. Herein is another of Mr. Burt's greatest gifts; by his power to suggest, by his challenge to the imagination he induces the reader to construct and to collaborate.

For at least a few critics *Le Panache* stands one of the best biographical stories of the decade. Though arguing that Hugh Craig might serve as the hero for a whole novel, one must admit that his portrait is as complete as one need wish or as a longer work could make it. He is a riddle man, one seldom attempted, never solved. The utmost an author can do is to record him, and to emphasize his ideal. This ideal is that of Cyrano de Bergerac, who hoped when he died "to sweep the floor of heaven with the plumes of his hat—his *panache"*; to keep such hope, Craig would wear a plume immaculate.

Mr. Burt's "story," then, is the life of a man or woman illuminated by a series of vivid flashes or by a single steady light.

Poignancy he achieves by denying a character something, the deprivation of which, under similar circumstances, would sadden him. Sir John Masters fell short of being a gentleman, as he also missed the love of the woman he had technically won. Knowing the magnificent villain has failed in a vital way, the reader cannot but pay him the tribute of pity, in spite of the contempt Burnaby justly manifests. John O'May, like Henry James's man of *The Beast in the Jungle,* missed the great thing—though what it was, or might have been, for John is difficult to say.

Perhaps the author relies too greatly upon the principle, "To determine your character's behavior at the crisis, put yourself in his place." Not that the portraits are less objective, but the initial presentation appears to spring from a single significant meeting or concept and to round to completion through the author's studying his own reflection. Sir John would hardly permit the self-betrayal set forth in *A Cup of Tea*.

In 1917 Mr. Burt entered the army as a private in the Aviation Service. The only story he published the year of the armistice, *Wings of the Morning* (*Scribner's*, July, 1918; reprinted in *John O'May*), in its soaring quality and exalted mood achieved after serious study of apparently earth-anchored Ann Graham, might be the narrative symbol of one who had learned superbly to wing the ether after trial runs over shard and clod. The war was not without meaning to the art of this author in other respects, as may best be found by reference to *Shining Armor* (*Harper's*, July, 1919) and *The Blood Red One* (*Scribner's*, November, 1919). The indirection of these tales, pursued through a means half allegorical, wholly idealistic, becomes a fine directness.

His fiction of 1920 reverts to his earlier manner, with a curiously provocative predominance of the "culture" element. *A Dream or Two* (*Harper's*, May,

1920) and *"Bally Old"* *Knott* (*Scribner's,* August, 1920) employ foreign settings and more than elsewhere show him to be of the literary family of Henry James, Edith Wharton, and John Galsworthy. His further kinship with them emerges in mood, deliberation, and easy dignity of sentence rhythm.

Each in His Generation (*Scribner's,* July, 1920) swings back to an eastern city—possibly New York—for its setting; and reveals the antagonism between successive generations, for its struggle or dramatic element. One may read to find the outcome of the conflict between temporal periods and race, or merely to find out whether Uncle Henry left his money to Adrian; but only a jejune reader would be satisfied with the latter, the outward, "story." In its originality, in its tour de force dramatization of a subjective theme, and in its technical finish, it is near the peak of the author's accomplishments. The Committee of Award of the O. Henry Memorial Prize, offered by the Society of Arts and Sciences of New York City, adjudged *Each in His Generation* the best story of the year. It therefore received the first prize of five hundred dollars for the best story by an American published in America in 1920.

Mr. Burt's sympathies and likes occur frequently throughout this recapitulation. Lest he seem, like a certain famous duchess, to have "a heart too soon made glad, too easily impressed," it is well to notice that he hates with exceeding definiteness a few things: "socialism, except as a club held over other forms of government; prohibition; militarism; land and water promoters (this comes from living in the West); automobiles; dirty campers (this includes picnickers who leave newspapers); and most churches ending in 'ist. Not the individuals belonging to them, but the policy of the churches. I think the last is perhaps the most serious question confronting America to-day, and I cannot understand why more people don't see it. Accentuated by the war, we are in for a knock-down fight between the sons of darkness and the sons of light. It's an age-long struggle. At present, the sons of darkness—materialism, hatred of beauty, narrowness, an unwitting socialism of the most irksome kind—are winning, and it seems to me that the biggest job any writer can undertake is to combat them, not by tracts, of course, not even with them very much in his mind, but by his attitude and everything he does. We have the loveliest country in the world, we are trying to make it materially and spiritually the most unlovely."

Volumes of stories by Mr. Burt:

John O'May and Other Stories, 1918.
Chance Encounters, 1921.

CHAPTER XXII

BY a pleasant coincidence the American who has received two prizes from a memorial to O. Henry shares with the older writer the birthplace of Greensboro, North Carolina. On March 17, 1886, four years after Will Porter left his native city, arrived Wilbur Daniel Steele. But whereas O. Henry's parents were at home in the South, and he was throughout his life essentially a Southerner, Mr. Steele's forebears belong to the East and he is himself a citizen of the world. His father, the Rev. Wilbur F., Professor of Biblical Science at the University of Denver, is in turn the son of the late Rev. Daniel, known within and without Massachusetts as a Greek scholar. Wilbur Daniel was born while his father was principal of Bennett Seminary (Greensboro), a position he occupied from 1881 to 1888.

From 1886 to 1907 Mr. Steele profited by the advantages of careful training at home and in the school room. When three years of age, he accompanied his parents to Berlin, at the University of which the Rev. Wilbur pursued his post-graduate studies. Young

Steele was placed in the kindergarten of Fräulein Froebel, niece of the great educator. His memory of this period is justifiably hazy, nor is it surprising that it has to do not with work but wholly with the fact of his aversion to the fat in the luncheon soup. In 1892 his father was called to the University of Denver, where he still remains, and it was, therefore, in the Western city that Wilbur Daniel received his academic education, attending successively grammar and preparatory schools and the university. As he says, himself, since his ancestors had been theologians it was ordained somewhat inconsequentially that he must become an artist. So it was, partly by choice, partly by coöperation with a sense of destiny, that he began his studies at the art school in Denver, making use of the night school and summer sessions.

After proceeding to his A.B. degree from the university in 1907, he went to the Boston Museum of Fine Arts, where he studied in the life class of Philip Hale, son of Edward Everett; in 1908-1909 he continued at Julien's, in Paris; in 1909-1910 he was a member of the Art Students' League of New York City. Although his taking a number of prizes may be regarded as indicative of ability in the field of pictorial art, Mr. Steele gradually turned to the story form of expression. In this preference he was encouraged by his friend, Mary Heaton Vorse. With only his third attempt at narrative, he achieved the printed page: *Success* accepted *On the Ebb Tide*. He believes, how-

ever, that his real start lay in *A Matter of Education*
(*Harper's*, 1911). When in 1912 *A White Horse
Winter* was published in the *Atlantic Monthly*, it was
at once realized, says Edward O'Brien in his introduction to Mr. Steele's first collection of stories,
Land's End, "that a new talent of great promise had
appeared in American short-story literature."

After *A White Horse Winter* followed a series of
five narratives set in the imaginary island of Urkey,
lying off the North Atlantic coast. Since these were
brought out at various times and places they may be
recalled here as *White Hands, Ching, Ching, Chinaman, Wages of Sin, Out of Exile,* and *Crocuses.**
These and his Provincetown stories, stories wherein
the native and the Portuguese divide interest of author
and reader, may be put down tentatively as constituting
the work of Mr. Steele's first period. A descendant
of the *Mayflower* pilgrims, he had turned to the land
of the Puritans for his material, and he had found
there an unexpected character contrast afforded
through the old stock and the new. It is recorded that
Longfellow was stirred by the memories of "Spanish
sailors with bearded lips," aliens in Portland harbor;
it is no less true that Joseph C. Lincoln and Wilbur
Daniel Steele have been moved by the juxtaposition
of the Latin race and the English in Cape Cod.

To the analyst, these early stories reveal the author's

* The last named, a two-part story, is scheduled for early issues
of *Harper's*.

inheritance; his own genius for depicting color, form, mood; and his skill in narrative structure. A strong theological flavor is manifest in the choice of certain of his characters, for example, Minister Malden, of *Ching, Ching;* in biblical references and allusions throughout a number of the stories, as in the title *For They Know not What They Do,** in fragments of church scenes and in echoes of the thunder rolling voice of the Puritan God. But this spirit is tempered and combined with the artist's love for vivid pictures, preferably pictures of the sea in storm. His sympathy with the unrest of nature has further witness in the title of his one novel (*Storm,* 1914). Since, however, our present concern is with his short stories, it need be remarked only that he has not succeeded, as yet, with the longer story, despite prognostications of certain critics, and that his characteristics are best exemplified in his briefer tales.

All the Urkey Island stories are told, logically, as if by "the Means boy" grown to manhood; for as they are of the past they seemed to the author best unfolded by one still living and familiar with that past. Through this boy, then, Mr. Steele delights in recalling † the shouting of the Round Hill Bars, a shouting that filled the bowl of the invisible world and rumbled in tangled

---

* Awarded a prize of $250 by the O. Henry Memorial Award Committee as the second best story of the year, 1919. The late Edward J. Wheeler, Editor of *Current Opinion,* declared it "head and shoulders" above other short stories of that year.
† *A White Horse Winter.*

reverberations: "I could see the outer bar only as a white, distorted line athwart the gray, but the shore-ward shallows were writhing, living things, gnawing at the sky with venomous teeth of spume. . . ." In this instance, also, is apparent that fine modulation or harmony whereby the real and the imagined perfectly merge. Says the narrator: "My mother used some-times to sing a little Portuguese song to my brother Antone, the baby. It had a part which ran—

> The herd of the King's White Horses
> Comes up on the shore to graze . . .

And so well has the author combined the boy's fancy of the ocean in frenzy as that of an animal gnawing with venomous teeth, the reader is hardly aware of the transition whereby the white horses of the bar pass into the splendid white steed that, washed ashore from the wreck, staggered up the face of the dune and stood against the sky. Further, the same tale illustrates the author's sense of structure. The salvation of the white horse would hardly be sufficient for a well rounded tale. With it, therefore, is inwoven the love story of the boy's sister, Agnes Means, and Jem Hodges, the owner of the white stallion. The narra-tive is not illustrative of Mr. Steele's procedure in composition; for though based on an actual occur-rence, it stands alone in this regard. One other story may be excepted, in that the hero of *A Devil of a Fel-*

low, Va Di, reflects a man of Mr. Steele's acquaintance.

Since in only these two instances has the author drawn upon life immediately, the conclusion is inevitable that he relies almost altogether upon imagination. Place or locale is the usual basis, but the evolution of the building process is confined to •the cerebrations of Mr. Steele. He says with too great modesty that this evolution is a matter of mechanics. He determines to write a story and gives himself up to meditation. The story comes. He cannot recall its genesis, save that he develops a mood from which the whole fabric seems to take shape. In former days this manner of creation would have been termed inspirational, a word of more exact application here than the word mechanical, but having always back of it—except in the assertions of literary mediocrity—hard work and knowledge of technique. If his method is in the least mechanical, it is because of the author's reliance upon mood, a mood which he from resolution or perhaps now with the ease of practice rigidly mantains. In 1920 I wrote in the Introduction to *O. Henry Memorial Prize Stories,* Volume I, "The tale predominantly of atmosphere, revealing, wherever found, the ability of the author to hold a dominant mood in which as in a calcium light characters and acts are colored, occurs so rarely as to challenge admiration when it does occur. *For They Know not What They Do* lures the reader into its exotic air and holds him, until he, too, is suffused, convinced." Stevenson practised this procedure, notably in *The Merry Men*, as he has told in one of his essays, nor is the work of Mr. Steele so reminiscent of any other author in this respect. Since he cannot recall following the example of the Scotch writer, however, Mr. Steele resembles him, out of doubt, only because of similar approach in workmanship.

Not Stevenson but Lafcadio Hearn is the writer for whose works Mr. Steele expresses enthusiasm. Between the author of *A Japanese Miscellany* and *Some Chinese Ghosts,* and the author of Provincetown and Urkey Island stories exists no obvious kinship, save in the apprehension and delicate use of the fanciful. Rather will *Down on Their Knees* and *A Devil of a Fellow* demand comparison with the fiction of Mr. Joseph C. Lincoln. Yet this challenge is met in a brief enumeration: Mr. Lincoln writes of another neighborhood in Cape Cod, both men relish the salt of locale and atmosphere, neither draws portraits—if they know it—of the living. Their styles are far apart. If Mr. Steele should ultimately settle upon a particular foreign soil and should emphasize his handling of the fantastic, he would afford reasons for the conclusion that he has, to a degree, profited by study of Hearn. His second period has inaugurated the possibility of such later deduction. As he was moved by the Portuguese of the Massachusetts coast, so he has reflected his visit to Bermuda in *At Two in the Bush,* has written of *Both Judge and Jury* in the West Indies, has forecast a trip to the South Sea Islands in *The Shame Dance,* and has interpreted to readers at home the Arab in Africa.

The Shame Dance, titular story of his second collection, entertains by suggesting the origin of a dance popular toward the close of the second twentieth century decade. It illustrates, further, the grip in which Mr. Steele is held by the magnetizing influence of place, even from afar. It offers an etymology, interesting if not philologically correct, "Shame dance, Shem-dance, Shimmie dance."

Perhaps the war had something to do with Mr. Steele's change of locale as a setting, though admittedly he has "finished with Provincetown," to the extent of selling his home there. After the United States entered the conflict Mr. Steele, asked to write articles on the American Naval participation, visited the North Sea, Dunkirk, Brest, and North Ireland. The results he utilized in *Contact!* published in *Harper's,* September, 1919. This work excited provocation among critics who like to consider the question, "What, anyway, is a short story?" Three out of five declared that its finely imagined situation and its maintenance of the struggle placed it in the fiction class and that of the short story in particular. But the editors, when questioned, wrote: "It is a faithful portrayal of the work done by our destroyers and therefore falls under the category of 'articles.'" And the author: "I am not quite sure what to say. *Contact!* was, in a sense, drawn from life, that is to say, it is made up of a number of impressions gained while I was at sea with the U. S. destroyers off the coast of France. The characters are elaborations of real characters, and the 'contact' told of was such a one as I actually witnessed. Otherwise, the chronology of events, conversations, etc., were gathered from various sources and woven to the best of my ability so as to give a picture of the day's work of our convoying forces in the war."

No better instance can be adduced than this for showing the reorganizing habit of the fictionist by which the record of fact is imbued with the feeling and coloring of fancy.

The Dark Hour, a conversation centered on the meaning of the struggle among the nations, was reprinted in O'Brien's anthology of 1918 as one of the best twenty stories of the year. Although it possesses literary merit, it is not a story; moreover, it displays its author in a philosophic rather than artistic state of mind. On his way home from France, Mr. Steele received news of the armistice. Its timeliness having departed, the rest of his war material was lost, temporarily at least, to the world.

In recent years, as has been indicated above, Mr. Steele has left far astern the curving peninsula of Cape Cod. Among the countries he has visited, and which have been summarized in preceding paragraphs, he has found North Africa fertile for his imagination.

"Kairwan the Holy lay asleep, pent in its thick walls. The moon had sunk at midnight, but the chill light seemed scarcely to have diminished; only the lime-washed city had become a marble city, and all the towers turned fabulous in the fierce dry needly rain of the stars that burn over the desert of mid-Tunisia." The story, *A Marriage in Kairwan,* presents the crisis in the life of an Arabian lady who elects for herself her lover's standard of morality, a standard, as the outcome tragically reveals, one for his sex alone. The thread of the narrative may be a trifle thin, though somewhat strengthened by the terminal shock (nowise dulled because the reader is subtly prepared for it), and it runs through a warp and woof Orientally splendid, heavy as cloth of gold.

Akin to this story are *The Anglo-Saxon, East and West, He That Hideth His Secret,* and *The Other Side of the South.* Tales of Arabian nights and days, they have in common with his preceding stories the elements of the strange and the fanciful. As in *The Woman at Seven Brothers* the ghost became for the author the best possible form of fairy tale, as in *Guiablesse* the jealousy of a ship for a woman constitutes the cause for conflict, so in *The Anglo-Saxon* the vision of the sands and the palm trees is the flotsam of memory by which the Anglo-Saxon recovers all his past.

He That Hideth His Secret brings together the Arabian and New York City, as *The Other Side of the South* performs a *tour de force* in a Civil War story. Over in Africa survives a blind one-time slave, whose story is told by the nephew leading him from place to place. It is the more diverting as a Steele story, in that the author has never revisited, in all his wanderings, the land of his birth; it apprehends the South of slavery through the author's interest in North Africa. A mighty compass, but he has fetched it round.

Although a tried device of the story-teller is that of creating a character who grasps the external world through fewer than the usual five senses, yet Mr. Steele has not emphasized the trick in *The Other Side of the South*. He has done so in *Footfalls*. Boaz Negro lived in one of those old Puritan sea-towns, which has become of late years an outpost of the Portuguese Islands. When in spite of blindness he relies on his ability to distinguish footfalls, he sets up suspense which is terminated only at the redemption of his son's name. Boaz's killing of the villain who had brought about the dishonor of that son is perhaps the best instance of surprise in all the narratives, if *For They Know not What They Do* is excepted. The latter story presents a most poignant instance of sacrifice: a mother, lovely and virtuous, recognizes that the curse of insanity obsesses her son. He has discovered that his father and his father's father committed crimes, knowing not what they did. His own life seems doomed. To save him from himself the mother avers that her dead husband was not his father. Of course, he learns long after that she had lied gallantly; but, then, his mother, from whom he had withdrawn himself, was dead.

Ordinarily, surprise is a tool this author handles with not more than casual concern for its incisiveness. His management of a single vivid moment is frequently more compelling. For instance, in *A Man's a Fool,* the narrator is rehearsing the struggle he and his brother Raphael endured with the *Flores,* and he has reached the point where the boom had broken Raphael's back: ". . . I get down beside my brother and I give him a kiss, and I see tears running down his face, and they was mine. And I says to him:

"'Wait! You're all right, Raphael boy. You'll be all right and you ain't hurt bad. It's all right, Raphael boy. Only you wait here quiet a second while I heave over that anchor and I'll be back.'

"I give him another kiss on the cheek, and then I tumble up forward and heave that anchor over. It never take me no time. I was back like that. But yet what little sea there was had shift him a mite on the deck, and I see my brother was dead."

The passage is rescued from the sentimentality, which might be otherwise charged to it, by the previous long struggle between the two brothers over a woman. This is the resolution of the problem.

In 1922 Mr. Steele first came into extraordinary recognition when the O. Henry Memorial Committee awarded him a special prize for supremacy in story writing from the year 1919 to 1921, inclusive. They summed up his abilities as lying in an individual temperament that invests the real with the color of romance, in a sense of correct architecture, in the happy knowledge of unique situations, in the climactic development of struggle or complication, in the power to move the reader's emotions, and in a satisfactory dénouement. All these characteristics are manifest in tales marked by a distinctive style, a style dependent upon seizure and conveyance of atmosphere.

Mr. Steele's volumes of short stories:

Land's End, 1918.
The Shame Dance, 1923.

Lightning Source UK Ltd.
Milton Keynes UK
UKHW011519050620
364505UK00003B/607